MATT JANSEN

THE AUTOBIOGRAPHY

WHAT WAS, WHAT IS AND WHAT MIGHT HAVE BEEN

WITH JON COLMAN

POLARIS
PUBLISHING

First published in 2019 by

POLARIS PUBLISHING LTD
c/o Aberdein Considine
2nd Floor, Elder House
Multrees Walk
Edinburgh
EH1 3DX

www.polarispublishing.com

Distributed by

ARENA SPORT
An imprint of Birlinn Limited

Text copyright © Matt Jansen and Jon Colman, 2019

ISBN: 9781909715851
eBook ISBN: 9781788851893

British Library Cataloguing-in-Publication Data
A catalogue record for this book is available on request from the British Library.

Designed and typeset by Polaris Publishing, Edinburgh

Printed and bound in Great Britain by Clays Ltd, Elcograf S.p.A.

CONTENTS

To Lucy

PROLOGUE

March 2013. England's latest goalscoring hope has emerged – the first of the clickbait era. And here's what he has to deal with. On the website of *The Telegraph*:

Harry Kane beware: 10 young English forwards who never matched the hype

I wonder.

Click

Danny Cadamarteri. I'm two years older than Danny, but I was still at Carlisle when he broke through at Everton. By the time Danny slipped down the divisions and landed at Carlisle, I had done the same and was playing for Chorley.

Click

Michael Bridges. We were in an England Under-21 squad together in 1999. Michael was tearing up the Premier League with Leeds. Then he had a series of injuries and he never got back to the same level. Also played for Carlisle. Is there a theme developing here?

Click

Ah, yes. Here we go. The half-and-half Uhlsport Blackburn Rovers kit . . . Floppy 90s hair . . . Looks like I'm in mid-sprint. Now, what does it say about me?

In the late 1990s, Jansen was one of the hottest properties in English football. Impressive displays for Carlisle earned the youngster a £1 million move to Premier League side Crystal Palace in February 1998, and less than a year later he was snapped up by Blackburn for £4.1m at the age of just 21. A mobile striker with a good eye for goal, Jansen was seen as a dead-cert for England, but despite being a consistently excellent option on Championship Manager, he never fulfilled his potential in real life. Injuries ravaged his time at Ewood Park, and after leaving for Bolton in 2006, Jansen retired from playing for eighth-tier outfit Chorley FC in 2010.

That's it?

A couple of transfer fees and a joke about a computer game? *That's* who I am?

There's no mention of the accident. *Injuries ravaged his time at Ewood Park.* How can they not mention the accident? It's no secret.

The accident split my life in two. Before and after.

Before: A young, free-wheeling footballer with the world at his feet. Coveted by Sir Alex Ferguson, manager of Manchester United. A goalscorer in a League Cup final. Selected by the England manager, Sven-Göran Eriksson, for his squad in the build-up to the 2002 World Cup. Denied a place on the plane to Japan by a knife-edge decision. But at the time I really didn't care. My time with England would come. I was as confident about that as I was about everything else, on and off the pitch. That's how I felt on holiday with my girlfriend in Italy. Then, on our last night, we hired a moped. At a crossroads, I nosed out and was hit by a taxi, knocking me across the cobbles and into a coma.

After: The same, but different. Back too soon, and with invisible scars. What had been natural was now painstaking. What had been instinctive now was daunting. Where there had been confidence there was doubt. I had been invincible. Now I was broken.

I was twenty-four when the accident happened, entering my peak years as an athlete.

At first I was puzzled by my new-found limitations. Then I became desperate. Desperation turned to a deep depression. I drifted away from the player I had been without understanding why. I was trying to prove to the world that I was still me, unable to come to terms with the change that had taken place.

It took me a long time to work it all out, and I needed a lot of help. The same is true of this book, and you will hear voices other than my own: family members, former managers and one of my old teammates. The result is my story. How a boy became a star; how his life was shattered in a split second; how he struggled to put it back together; and how he found a way back out of the darkness.

ONE

THE HAPPIEST MAN IN THE WORLD

Where shall I start? Let's go back to 2002, and a few weeks that changed my life.

In the middle of March, I played through the niggling feeling of a hernia and scored a consolation goal for Blackburn Rovers in a 3–1 defeat against Leeds United at Elland Road. It was my fourteenth of the season, and I later learned that Tord Grip, the England assistant manager, had been in the stand.

Maybe, maybe . . .

The talk was that England were considering me for their friendly against Italy as the countdown to the World Cup in Japan and South Korea went on. I had been given no hint or inkling, but reporters were keen to know my thoughts on the matter at full time.

I said all that I could. 'I know if I'm playing well enough, then I'm sure I'll be included. If I'm not, then that will be it for me as far as the World Cup goes. If that's the case, then I've got to look forward to trying to break in in the future.'

If the words come across almost casually on the page, it's because I was completely relaxed about the idea. It was an exciting thought, and I can't pretend I didn't leave Leeds wondering, but it was very late in the day. Uncapped players don't often sneak into a World Cup squad at the last minute, and Sven-Göran Eriksson, whose qualifying campaign had included a 5–1 win in Germany, which felt worthy of a national holiday, didn't seem the most impulsive of managers.

The squad was announced a few days later and my name wasn't there. No worries. I could live with that. Life was still pretty good.

A couple of weeks later, the Blackburn Rovers club doctor, Phil Batty, approached me at the training ground.

'Don't suppose you were drinking yesterday?' he asked.

'No, why?'

'Oh, nothing. Well, just think about being careful. You never know about England. That chance might still come. Just make sure you look after yourself.'

Maybe Phil knew which way the wind was blowing. I suppose word gets around in football, but after missing out on Italy, I wasn't exactly on tenterhooks when I flopped on to my sofa and performed the reflex action of switching on Sky Sports News.

Another England squad announcement was coming up, for the final friendly before the World Cup: Paraguay at Anfield, on 17 April. With Sky Sports News, you know that if you miss it the first time, you'll catch it again a dozen times within the hour. I didn't have long to wait. I heard them say my name, but it didn't hit me until I saw the graphic on screen.

Goalkeepers: *David Seaman, Nigel Martyn, David James;*
Defenders: *Gary Neville, Phil Neville, Wayne Bridge, Danny Mills, Jamie Carragher, Gareth Southgate, Sol Campbell, Ugo Ehiogu;*

Midfielders: Paul Scholes, Steven Gerrard, Nicky Butt, Joe Cole, Trevor Sinclair, Frank Lampard, Kieron Dyer, Owen Hargreaves, Danny Murphy;
Forwards: Michael Owen, Robbie Fowler, Teddy Sheringham, Darius Vassell, Matt Jansen.

There are moments in life – rare, beautiful moments – when electricity judders uncontrollably through every fibre of your body. Your chest is so tight you can barely breathe. The world tips and spins, you struggle to focus. But there it was. My name.

'Matt is doing very well at the moment, and deserves his chance at international level,' Eriksson said. 'His form last season was good, and this season he is playing better than ever.'

He made it pretty clear that I would play at least some part in the game.

I couldn't wait to tell Lucy, my girlfriend, and for the rest of the night my phone didn't stop buzzing. Eventually I got through to Mum and Dad, whose heads were in the clouds. My dad had often told me that I had never seen him cry, but that would change the day I played for England. I knew straight away how much it meant to him.

The itinerary arrived in the post, each letter headed with the Three Lions crest. We were asked to meet at Carden Park Hotel in Cheshire on Monday afternoon. There would be a training session at Wrexham's Racecourse Ground, the first fifteen minutes of which would be open to the media. The following day, at 4.00 p.m., we would be training at Anfield.

Another page offered a map of Liverpool's stadium. The thought of playing there, for England, with a full house on your side . . .

A further letter set out the formalities in the event of being called for a random drug test. Another document explained that everyone in the squad would undergo a fitness test. I was in the 8.30 a.m. group with Wayne Bridge, Nicky Butt, Jamie Carragher and Owen Hargreaves. 'Please bring trainers and boots.'

The small print held a lot of fun details. If we were approached for autographs, we were recommended to personalise them, to restrict onward sale by professional signature hunters. A letter from FA chief executive Adam Crozier warned that 'under no circumstances' would alcoholic drinks be allowed 'without the express authority of the head coach'. The FA would cover the cost of non-alcoholic drinks, newspapers, videos and use of the gym, but not golf fees or hire. Also, we were not to swap shirts with Paraguay players until both teams had returned to the dressing rooms at full-time. We had to wear Umbro gear at all times – and also watch what we said in post-match interviews.

As it all sank in, I realised that it wasn't just my summer that might be affected by my participation at the World Cup. I was due to be an usher for my brother, Jo, at his wedding in Canada. I checked the calendar. His big day was scheduled three days after England's third group game, against Nigeria in Osaka. If all went to plan, I wouldn't have a hope of being by his side.

A crazy thought. But I knew he would understand.

Carden Park, set in masses of countryside, was a suitably luxurious setting for the squad's get-together. I couldn't keep the smile off my face as I walked through the lobby and was greeted by members of the England staff and some of the players. A few of the protocols were explained again, a small pile of kit was handed over, and I was shown to my room. I lay on the bed to contemplate life. More time must have gone by than I'd realised when there was a firm thump on the door.

I opened it to find Ray Clemence, the goalkeeping coach, wearing a serious expression.

'You know there's a meeting now, don't you?' he said.

Okay, being late for your first team meeting as an England player isn't the ideal start, but as I went downstairs and entered the designated room, nobody seemed too fussed. Most of the players were there, including David Beckham, who was with the squad despite being injured. He turned around and smiled at me.

Eriksson was at the front of the room. 'Hello, Matt,' he said.

I found a seat and listened as Sven spoke briefly about the plans for the next few days. His manner was very easy-going. There wasn't any hint of stress about him. Wasn't the England job supposed to be the hardest in the world?

We ate, and then it was off to Wrexham, where training was taken by Sammy Lee and Steve McClaren. Sammy, who was extremely chirpy, assumed a natural control of things, while Sven walked around the pitch, watching, not saying much.

I felt a surge of pride as I pulled on the training kit. I can still see it: the navy shirt, the name of the sponsor, Nationwide, in white, the Umbro logo, the Three Lions. It was a badge of honour, but I had long gone past the time when I would have felt unworthy of being in the sort of company I was now keeping. That day, everything felt perfect. I was desperate for the ball and ready to work hard. And maybe show off a little, if the opportunity arose.

The standard was high, the sharpness another level. I was impressed by Owen Hargreaves' technique and awareness, while Michael Owen was seriously rapid. As we moved into phases of play and small-sided games, the drills were arranged so that I was playing alongside Michael, or just behind him.

Was that a hint at the plans for Paraguay? It certainly seemed geared that way. Michael's movement was electric. He was one of the best strikers in Europe, and we linked up well. I scored a few goals and when the session finished, I had an overwhelming feeling that this was my time.

Back in the hotel, I was passed a bundle of fax messages, many of them from old schoolteachers and coaches. I also faced the media in an official press conference, and you can imagine how pleased Sky Sports News were when I told them exactly how I had learned of my call-up. That soundbite was quickly included in their eternal loop.

I had never felt more positive. The next day couldn't come quickly enough. The chance to nail things down at Anfield. Nothing could stop me.

It came upon me slowly that night, and then seemed to take over my body. First, a queasy feeling, followed by the shivers. I sat on my bed and waited for the room to stop wobbling, then jolted to my feet and ran into the bathroom to be sick.

I was shaking and sweating, my vision was blurred and, as the minutes went by, my head felt so cloudy that I thought I was going to start hallucinating. It was like being hit by a sledgehammer. I collapsed into bed for a restless and fitful night's sleep.

The next morning, I felt no better. I called for the team doctor, who quickly came to examine me.

'Yeah, you're not good.'

What about training? What about the game? I can't be ill!

A short while later, there was another knock, and then the door opened. As Sven walked in, my instinct was to get out of bed and attempt to greet him.

I threw back the covers and gingerly got to my feet. Sven looked at me, frowned and raised his hands. 'No, no,' he said. 'Don't get up. Stay there.'

I did as he suggested. There was certainly something surreal about sitting on my bed in only my boxer shorts whilst speaking to the England manager, but I felt too weak to register any embarrassment.

I told him how rotten I felt.

'Don't worry,' he said. 'We will make sure everything is okay for you. Just make sure that you get better.'

As he left, and the door closed, I raced to the toilet and threw up again.

When I was diagnosed with a severe bout of gastroenteritis, it was clear that I couldn't stay at Carden Park any longer. As the rest of the squad were conveyed to Liverpool, Jay Bevington, my brother-in-law and agent, arrived to collect me. I was still shaking and struggling to stand up as he helped me into his car and took me home to Manchester.

The next day, Phil Batty visited in order to attach an intravenous drip. The first attempt was unsuccessful, as the needle penetrated my skin, only to come out the other side.

'Oops. Let's do that again.'

The second effort was a success and, as the antibiotics entered my system, I switched the TV on and struggled to pay close attention to England's 4–0 victory over Paraguay.

There is no point in pretending that I wasn't devastated to miss my chance, but I told myself that events had been out of my control. It was nothing more than bad luck, and anyway, did I ever *really* think I was going to be on that plane to Japan? I would just have to get back on the pitch for Blackburn, play as well as I had been playing all season, and take whatever came my way.

As I recuperated, I read a couple of articles criticising me for pulling out. It was typical tabloid rubbish. Steven Howard in *The Sun* was one of the main culprits. 'Most people would give their right arm to play for England' – that sort of trash. They wrote it without any idea of how ill I'd been, or how I felt about it. I wouldn't have been able to stand up on the pitch and I might also have infected half the squad.

Why on earth would I make an excuse not to play for England? This had been my only chance to impress the national team manager who was about to select his World Cup squad. And on top of that, I was due £1 million from Adidas the minute I gained my first cap. Who in the world would turn all that down lightly?

I threw the papers aside. Even when I realised where the illness had come from (Jay's eldest son had just got over a horrible virus – our apartments were connected and we spent a lot of time together), I knew there was more to gain from looking forward than back.

I missed Blackburn's next game, at Middlesbrough, but was fit enough to return against Newcastle at Ewood. I wasn't at my sharpest, and had lost a stone in weight, but five days later I felt like my old self again, scoring at Everton in a victory that meant we were safe for another season in the Premier League.

Our next game was also on Merseyside – by sod's law, I was going to play at Anfield, after all.

Eriksson was due to name his World Cup squad the following day. I hadn't given up all hope, but as we arrived in Liverpool I strongly suspected the footballing highlight of my summer would amount to a hernia operation and watching the tournament on television.

We warmed up, had our team-talk and then lined up at the mouth of the tunnel. Graeme Souness, our manager, came out of the dressing room and beckoned me to one side.

'Listen,' he said quietly. 'Sven's here and I've just been chatting to him. He's told me not to say anything, but don't go getting injured, because you're going to the World Cup.'

He concealed his smile just enough not to give the game away to anyone else. I'm not sure my feet touched the floor as I glided out on to the pitch.

Souness certainly knew what made me tick. I knew he was delighted for me, but he also had selfish reasons for breaking Sven's promise, because he realised how my ego worked. Anfield was always a great place to play – even more so when you've got wings. I didn't play to avoid injury – I was completely convinced that I was untouchable. Ten minutes from time, I crept on to a cross from Keith Gillespie and passed it into the net to make it 3–3. Party time.

Not quite. Emile Heskey scored a last-minute winner for Liverpool. But I was happy with how it had gone for me. Sven had seen me score, I had come through it unscathed, and now it was just a case of waiting for the call.

That night I went to a Chinese restaurant in Manchester, Yang Sing, and chatted to Lucy and Jay about everything that was about to happen. The announcement, the plans, the formalities. I couldn't wait.

We were due in for a light session the next day. The television sets in the canteen were mostly locked on the usual channel. When I arrived, Souness said I could watch the screens while the others went outside for a game of head tennis. There was no immediate sign of the announcement, and eventually Souness poked his head around the door.

'You may as well come and join in,' he said. 'You've nothing to worry about. You know you've made the squad.'

I did as he suggested, then came back inside an hour later to find the news had still not broken.

'Stop worrying, will you?' Souness said.

'I'm not!'

I showered, changed, got into the car and turned the radio on. I was halfway home when the sports bulletin led with the news that Sven-Göran Eriksson had named his twenty-three-man squad for the World Cup finals. Finally! Captain David Beckham was included as he recovered from a broken metatarsal, while the veteran Arsenal defender Martin Keown had been preferred to the uncapped Matt Jansen.

Come again?

I called Jay and asked what was going on.

Eventually the story was pieced together. It turned out that, while I was scoring in front of Sven, Tord Grip had watched Arsenal win the title at Old Trafford. They had met on the journey home, and the assistant had convinced his boss to take the supposedly safer option of an extra defender.

You might think I went home, cried myself to sleep and spent the next few weeks sticking pins in a Tord Grip voodoo doll morning, noon and night in a bid to alleviate the unbearable personal torment. But that's not how I felt.

I was certainly confused, and deflated, but the more I thought about it, the more I started to lift my sights again.

It wasn't the end of the world.

It had always been a long shot.

Keown had played over forty games for England. I had played none, and I'd still come so close to being on the plane. That told me it was only a matter of time. I could live with the disappointment when it was clear that, once the friendlies and qualifiers came around next season, I was bound to get a proper chance. Sven liked me, that was obvious, and what international manager doesn't try new ideas immediately after a big tournament?

I would give him no choice next time.

Blackburn's last game of the season brought Fulham to Ewood. From the moment I woke up, things felt strangely different. As kick-off approached, I had a clear sense that something was missing.

My nerves. They had completely gone.

The usual churn, the flutter of butterflies that stopped me eating for several hours before a game; the anxious sensations I'd felt ever since I had started playing football. For the first time in my life, none of it was there.

It was an end-of-term game that carried no pressure for either side, but this was more than that. I'd never felt like this before a game and it had to be about what had happened with England. I knew that I was an international player in all but name. I'd had the best season of my career, scoring sixteen goals in the Premier League and one in our League Cup final win over Spurs. In Lucy, I had found the one.

I felt invincible on the pitch that day. I played with a smile on my face until I was subbed with fifteen minutes left of a 3–0 win. Maybe it would feel this good every time from now on.

Maybe.

Lucy was completing her languages degree at the University of Manchester and was practically fluent in Italian. With her exams finished, we had the opportunity to take a short break before heading on to Canada for Jo's wedding. I'd always fancied Italy. Lucy had spent an enjoyable time there as part of her studies, and we decided to see Rome.

Although we hadn't been dating for long, I sensed a connection with her that I hadn't known with anyone else. It felt like I'd found what I'd always been looking for.

After checking into the Hotel Eden, near Rome's Spanish Steps, we went for a walk in the sun. It was on one of these strolls, around the great city, that I said out loud what I'd been feeling.

'I'm the happiest man in the world,' I announced. 'I'm actually the happiest man in the world!'

On our travels around Rome, we took in all we could: the cafés, the bustling streets, the shops, the Colosseum, the Pantheon. It was very hot, a little hazy and smoggy, but we were young and fresh, living a dream life. In a new relationship, and earning a decent wage, I was also feeling a bit flash. Somewhere near the Pantheon, we paused at a café for a drink. After finding a table, I got up to go to the loo. 'Order whatever you like,' I told Lucy.

She suggested a glass of champagne. 'We might as well get a bottle,' I said.

When I returned, we were joined at our table by a bloke with a violin, swiftly followed by an ice-cold and expensive bottle of Cristal.

'You won't like it – too sweet,' I said. Lucy was determined to try it, but after a couple of sips her face soured.

As the bottle was now open, it was too late to replace it. We turned to the next table, where another couple were sitting quietly, and caught their attention. 'Would you like a bottle of Cristal?' Lucy asked. They accepted the unexpected gift graciously, and we decided to go somewhere else.

I'm the man. Giving away the most expensive champagne in Italy without a care in the world!

By this stage in our trip we'd already been on a scooter. When in Rome, do as the Romans do. Getting a taxi from the airport to the hotel, through a city where bumps and bashes were par for the course, had felt much scarier than negotiating the streets on two wheels.

We'd hired this particular model, a Honda 250, from a garage on the side of a street in Piazza Barberini that afternoon. We just rocked up, gave a few details, paid 103 Euros, strapped on our helmets, and off we went. We had taken the scooter up to the Trevi Fountain and ridden it to another of the great monuments at Piazza Venezia. The next day's plan was a trip to the Vatican as a last hurrah before leaving – not that I particularly wanted to leave. 'Should we stay a couple more days?' I suggested, only half in jest.

A while later, we returned to the Hotel Eden, which had a

gorgeous terraced restaurant, with beautiful views. In Italy there is a custom of going for an evening stroll after dinner – *fare un giro*, Lucy tells me, which essentially means heading out for a bit of a walk, getting a *gelato* or a coffee, having a chat and mooching around as the sun settles. Lucy was very much in Italian mode and, after we had eaten, she was eager to go back out, but on the bike.

I wasn't so enthusiastic, as I'd been on the Honda all day, but she persuaded me without too much of a fight.

We didn't get very far when Lucy, riding pillion, felt her helmet fly off. We parked up and tried to find it, without success. There were some police officers at the side of the road, and they made it clear that we couldn't be riding around Rome without head protection. The hotel was very close, a few hundred yards away, and the officers accepted our suggestion that we would ride back up the road and only come back out on the bike once we had sorted the helmet situation, even if that had to be the next day.

Before setting off, I removed my helmet and offered it to Lucy. 'No – you're driving, you're at the front, you'd better keep it on,' she said, handing it back.

We had to drive up a cobbled road, turn right, navigate a crossroads, and head up to the hotel. A straightforward journey – by Roman standards.

There is no such thing as a deserted street in that city and, at this particular crossroads, cars were parked on every corner, virtually touching each other. If you think of how a child might draw the sun, with lines sticking out to indicate rays, that's how they were protruding. As a result, visibility around the corners was poor.

In Italy, when both sets of lights flash amber, that's your cue to edge towards the junction and judge whether it's safe to go. At no point did I feel we were travelling at a risky speed. As we approached, I pressed my foot on the pedal and moved forward, leaning out, and something flashed across from the right. And then I don't remember anything.

TWO

BANG-BANG MAX

It would be easy to say I got on the scooter in the first place because I felt invincible, because I sensed no danger in the riskiest of activities. It sounds good, but it's not true. Climbing on to the bike with Lucy didn't feel daring or foolhardy. It was just the best way of negotiating a busy and unfamiliar city.

It's taken time for me to look at what happened from a distance and come to this conclusion. In the years following the collision, when my life became a torment, it felt at times as though regrets were all I had. I chewed them over, fought them and, at my lowest, lost hands down. There were so many moments when I blamed anyone and everything. I fooled myself into thinking that the answers were hiding in plain sight. When I failed to regain the old magic on the pitch, failed to convince everyone that I was brain-damaged and then tried different ways of blurring the edges, I was followed around by two phrases: *what if* and its close friend, *if only*.

I know now that the accident didn't occur because of a reckless act, by ignoring risk because I felt that nothing could go wrong.

It was an accident. It could have happened to anyone. The decision to get on a moped was not fuelled by adrenaline in the same way football was.

The places where there was an advantage to fearlessness were the stadiums where ruthless and rough defenders tried to intimidate me. They were the grounds of the lower leagues, where heavy challenges and swinging elbows told me I was winning the battle. They were the penalty areas where a cross rewarded the gamble of a confident leap in the air.

I was never one for damage limitation. On the pitch I was a show-off, happy to pay the price of a bruise for a chance to emulate my idol. On a black VHS tape that was never out of the recorder, he slalomed around opponents, tumbling under violent tackles, emerging with scarred legs and the World Cup in his hands.

The official film of the 1986 World Cup was, appropriately, called *Hero*. In theory it was a review of the tournament, but mostly it was a celebration of a genius. It started with footage of the best goal ever scored: Diego Maradona gliding through a queue of lunging English defenders before feinting past Peter Shilton and guiding the ball home for Argentina. It covered the group stages and knock-out rounds, yet there was nothing as fascinating to my nine-year-old eyes as the way Maradona made the film his own. It was an era of cynical defending yet, as he crashed into the baking Mexico pitches and then got up again, appealing theatrically to the referee before going on to bamboozle more opponents, one thought stayed in my mind: he won. They lost. Skill beat muscle. Flair beat brawn.

I remembered this when, as a teenager in the playground at Newman Catholic School in Carlisle, we played a version of the game that would be outlawed by the Department of Education today. Hack Football, it was called, and either you found a way of dealing with a boot heading for your shins, or you vanished.

On the concrete yard, teenagers imposed themselves with testosterone and aggression. It encouraged strength, balance and courage.

As I passed from the yard to the professional game, I never shied away from that side of things. Hack Football shaped me, helped me stand up to attack and to calculate danger. It also taught me to be a little more cunning than I had been when I was little, frequently bashing into things and cracking my head open.

In my earliest years, Mum found it appropriate that I enjoyed attempting the opening syllables of the chorus to the Beatles song, 'Maxwell's Silver Hammer'.

Bang, bang, Maxwell's silver hammer
Came down upon her head
Bang, bang, Maxwell's silver hammer
Made sure that she was dead.

'Bang, bang, Max . . . bang, bang, Max . . .' was all I could muster. Enough for a lifelong nickname, Max, which was doubly convenient given my father was also Matt – or Mat, to be precise, short for Mathieu.

My grandfather was Dutch – from Maastricht – and came to England shortly after the Second World War. He met my grandmother in Worcester and Dad was their firstborn. Granddad clearly had the first choice of names, and Grandma second. Dad was christened Mathieu Gerardus Louis. His younger brother is Peter Harry John.

Dad grew up in Worcester. He played semi-professionally for Worcester City, and also Bridgnorth Town in the Midland Combination. He was once scouted by West Bromwich Albion but, because of a chequered disciplinary record, they wouldn't touch him. On the pitch he had an aggressive streak. He once turned out for his brother's team while my mum was in labour with Clare, my sister. As he went for a header he took a boot in the face, and in Clare's first photographs there's this gruesome figure with purple eyes, a broken nose and a bruised face.

He met Mum at a friend's party in Worcester. She was a nursery nurse and he was unhappy in his career as an engineer. They first moved to Cumbria to manage Fallbarrow Park, a Lake District leisure pursuits centre. Then Dad decided he wanted to join the police. After applying to several forces, he heard from Cumbria first. Initially he was posted to Windermere, then Roadhead, and then Wetheral, a secluded, affluent north-Cumbrian village through which runs the River Eden. My earliest memory is of being rescued from its pitiless currents.

I was barely three, out walking with my brothers, sister and uncle Edward, who was throwing sticks for his collie. The dog fell foul of a strong current and had to be hauled out of the river. As everyone retreated, I paddled further in and was swept under. My brother Daniel raised the alarm, and Eddie wrestled off a backpack that he had been using to carry my younger brother, Jo. He reached in where I had gone under and pulled me out. That was Bang-Bang Max's first great scrape.

There was the time I challenged one of my siblings to a race only for my legs to plunge through the bars of a cattle grid. The time I put my head through a broken window and, flinching as Jo pretended to throw a stone, cut my face open. At school, a routine eye test found the vision in one of my eyes to be very poor. I wore patches and glasses to correct the problem, but these didn't slow me down. Adults called me The Exocet for the way I tore around.

The search for a house in Wetheral led my parents to a place directly beside the old train station, which had been closed down in the Beeching cuts. It had been the old stationmaster's house. Mum cried when they bought it because it needed so much work, but the field outside the back door, owned by our neighbour Peter Tyson, provided me with my own personal football pitch. Dad set up some goals and would challenge me to do ten kick-ups for the prize of a fifty-pence piece. The bar was then raised to fifty kick-ups.

We were a competitive family. Danny, my older brother, was talented in most sports, but lacked aggression. Jo was the opposite. I had both, while Clare inherited a little more from Mum, who has a gentler nature. At Butlin's, in Ayr, we entered a family team in the five-a-side tournament. We put Clare, the oldest of the four of us, in goal and, after losing the final, we gave the poor girl such a bollocking. That's just how we were.

We didn't have a lot of money for exotic foreign holidays, so when we took the caravan to Scotland, or Dorset, or did a house swap with another family in Kent, we would hit the beach and have races and long jump contests. Jansen Sports Days, we called these – or, after watching the athletics from Seoul in 1988, the Jansen Olympics. At night there would be domino championships, contested with the same passion.

At Cumwhinton Primary School I was fortunate to have a headmaster who understood my growing passion for football. Ken Boyd, a big Newcastle fan, had played at semi-professional level and always played football with us at break. It was only a small school and, if we were getting rowdy in class, he would sometimes take us outside for a game, to burn off energy. At the end of a school day, while I was waiting for Mum to pick me up, Mr Boyd would join me in the yard to play headers and volleys.

At home, I played endlessly against the wall – this was where I practised the most. Sometimes the ball disappeared on to the train track where we were forbidden to venture. If nobody was watching, I would sneak on to get it back. Other times, in next door's field, the four of us kids used hay bales as goalposts in super-competitive games.

At the age of eight, I pestered my dad to let me play in an under-11 friendly involving Danny. It was at Warwick Bridge, another village to the east of Carlisle, and their team was run by a policeman of Dad's acquaintance. He describes his Eureka moment, when a bigger lad crossed the ball, and I rose above a defender to head it in.

I enjoyed protecting the ball, passing it, beating players, rolling with challenges. I also had that nickname. Mum, on the sideline, had been screaming, 'Come on Maxi! Come on Maxi!' Afterwards, when the opposition manager was asked to pick his man of the match, he said: 'Maxine'. There's a newspaper cutting that also names Maxine Jansen in a team photo.

These were my unlikely beginnings in the game. Later, in the Cumwhinton school team, which was also run by Dad, we played nearby Great Corby. They were benefiting from the coaching acumen of Bob Stokoe, who was nearing the end of his third and final spell as manager of Carlisle United. I scored a hatful of goals and the story goes that, as we all came off, Bob approached Dad. 'Wrap that left foot of his in cotton wool,' he whispered, 'because it will make him a living from the game.'

Things like that must have stuck with Dad. The better I got, the more he encouraged me, even if there were times when his determination came out in stern ways. Dad would sometimes read an article or see something on the television about health or science and just buy into it completely. This cost me when, having apparently heard a scientist on the news claiming that cheese was bad for you, he caught me eating some before a junior game at Wetheral. He went ballistic, launching a chair in my direction. 'What the hell are you doing?' he shouted. I scored a hat-trick in spite of consuming the evil cheddar.

I was part of Carlisle United's school of excellence now, in which Dad also coached, with sessions in the Neil Sports Centre, the club's indoor training facility where the old artificial surface shredded your knees. The coaching was fairly basic – simple drills, old-school, technique-based stuff, ending with five-a-sides. The balls were as hard as cannonballs, and there could be thirty or more kids crammed into the Neil. Organised chaos, but I loved it.

We continued playing for our local clubs too and, after being chosen as player of the tournament at an event in Kirkbride, my prize was a new pair of boots. Clive Middlemass, the new manager of Carlisle in 1987, walked up to our house by the train track and tapped on the door. In his hands were two shiny Reebok boots.

'There you go, son,' he said, holding them out.

They were black, with a flash of green. I only had to imagine wearing them to think that I would look, and therefore play, like a professional.

I was amazed the Carlisle manager had come to our house to give me this treasure. Clive was a kindly, genuine man, with a warmth that was carried by his Yorkshire burr. As my career developed I felt my ego was like a snowball, something which was tiny to begin with but, as life rolled on, grew and grew. That might have been the first time I puffed my skinny little chest out a few millimetres more.

Austin Friars did its best to deflate it again. This was the private secondary school in Carlisle that came after Cumwhinton. Danny had won a maths scholarship there, and my parents, despite the heavy cost, resolved to give me the same opportunity, but it wasn't the place for me. The head of PE was a tall, fair-haired and strict customer called Dudley Smith who took every opportunity to announce his disdain for football. Games in the yard drew a sharp rebuke . . .

'This is a rugby school. That's the wrong-shaped ball, Jansen.'

You had to play rugby, no ifs or buts, and I quite enjoyed it – scrum-half was my position – but Smith was always keen to make his point, especially if he felt you had hit the turf too easily, or were exaggerating a tackle.

'Oh, get up – stop acting like a soccer player!'

It was hard not to smile, then, when the weekend came and we went to Brunton Park, spotting Smith's familiar features in the crowd.

I found an outlet in other sports, such as athletics, where I broke the county high jump record. Smith showed a kinder side when praising achievements like this. In class, though, discipline was rigid and teachers ruled by fear.

In my second year, Dad spotted an advert for a schools five-a-side tournament in the city, and suggested I entered with some mates. He approached the headmaster, Father Tom Lyons, because he knew that Father Lyons was a big Celtic supporter, and asked for permission to form a team. Father Lyons readily agreed and my dad started to come down once a week after school to put us through our paces in the gym.

We didn't imagine we'd stand much chance against schools with hundreds of football-playing Carlisle lads. But we ended up winning it. On top of that, we progressed to the national finals and finished as runners-up. Friars was the sort of school where you could gain a mention in morning assembly just by winning a game of draughts in after-school club. But our status as national runners-up in football? Not a word.

I hated the school for other reasons, too. Quite why I became the target for a handful of bullies in my year I don't know or understand, but they certainly made it their business to make my life unpleasant. It ranged from annoying, niggly little things – stealing my stuff, pushing me when we were in a line, standing on my toes – to nastier incidents.

The worst was the time four or five of them dragged me upstairs to the top of the building at the end of a school day. They forced me into the toilets, held my nose and prised my mouth open before one of them hacked up a huge greenie and spat it down my throat. They then left, laughing, leaving me shaken and retching as I scrambled to the sink to wash my mouth out, before trudging downstairs to wait for Mum to pick me up.

It was a miserable time, but I kept quiet about it. Maybe I felt it would have been weak to speak up about it, or I wasn't confident enough in myself at that stage to do so. Maybe, with my under developed ego, I was also asking myself: why am I so unpopular?

All in all it was a horrible period in my life and one more reason to despise Austin Friars. I always made it clear to my parents that I didn't like it, and there were even times I'd cry at the prospect of having to go into school, but they didn't know exactly why I found it so unbearable. Hence their response was always, 'Not everybody likes school, but you still have to go'.

It was, then, with some relief that, three years in, Mum and Dad took Jo and me out of Friars – mainly for financial reasons – and sent us to Newman, a comprehensive that just felt, well, more normal. I didn't have any bullies on my case, for one thing. And at Newman it was all about football – we played every chance we got.

There were some rough lads at Newman and Hack Football there was a brutal game, but that was the sort of examination I loved trying to pass. In class, I wasn't such a great trier. Mum always placed great emphasis on education, but I didn't have any academic instincts. Homework was something that just had to be done, projects were there to be finished at the last minute, revision was a nuisance to be sacrificed when there was football to be played.

I represented the school team, turned out for Denton Holme and the ex-servicemen's club in the city, and also played in police tournaments, through Dad's connections. In the Carlisle United school of excellence, meanwhile, there were some useful players, among them a lad called Steven Holt, who was rated higher than his younger brother, Grant. Another name on local lips was Rory Delap, from Great Corby, who was fifteen months older than me. We played in the same Denton Holme team and, although we were oblivious to it, there were scouts in the area who would monitor talent and recommend lads to Carlisle.

Bigger clubs also had eyes in the city. There was a bearded guy who did some scouting for Manchester United and, in my early teens, I was invited to spend a few days there. The prospect didn't excite me as much as it should have. I was quite shy, reluctant to step out of my comfort zone. It didn't help that, upon arriving, we were shown to some fairly horrible halls of residence-type accommodation. I remember Alex Ferguson and his entourage coming down to watch one of the games I played in, and I was mixing with other lads who were supposed to be future world-beaters, like Marlon Broomes – a big, well-developed man-boy – and the McNiven twins, Scott and David.

Next was Ipswich, which was a little more welcoming. For much of Bobby Robson's reign they had benefited from a Carlisle-based scout, John Carruthers, who had sent talent like Kevin Beattie to East Anglia. He recommended me to the club along with another promising lad from the north called Michael Carrick, the pair of us travelling from Newcastle by train. I have one memory of Ipswich's training ground that will never leave me, and it is of me on the left wing, and Robson, now England manager, watching on the touchline. As I ran past him, he caught my eye.

'See that lad there?' he said. 'Just go inside him.'

I followed his tip. Seconds later I received the ball, beat an opponent, and shot into the top corner. Jogging back, I looked up.

He winked. 'Well done, son.'

I treasure that wink, and those words, and according to Dad

they were followed by a phone call, urging me to spend more time at Ipswich. The truth is that that sort of upheaval always felt a remote possibility to me. I was a homebird, with limited horizons.

While I also had north-west regional trials under the FA National Schools set-up, with names like 'James Carragher' on the team sheet, it was assumed that, if I was going to further a football ambition anywhere, and prove myself good enough for a YTS future, it would be at Carlisle. That was fine by me, although there were other adventures available. In the approach to the 1990 World Cup, you couldn't move for little red footballs stamped with the Coca-Cola logo. They were promoting a skills competition for kids under eighteen – 'Soccaball' – and the overall winner would scoop tickets for Italia '90.

I was outside after school every day with that little ball, practising and perfecting the skills. The rules were that if you demonstrated them all in one go, you got ten points. Two goes and it was five, and so on. I was successful in the regional finals at Gateshead, then progressed through the north of England stage, and that resulted in the daunting prospect of the national final, live on TV, on a bizarre and colourful show that dominated millions of young lives: *Wacaday*, starring Timmy Mallett and Michaela Strachan.

We were invited to stay at the Midland Hotel in Manchester, with the competition to be held at Granada Studios the following day. In the hotel, we were introduced to a bearded and slightly bloated Irishman who was regarded by Dad with awe. I had heard of George Best, although had never seen him play, and after posing for photos with him, I remember Mum and Dad constantly urging me to ask him to sign something. I was shy and reluctant.

The final saw three contestants competing for the prized tickets, ending in a sudden-death, keepy-uppy decider. Under the bespectacled eyes of the lurid-shirted Mallett, we juggled the little red ball from one knee to another, one foot to the next, until I finished a narrow second. I missed out on the World Cup trip, but the runner-up prize softened the blow: two season tickets to the English club of your choice.

Presumably expecting me to choose Manchester United or Liverpool, Mallett and co were a bit surprised when I asked for Carlisle United – so much so that I was given six season tickets for Brunton Park, not two. They were slightly cheaper, I guess.

This prize took me into Carlisle's ground more often. I became more familiar with the stadium's shape and sounds, and with players like Keith Walwyn: a big, experienced striker who was standing out in a struggling team.

My horizons extended as far as that blue jersey. I had no notion of going to the top flight or playing for England. What I had, though, was an obsession that continued to be fed. While Danny, who was also in the school of excellence, didn't make it – Dad, as that age group's coach, made the tough decision that he wasn't going to be good enough, and any other conclusion would have cost him credibility among the other coaches and parents – I was now becoming ingrained at my club.

Danny was laid-back enough not to take it too badly, and if anything preferred rugby, while Jo found his own path with the Army cadets. I, though, was perfectly happy growing further into the game, marching on in my brilliant Reebok boots.

THREE

WILLY WONKA

Before Clive Middlemass brought me those boots, I had worn a basic pair, called Mercurys, made of cheap plastic and presumably bought from the local market. The Reeboks that were handed to me by Carlisle's manager gave me a taste for the finer things. And what teenage boy doesn't want the best new stuff?

'You'd better earn some money, then,' my parents told me. I did a paper round in the village – four huge bags I could barely lift – and later a job in the kitchen in Wetheral's Crown Hotel. I got a £5 note for six hours of peeling a mountain of potatoes and carrots and cleaning the pots. It wasn't inspiring labour, but I was learning that nothing was coming my way without hard work.

I had signed schoolboy forms with Carlisle at fourteen and I was moving through the age groups. Dad was coaching a good crop of players in the under-16s. After one of their games, at Liverpool's training ground, their coach – the legendary Steve Heighway, a double European Cup winner in the great Liverpool team of the 1970s – told my dad his team, which included the future first-team winger David Thompson, had received a football lesson from the Carlisle side.

Dad always said the hardest part of his role was telling young lads they weren't going to make it – those were tough conversations to have with kids and their parents. Carlisle produced some fine players during that period, but it is not a precise art and there are always those who develop a little later – after the club has made their decision. Grant Holt was one such player. His dad died young, from cancer, and Grant dedicated himself to making George proud. After being released by Carlisle, he established himself at Workington, Halifax and Barrow. His commitment never wavered and he eventually reached the Premier League with Norwich and made a very good living out of the game. I can't think of a better example of determination, of believing in yourself. And he was one Carlisle didn't fancy. It came down to the decision of coaches who were watching young players over a relatively short period of time and making a largely instinctive decision.

I'm three and a half years older than Grant and my class of players pushed through sooner, at a time when the club needed something to get behind. Carlisle were skint and struggling at the start of the nineties, but in 1992 they were taken over by a man who could sell dreams like Willy Wonka. I remembered, three years earlier, watching Michael Knighton on *Match of the Day*, juggling the ball at Old Trafford and shooting into the net at the Stretford End as an elaborate build-up to his doomed takeover of Manchester United. Yet now he was on the front page of Carlisle's evening paper, hailed as Mr Moneybags, declaring that there was now 'only one United', and they played at Brunton Park.

Knighton arrived with promises of reaching the Premier League within ten years. He was pinstripe-suited, had a megawatt smile and was incredibly charismatic. I first encountered this charm machine when I chose Carlisle United as the subject of a project for my business studies class. My choice of topic was just a way of spending more time at the football club, and it also earned me an audience with Knighton.

I was fifteen and I was in awe as he talked me through his vision for the club: a grand new, all-seater stadium, surrounded by enviable facilities snaking from Brunton Park up to the nearby M6 motorway. He was an eccentric and he had supporters of a bankrupt club eating out of his hands. As he spoke, I noted down his take on Carlisle's financial position. I wrote: 'I think he enjoyed the position he was in'.

I certainly didn't appreciate how central Carlisle's Mr Wonka would become both to my career and to one of the biggest decisions of my life.

Joining the YTS set-up at Carlisle was a natural step. I had played for the youth team at fourteen and had also been with England's Under-16s by this point. The future was starting to become a little clearer, but Mum, who was not a sporty person and found it harder than Dad to envisage a career for me in football, was determined that I shouldn't abandon my education. She threatened to pull me out of the club if they didn't agree.

My parents had invested a lot of money and effort into getting the best possible education for all of their kids. Mum must have been persuasive because, as I started life as a full-time youth player at Carlisle, I was also asked to attend St Aidan's, another school in the city, to study A-level PE. I also enrolled in night college to take psychology and sociology.

I appreciate why Mum wanted me to do this, but I can't say I was any more committed to my studies than I had been at school. I hated having to do any form of revision and often dodged it, while the PE course was a joke. You had to do practicals, but I found it hard to find the time, as I was spending so much of my week at Brunton Park. Thirty per cent of your overall grade was decided by your performance in two sporting disciplines of your own choice. For some reason I wasn't allowed to pick football, so I chose swimming and athletics. After explaining why I was finding it hard to keep up with the course, I was eventually asked to give my time for the 100m in both disciplines, without being measured by a teacher. Thinking on the spot, I said something like 10.8 seconds for the sprint and an equally unlikely time for the swim. The marks were taken on trust and, because they counted for about twenty-five per cent of the overall examination, they helped me towards a C grade – I still don't know how they bought the idea that I was some sixteen-year-old blend of Carl Lewis and Michael Phelps.

By this time Knighton's rebuilding of the club appeared to be going well, and Carlisle were emerging from a dark period with a brighter team, led by the Yorkshireman Mick Wadsworth. The YTS set-up remained what you would call 'traditional'. The facilities were basic, and we were required to be skivvies for the first team: washing showers, cleaning toilets, digging weeds, hosing down stands and helping with the laundry. Although I was fortunate to be responsible for cleaning the shooting boots of our top scorer, David Reeves – a decent guy who tipped well at Christmas – the environment also bred an element of fear.

As a YTS player, you knew your place – and also accepted that you were fair game for the first-team lads, who would bully and abuse you while you were carrying out your chores. It was a blunt introduction to professional football and nothing was more terrifying than the initiation ceremony demanded of every youth player.

First, there was the build-up: a few days for the fear to set in, days when senior players found you in a corridor and gave unnecessary reminders that you hadn't taken your turn yet.

Then the nights, when sleep was disturbed by the thought of what was to come.

Finally, the day itself. There was no escape when you were

frogmarched into the first-team changing room, stripped of your clothes down to a slip that covered your modesty, ordered to stand on a medical bed and, in front of the gathered professionals, state your name and the song you had chosen to sing. It is the sort of ritual that would probably land a club in hot water these days. I opted for Mark Cohn's hit, 'Walking in Memphis', and as I nervously sang the opening lines, the flak was physical and relentless. I can feel the tremors now . . .

Put on my blue suede shoes . . .
They're hurling bananas at me.
. . . and I boarded the plane.
Now they're approaching me with boot polish, and Vaseline, rubbing it all over me.
Touched down in the land of the Delta blues . . .
What's this? Oh, a sweeping brush, and the broom handle is heading for my arse.
. . . in the middle of the pouring rain.
Finally, water and other drinks – I hope they're drinks – are tipped over my trembling head.

I hurried through a few more bars, bruised and smeared. Then a massive cheer went up and everyone joined in. The relief when the ordeal was over is impossible to describe. Then, like pass the parcel, it was a case of transferring the fear on to the other boys who still had it all to suffer.

We had no choice but to accept it. We still looked up to those first-team players, still saw them as characters rather than bullies. And so when we actually played football it felt like a great release.

Looking back all these years later, that initiation ceremony may sound brutal, but it was the norm. It's what you had to do. Nowadays it's different – when I was manager at Chorley, all a new player had to do was stand at the front of the bus on their first away trip and sing a song down the microphone, and he'd get clapped or booed, or people would sing along with them. Back then, though, the custom was that you were terrified of the first team. I didn't feel violated or abused in any serious sort of way. More than anything, I yearned to be a first-team player, and you didn't want to be that person in the dressing room who complained about it. When I was watching the others lining up to go through it, we would be asking each other, 'What are you gonna sing?' and so on – and yes, there was a huge feeling of relief when you did it. But there was great banter there as well.

I can't remember exactly how far the broom handle went, but it was there. If someone from the football authorities watched it today, there would probably be people locked up – but it was all part and parcel of what went on. If I was fearful of the first team, I also respected them. It was a hierarchy thing too, I suppose.

I think too much of that has gone from professional football now. You can argue that what happened to us was over the top – although if you go back another twenty, thirty or forty years it was probably worse – but surely there is a happy medium that could be found between rituals like that and today's culture, where you have young players strutting around on massive contracts, having never kicked a ball for the first team, thinking they've made it. YTS players of today are driving BMWs; we were on £27.50 a week (£5 of which I had to give to Mum). They're indulged with the very best facilities; our gym had three machines, all broken, and one punching ball. Everything's done for them now and they're wrapped in cotton wool, and I don't think it's a good grounding. What happened in the dressing room that day didn't leave lasting scars, but did leave in me a clear feeling of frustration that young players now don't have that respect for the first team. It makes me feel that some risk being lost to the game because things are too easy, too early.

Ultimately, I wanted to be a professional footballer and was driven to get to the stage where people looked up to me as one of those guys. That environment was part of what pushed me. If I'd had the benefits today's young players get, would that have helped me? Would I have tried as hard? Would I have been as grounded, and had the same desperation to do whatever it took to climb that ladder?

We had a good youth side and we held our own against bigger clubs. On the training pitch, though, I started to feel my little snowball ego shrink. Why? In the amateur leagues, I'd stood out. Now I was at the bottom of a different ladder. I was training with the under-18s over here, and the Carlisle first team were training over there. It felt miles away. I'd become accustomed to praise and attention. Without that, doubts crept in and I found that my glass was half empty.

Am I actually going to make it?

Am I going to be strong enough?

Am I too small?

This was the first time I had to confront that kind of pessimism, but it wouldn't be the last. Whenever I felt I was falling short of the absolute peak of where I could be, that would fuel my self-doubt.

Maybe I'm not going to be a footballer.

Maybe this is all a bad idea.

Maybe I'll be a postman or something.

At one point, weighed down by teenage angst, I approached Dad and suggested I might pack the game in. We sat down and talked it through. I realised I couldn't bring myself to walk away. Or maybe I didn't have the balls to do it.

I needed to restore my self-belief and that could only come through a gradual process of playing better, scoring goals and silencing the sceptical voice inside my head. In this regard, my youth coach, David Wilkes, was the perfect mentor. Wilkesy, a former Barnsley player, had gone into coaching after injured knee ligaments cut short his career. He was an easy-going, soft-natured, nice guy who praised and encouraged me relentlessly. He thought I was a superstar and told me as much. And that's what I needed to hear.

There were times when I wished I'd heard it more from others – even from Dad, who I'd seen shaking his head at me in the rear-view mirror when we were driving home after a youth game and I'd played badly. The truth is that I only ever wanted to please my dad, and this was at the heart of my relationship with him as a boy. At that age, you just think your dad's brilliant. You idolise him, he's your hero. That's how I felt.

He was from a council estate and had a bit of a rough background. He was a bit of a warts-and-all man, although I think my mum was a good influence on him in terms of settling him down. He was a rough diamond, essentially. As a footballer himself he was a better player than he became, and maybe he then started living his life through me. He came to watch me play everywhere, and he certainly knew the game.

Because I was so desperate to please him, any time I didn't play brilliantly, I was gutted. He would praise me to the hilt when I'd done well, but he wouldn't hide his disappointment when I hadn't.

Although I was devastated any time he expressed that disappointment, I can't look back and say it was a bad or negative thing for me. Had he been different, softer, maybe I wouldn't have been as driven in my career. If he'd responded to a poor performance by saying, 'Ah, don't worry, it's just about the taking part,' I might not have gone as far as I did.

His attitude, his parenting in that way, the man his own background had forged, possibly made me. It may have been why I had the grit and determination I did. It's very hypothetical, rather than something you can judge in black and white, but my own view is that, instinctively, I probably had a bit of my mum's personality in me – soft, possibly too nice – and Dad had the drive that was needed to push me. I can't criticise him for that.

I can remember one time in my professional career when I reacted differently to Dad showing his disappointment. It was after a game at Walsall – I can't remember who for – and the family had come to watch. I hadn't had a brilliant game, and Dad made his disappointment clear. 'All your family's come to watch, and you play like that?!' he said. By then, in my early twenties, I was old enough, confident enough and established enough to brush it off. Inwardly I told him to get lost. This was evidence of my snowball growing, my inner belief and confidence swelling, my invincibility forming.

Above all, though, Dad was probably responsible for that snowball in the first place, for that bit of hardness. Ultimately, I was a success as a player, and what happened when I was younger led to that.

That competitive edge, the will to win, made me part of the most talented crop of young Cumbrians that Carlisle United had seen. A bunch of slightly older lads had already progressed into the first team – Rory Delap, Jeff Thorpe, Darren Edmondson, Tony Hopper and Tony Caig – and not far behind were Paul Murray, Lee Peacock and Will Varty. Scott Dobie and Paul Boertien were emerging from the years below me, while Neil Dalton, who eventually became the club's physio, also possessed a promising left foot. It was a collection of home-grown players that ought to have been the backbone of a forward-thinking club for many years.

With Wilkesy stroking my ego, I progressed well in the youth team, and made it into the reserves. I had passed one level, so maybe I could make the next step, after all. The reserves normally included a combination of youth players and older first-teamers. On the pitch, disgruntled veterans on one side would seek to dish out a few lessons to the youngsters trying to make their way on the opposing team. Against Wrexham, Joey Jones, the former Liverpool defender whose reputation for munching strikers defined his career, embarked on a one-man campaign to boot me all over the park. He smashed me, time and again – but I found that I could handle it. In my mind, I went back to Hack Football. I was used to someone coming for my shins, I relished the chance to show them that a smaller, lighter lad could overcome them with skill and balance. I was up against one of the toughest players of his era, a European Cup winner old enough to be my dad, and I wasn't a little bit scared.

In season 1994/95, the first team won the Division Three championship and reached Wembley for the first time, in the AutoWindscreens Shield. The city celebrated and Knighton was anointed as a messiah.

I had trained a few times with Wadsworth (director of coaching, not manager) and his first team. Wadsworth, a confidante of Bobby Robson from previous roles at the FA, was known as a progressive coach, and he had galvanised a fine team at Carlisle. However, he was not a man-manager. He could be extremely abrupt, and many young players regarded him with trepidation. In one of my first sessions with the top team, I realised our styles might not be perfectly matched. I received a ball at pace and controlled it instantly on my left. I shifted to the side and, with the outside of my left boot, bent the ball in a perfect arc for Reeves to head it home.

The other players were complimentary – 'Oh, Janny, what a ball!' – but then Wadsworth blew his whistle.

'Janny, what the hell are you doing?' he barked. 'That's so amateurish. You should be using your right foot there. How will you ever get better if you don't use it?'

Maybe it was his version of reverse psychology. Maybe it worked with other players. But it didn't do it for me. I wanted him to say I was fucking brilliant, to build me up to the stars.

Lads were uneasy about knocking on Mick's door, because

you were never sure what you were going to get. I guess some managers deliberately create that sort of distance, but the youth players would often discuss how odd we thought he was. You never felt like you were impressing him. You could be with the first team, and then be dropped back to the youth ranks without explanation. It's true, though, that being treated like that gave me a burning drive to prove him wrong and show how good I could be – which could have been his intention all along.

As my progress quickened, my two-year YTS contract was halved so I could be moved on to professional terms ahead of schedule. But when it came to negotiating my first pro contract, the club became difficult. We weren't asking for the earth, but Dad wanted to make sure I was being paid fairly for a player my age at a club the size of Carlisle.

One day as these discussions were ongoing, I went on to the training pitch and was spotted by Wadsworth, who was talking to his centre-forward and raised his voice as I passed. 'Fucking hell, Reevesy, this kid thinks he should get as much money as you!'

That made me anxious, as did the negotiation process. Knighton drove a hard bargain and his final offer was deemed unacceptable by Dad. I turned up for a reserve game and started getting changed, only to be told by Mick's assistant, Mervyn Day, that I wasn't going to be involved. I had to throw on a coat and sit in the dugout. Wadsworth appeared at my side.

'Here – tell your fucking dad that if all this carries on, you won't be playing for Carlisle,' he said.

I went home upset. Dad had consulted the Professional Footballers' Association and was confident of his position. He went into the club and laid it straight with Knighton: either I would be looked after properly, or we would walk.

Within two days the offer was amended – yet even then it wasn't straightforward. Initially Dad requested a copy of the new terms from the club secretary before signing, but that request was refused. Quite reasonably, he walked out without signing it. Within fifteen minutes there was a phone call from Knighton, citing an unfortunate misunderstanding, 'And of course you can have a copy, Mr Jansen.'

Eventually the contract was signed and I was on a lucrative deal worth £175 a week (plus goal and appearances bonuses), but it had seemed an unnecessarily stressful time.

Midway through the 1995/96 season, Wadsworth quit to become assistant manager at Norwich City. Day took over and, although the club failed to avoid relegation back to the bottom tier, the new boss was more my kind of manager. Mervyn, who had played at a high level, was more of a people person – serious, certainly, but urbane and warmer of nature. We got on well.

In his first pre-season, Day involved me in a few friendlies, and on one warm evening at Brunton Park I took what felt like an unprecedented stride. Bolton Wanderers were the visitors and the game marked the ceremonial opening of the club's new East Stand: a modern-looking structure which Knighton had built several yards out of line with the pitch, intending to develop and move the rest of the stadium with it.

I was brought on late in the second half, with the game scoreless. We were awarded a free kick on the right, close to the Paddock terrace which was known for attracting the more straight-talking members of the club's fanbase. I took a lot of set pieces in training and I took the ball. Dean Walling – a defender with a goalscoring knack that brought him cult status in Cumbria – whispered in my ear.

'Just do what you do, Janny. Hit me at the back stick.'

My inswinging delivery was perfectly aimed, and Walling glanced it home.

What happened next was incredible. Instead of crowding around Walling, all the players ran for me. As they hugged and lifted me, and shouted praise in my ear as the crowd went ballistic, it was as though a bright light had been switched on in my head.

This is what I want.

Footballers I looked up to were rushing towards me and lifting me in the air. For what? One decent free kick? My snowball ego rolled on.

Yes! I can do it! And it feels amazing!

The new season saw Day introduce a progressive 3–5–2 system, with a team that accommodated several home-grown players among older heads like Walling, Steve Hayward and Warren Aspinall. I began to make my mark: first my debut, in a League Cup tie against Port Vale; then on as a sub against Mansfield in the league; my first start, against Cardiff, when a couple of old-timers came for me, and I left them skidding on the turf. Mervyn told the press that he was obliged to protect me, so I wouldn't be starting every week. I wasn't yet in a position to hammer on his door, but a young ego is a tender thing, and any time I returned to the bench, or was omitted from the squad completely, it felt like another knock. I needed that snowball to keep rolling. When it stopped, the worries started again. Where this aspect of my personality comes from, I can't honestly say. I needed to feel like the best to maintain any confidence about the future.

There was a clamour from some supporters for Day to give more chances to the skinny kid with the quick feet, but Carlisle were at the right end of the table and the situation didn't really demand it. I had to accept what I felt was stilted progress, and so when I achieved another big dream – my first professional goal – it was not as joyous as that lightbulb moment against Bolton.

For the record, it came at Hull City, at a crucial stage in a promotion challenge which was surviving a few weird background noises, such as Knighton's claim, reported in the local *News & Star*, that he had spoken to aliens. Compared to that, the football pitch was an arena of sanity. At Boothferry Park, I came on to replace Chris Freestone and, in the ninetieth minute, found myself in the centre of a parted sea of defenders as Aspinall crossed from the right. I steered a simple header home and was briefly lost in celebrating our 1–0 win. But later, as I dwelt on things, I wasn't as happy as you might imagine.

I wasn't comfortable. I wasn't the best. I was a substitute, around the edges, not playing regularly and – come on – it wasn't even a brilliant goal, was it? Not enough to announce my arrival. Those were my feelings as I sat with my teammates on the coach on the way home as the matchwinner. I felt the same way as we got over the line to achieve promotion and even as I got to play at Wembley that season.

Okay, that wasn't *entirely* bad for the ego. In the AutoWindscreens final against Colchester, with the game tied at 0–0 in extra time, Mervyn sent me on to play twenty-five minutes on that famous pitch. I knew, as we encountered scores of well-lubricated Carlisle fans in every service station on the long way home from our penalty shoot-out victory, that I had been involved in a special day. We were pulling decent crowds and the city seemed to be enthralled by the thought of what could happen next (Martian encounters notwithstanding).

We had won promotion and I had played at Wembley. I had scored for the first team by the age of nineteen and earned a renewed contract of £400 per week. I had trained with England's Under-19 team and, if reports in the press were to be believed, been scouted by Manchester United. Yet something was missing. It was the spotlight, the feeling that I was the star, the one, the main man who people couldn't wait to watch on Saturday. That feeling was my drug.

I needn't have tormented myself so much. It was coming.

FOUR

ON STAGE

Someone must have pressed the fast-forward button in the summer of 1997. After wondering and worrying about my status, things suddenly sped up.

First, I bought a house. Okay, it was only up the road from Mum and Dad. And okay, I still always went to theirs for my tea. But it was an investment, another step on the road to maturity. Then came the big breakthrough I'd been craving.

I came on as a substitute in Carlisle's opening game of the 1997/98 season at Southend and did well. 'This is the season I want to make it,' I told the *News & Star* afterwards, and I kept my foot hard on the accelerator from there. I scored a consolation goal against Bristol Rovers and, while results were not sensational, a regular place in the side was finally mine. Very quickly there was talk of scouts at our games and, at a home match against Wigan, it emerged that Ron Noades, the Crystal Palace chairman, was in the crowd.

I wasn't the only young player at Carlisle drawing interest. Newcastle were looking at Will Varty, the centre-half. Rory

Delap was firmly established in the first team, while Paul Murray had already left for QPR the previous season. I liked the idea that people were coming to watch me. It started to feel like it had felt in the playground, or at Denton Holme, when I was the star. The thought really pushed my buttons.

Mervyn didn't hold back with his verdict on my displays. 'I don't think there's a better young player in the country,' he said in one interview. That was music to my ears, but it also put me in the sights of opponents who liked the idea of chopping me down to size. I took a few bruises from an encounter with Graham Taylor's Watford, for whom Robert Page dished plenty out, and more still when we played at Blackpool's Bloomfield Road.

The game had been put back twenty-four hours as Princess Diana's funeral put the country on pause. When we finally made it to the seaside, the Blackpool midfielder Gary Brabin had his crosshairs trained on me. We went behind early on, but I was still giving them the runaround when his opportunity came in the centre circle. After failing with a few scythes, Brabin came into me with a high tackle, and then clotheslined me with his arm for good measure. He absolutely pounded me to the turf.

As the lads rushed over, both to check on me and to confront Brabin, I was out for the count. I had only just started coming round when Neil Dalton got to me. This was one of Dolly's earliest games as physio and it must have been daunting to have to wade into that sort of melee to sort out a teenager who was barely conscious. He sat me up, threw some water over me and eventually helped me to the side of the pitch for more attention.

I was woozy and unsteady, but this was 1997, and protocols for head injuries were not as they are today. I felt the fizz of smelling salts in my nostrils, another splash of water, and back on I went. Another difference in the game as it was back then: Brabin stayed on the pitch. I wasn't intimidated by him, though. The opposite was true. I heard Dad's voice: *It's because they can't stop you any other way.* I remembered Hack Football, and the bruises Maradona wore like badges. I thought of the crowd *oohing* and *ahhing* as I stayed on my feet as the tackles flew in. I've since seen Brabin on the coaching and managerial circuit. We've laughed about that afternoon, and he also confirmed what I knew back then. 'It was the only way I could stop you,' he said.

Mervyn was also a marked man, not that he realised it. Knighton fired him after that Blackpool game in a move that stunned everyone else at the club. We hadn't started the season brilliantly, but we had only just been promoted, and Mervyn was still very well liked both in the dressing room and the city. Knighton came up with some stats about how many points he had failed to win over a particular period, along with arguments about tactics, but it seemed there had to be more to the decision.

Mervyn was a popular guy, who had his own radio show in Carlisle. Perhaps he was stealing the show.

His sacking is viewed by many Carlisle fans as the start of the club's decline under Knighton, which became bitter and almost fatal.

I felt for Mervyn, but for a nineteen-year-old in a hurry, it wasn't something that chewed me up. It did not deter me from the path I felt I was on, or the speed of progress I was finally making.

Mervyn Day: We were quite fortunate in the crop of young players we had in that period. Paul Murray, Rory Delap, Lee Peacock, Tony Hopper and Will Varty were very much part of the first-team squad and it was an exciting time for them all. Paul was sold to QPR for a lot of money, and we felt Delap and Peacock could certainly go higher, too. Matt, though, was one we thought could go all the way.

When I was assistant manager to Mick Wadsworth, I always used to watch the under-18s on a Saturday morning when the first team were at home. Matt would often shine in that side and, when I ran the reserve team in midweek, he came to play for me. David Wilkes was always pushing us to play Matt even when he was very young, because he had so much ability and balance. He could get past people in really tight areas – he could beat someone in a telephone box if he had to – and also had that burst of pace to get away from the opponent. When you have that sort of quality, no matter the level, you are always going to stand out.

In my first full season as manager, Matt was on the fringes of the team. A concern with all young players, especially ones who are physically slight and have that degree of flair, is not to burn them out. At that level, players like that also can become targets for defenders who feel they can be kicked out of a game. Matt was very durable and could take a tackle, but we felt that, if we got promoted, it would be the following season, at a higher level, when he would be ready to shine.

Although we had lost a couple of key players, we felt that, given enough time and stability, we could have been successful. As it transpired, Michael Knighton lost patience after a handful of games, sacked me, took over himself, messed it up and they got relegated.

Matt, though, made his mark before and after my departure. My last game, at Blackpool, was telling in terms of the reputation he was gaining, in the way that Gary Brabin absolutely flattened him, totally off the ball. There was a polite exchange of views between my coaches and Blackpool's manager, Sam Allardyce, as Matt lay on the floor. It was a particularly awful challenge, one that could have done Matt serious damage. When you have talent like that, you need referees to be strong and on top of the situation. If not, there is risk.

Challenges like that did not dissuade Matt. He would always want the ball, regardless of whether he was being marked, had been kicked, or had been having a bad time otherwise. Matt was doing it competitively in men's football at a time when you were allowed to tackle, and you were allowed a couple of free hits before you got a booking. It was tougher, physically, for players of Matt's ability and stature to stand out, yet he did.

My assistant Joe Joyce and I recognised that Matt was a free spirit and, when he was on the pitch, we tried to ensure we had a framework to get the best out of what he could give us, and – with respect to him – cover up his deficiencies without the ball. We had the likes of Steve Hayward, Warren Aspinall and Paul Conway in midfield, experienced players who worked very hard, and while Rory played wing-back on some occasions and up front on others, he was as honest as the day was long and worked his socks off. Having those elements in our side meant that, when we needed something different, we could readjust. To Matt the instructions were simple. Do what you do. Give us a spark.

I can't say I noticed anything of what he has said about being a glass-half-empty person who took time to feel like he belonged at first-team level. I saw a lad who didn't seem to have any doubts about his ability, which is why we pushed him to the fore. If he had crises of confidence privately, it wasn't apparent on the training field or on a match day.

I felt Matt was a Premiership player, and possibly an England player, in the making. It was just about him finding the right club, and the right team, that would showcase what he could do.

We knew, from his early days in the side, that other clubs were watching, and although we tried to keep players as long as we could, Carlisle were ultimately a selling club. It was the nature of the beast, and Matt was always going to go to one of the top-flight clubs; it was just a case of to whom and for how much.

If you asked me for one abiding memory of Matt – other than him being flattened by Brabin – it would be this: a reserve game, played on the training pitch behind Brunton Park, when he scored a quite unbelievable goal. He must have beaten five or six players and then stuck it in the top corner. I say unbelievable, but in hindsight it was perfectly believable, because it wasn't a one-off with Matt. He used to do it quite regularly in training. It was the nature of the talent he clearly had.

This must simply have been my time, my moment, because when we went to Wycombe a few days later under the stand-in management regime of David Wilkes, coach John Halpin and one M. Knighton, we smashed them 4–1 and I had the game of my young life. I was suddenly comfortable, and confident, with no trace of uncertainty about my place at Carlisle, or as a professional. It was as though I had evolved overnight.

I was on fire. I scored two headers, tore the home defence to bits and I knew I was the best player on the park. In the past, I had always deferred to senior players and never made much fuss when I felt I needed the ball. At Wycombe, I was bollocking much older and more experienced players if they didn't give me the pass I wanted. Steve Hayward, our captain and midfielder, had a natural authority and was also one of our best players, but that didn't matter.

'Give me the ball, Steve . . . give me the fucking ball!'

I didn't give a toss who was captain, who was manager or who was wearing the other ten shirts. I was only thinking of being man-of-the-match.

While Knighton, inevitably, took the acclaim at full-time, bowing to the fans and claiming ominously that he had 'never believed in managers' I knew what had really happened. From now on, I was going to be Carlisle's best player in every game. When I saw a mark of ten out of ten next to my face in Monday's paper, it underlined everything.

I'd cracked it.

I was a different man. If something went wrong, I would no longer gaze in the mirror and assume it was my fault. If I miscontrolled the ball, the person who had passed the ball was to blame. If I was tackled, the other players must have been in the wrong place. If we lost, it was in spite of my performance. If I was on the bench, the manager had lost his mind.

Off the pitch, things were different. If there was a fete at Wetheral, or a similar function in Carlisle, and the organisers wanted the emerging young United star to make a guest appearance, I would often shy away or ask Mum to make an excuse for me. On the grass, it was a different world. It was my theatre.

This new wave of self-belief helped me to survive the increasingly curious goings-on at Carlisle United. Knighton's decision to put himself in charge attracted lots of controversy, even if he didn't actually run the team. Mostly it was Halpin and Wilkes who took training, organised us, and tried their best to keep things as normal as possible.

Halpy, an ebullient Scot who had been a fine winger and was also at the forefront of the club's community work, spoke a player's language: clear and straightforward. Wilkesy was quieter, the nice guy – great for my ego as he was always talking me up, but never in a million years a first-team manager. He was just too laid-back and cheerful for that, and so it was completely bizarre when, at half-time in one particular game, he just lost it. All the players were shaken into silence as Wilkesy launched into a swearing fit – so out of character that it appeared almost staged. It seemed like it was something he thought he should be doing, because we were losing and he was supposed to be manager. After he had ranted and cursed, he stalked off into the showers. The rest of us couldn't help sniggering into our hands – but I also felt for Wilkesy. He'd been so good to me throughout my young career, and I still thought the world of him. The truth is that he had been thrust into an impossible position under Knighton, and maybe that dressing room reaction was down to the pressure of the unusual situation he found himself in. It just wasn't right.

Knighton's own input was minimal. He would come into the dressing room and give a thirty-second spiel, but it was just sales patter. It bounced off most of us. He watched training a few times, showing face – particularly when there were cameras around – but he certainly didn't take sessions or sort tactics.

A couple of years earlier, things had been a little different. When I think of Knighton now, I remember how he had joined in with the occasional youth-team session, living out whatever dreams had faded when his own playing days had stopped. By this stage, however, his proximity to the players seemed for show, or to prove a point of some sort. To me and the other players, he was still the chairman – and for all I cared, he could have been Prime Minister. I was flying, starting to touch the feeling of invincibility I was always striving for. That's all that mattered to me.

Steadily, the interest grew. After a cup tie against Tottenham, their chairman Alan Sugar said nice words about me in the press. After getting the winner at Brentford, Alan Brazil was in the paper, urging Ipswich to have another go for me. 'He reminds me of Gary Lineker – with more skill,' he said.

There were also rumours that Newcastle were looking at me, and that was particularly interesting, as I had often been to St James' Park with our family friend, Ian Gascoigne, in the era of The Entertainers: Cole, Shearer, Asprilla, Lee, 5–0 against Manchester United and all that. Ian had bought me a Newcastle shirt when I was younger and if I'd had my pick of the big clubs at this stage, I would have found it hard to say no to the black and white stripes.

That winter, though, I was linked with several others: Derby County, Manchester United, Liverpool and West Ham. Although we were bottom of the league, I knew I was the centre of attention and I absolutely loved it. This isn't the case for all young players who find themselves in demand. Paul Murray once described how, when the same clubs were circling Brunton Park for him, Knighton had approached him in the dressing room and told him that Roy Evans was there to watch. If he performed, he'd be getting sold to Liverpool. That wasn't what Muzza needed to hear. He was always destined for good things, but Knighton's pep-talk scrambled his mind, and he had a stinker.

He did get a decent move in the end, and at QPR he made it into the England Under-21 and B teams. I was a bit envious to see him playing at those levels, but soon the reports and rumours turned into something more solid. That December, Knighton agreed to a request from Derby for Rory and me to train with them. Knighton didn't describe it publicly as a trial, but that's basically what it was. Try before you buy.

It's not something you often see today, a club's best young players shunted around the country bang in the middle of a season. I can't imagine Mervyn would have let it happen – why would any manager want his best players risking injury and distraction on someone else's training ground? But as Knighton was now effectively in charge, there wasn't anyone to challenge his authority.

Around Christmastime, we were both dropped off the team bus on the way back from a Carlisle game, and got on the Derby County coach. They had a great side then, including Paulo Wanchope, Igor Štimac and Stefano Eranio and they were up there in the Premier League under Jim Smith and Steve McClaren. Rory and I trained with them for a couple of days, and then played in a game with a mixture of first-team and reserve players. Strangely, they played me at left wing-back, but nevertheless they made it clear they wanted to sign me. Knighton, though, said no – he wasn't happy with the fee they'd offered. They had better luck with Rory. He joined Derby in February 1998 for a reported six-figure sum.

So I came back to Carlisle, played again – and then I was off again. I didn't realise it at the time, but I was one item in an ongoing auction, that great wave of Cumbrian talent being sold off. I've often wondered how far the club could have gone if we had all been kept together. Next, Knighton informed me, it was Manchester United.

I travelled to the Cliff, their training ground, with Dad and we were collected by Ben Thornley, a member of the Class of '92 whose career had been hampered by serious injuries and who would leave United at the end of that season. We were introduced to the Neville brothers, Gary and Phil, and they took us to San Carlo, a little Italian restaurant, with some of the other players. The owner was Manchester United mad and, when he realised I was with their squad, he made a real fuss of me. We had our meal and a walk around town, and I was picked up and taken to the hostel-type digs where I would be staying. There were no home comforts or any of the trappings you'd expect from being courted by the biggest club in the country.

On the training ground it was better. I felt like I did well, mainly under the eye of Brian Kidd, and after a couple of sessions with the younger players and some of the reserves, he approached me with six words that must have put joy and fear into hundreds of young lads before me.

'Mr Ferguson wants to see you.'

I walked up to his office nervously, tapped on the door and opened it to find the great man behind his desk.

Like my digs, the manager's room was not as plush as I'd expected. The blinds were the grey kind you'd find on an industrial estate, and some of the furniture was basic. I had a split second to register this before he beckoned me in, smiling, and asked me to sit down.

'So, are you all right, son?'

'Er, yeah, I'm okay, thanks.'

'Well, we're very glad to have you here, and from what I hear you're doing very well. Now, are Ben and the boys looking after you?'

'Yes, they've all been fine.'

He chatted to me for a few minutes and was warm in his tone. Although he was probably giving my character a thorough once-over, it didn't come across that way. We didn't talk for long but he left me with some encouraging words when it was time to go back outside.

Eventually I got to train with the first team – Peter Schmeichel, David Beckham, the Nevilles, Ole Gunnar Solskjaer and so on – and, as unlikely as it might sound, it didn't faze me. I didn't feel like I was in the wrong place.

Ferguson had been watching from his window and appeared at the side of the pitch for the final twenty minutes of the session. The only time I was reminded of my place was when I hurt my knee and had to go for treatment from the physio, Dave Fevre. I was kept waiting, as the first-team players, Fergie's crown jewels, walked in and jumped ahead of me in the queue.

When Dave later joined Blackburn, he told me how one of those gems had been impressed with what he had seen.

'Who the fuck is this kid?' Roy Keane had wanted to know.

Whether I would be able to give Keane his answer wasn't clear as I returned to Carlisle. The experience, though, had opened my eyes. And I had yet another trip in store. Ron Noades was firming up Crystal Palace's interest and I had been invited to meet the chairman of the London club.

I travelled to the capital on the train, and this time, because Dad was unable to come because of work commitments, I had Knighton for company. We were due to meet Noades and receive a guided tour of Selhurst Park and the Palace training ground, but first I had to make nervous chit-chat with the chairman all the way to the big smoke. When we reached our hotel, he led me to the check-in desk. After the paperwork and formalities, a key was presented. Knighton collected it and turned to me.

'Come on, then.'

I followed him quietly, down the corridor and up some stairs, until we reached his room. He turned the key.

'Come on in. We'll go down for dinner at eight.'

As he opened the door, it dawned. There were two single beds in the room. The only room he had booked.

So began my journey of discovery to Crystal Palace – in an enclosed space with Michael Knighton. I spent the night wishing the budget had stretched to a second room and counting the hours until the morning.

Fortunately, things were more enjoyable once we met Noades the next day. Not only did he show me every last corner of Selhurst Park and the new training facilities, he also took us around both his golf courses, before welcoming us back to his house for dinner with his wife, Novello, and their kids.

He really made a fuss, and this personal touch hit a chord with me. While Manchester United had seemed quite formal, with Noades it didn't feel like I was in a Premier League environment. It felt more like a family experience than a football club trial. It was a homely introduction, comforting, and that made a difference to my thinking when the time came to make a decision.

While I hadn't thought of travelling from club to club as a particularly negative experience – I was still in my bubble, the talk of the town – Dad took a more practical view. To him, it was apparent what Knighton was up to, touting me around. He knew that some sort of decision would eventually have to be made.

'Either offer him a new contract,' he told Knighton, 'or agree to sell him.'

By this time, I had acquired a proper agent, the former Arsenal and England striker Tony Woodcock. He was based in Germany a lot of the time, which wasn't exactly convenient. As a result, Dad still did a lot of the talking. After a few weeks of shadow-boxing, Knighton finally informed us that two acceptable bids were on the table. They had been made by Crystal Palace and Manchester United, and I would have to choose.

Knighton, like many negotiators in his position, had been playing one against the other for a while to try to get the most for his asset. Derby had pulled out of the race, with Jim Smith unwilling to meet the £2million price Knighton had demanded, but Noades and Ferguson were staying the course. I had happily kept on playing for Carlisle as all this happened around me, but my mind was focused by the big decision I now had to make.

I had loved it at Palace. But Manchester United were Manchester United. I sat down with Dad and discussed the pros and cons. Palace were at risk of being relegated, but the chance of regular first-team football was greater than at Old Trafford, where there were so many stars. Under Fergie, it would probably be reserve-team football and the odd cup tie until I made my mark.

You might have expected a parent to try to sway their boy towards Manchester United, because it was much closer to Carlisle and the bigger and more glamorous club. But Dad didn't.

'It's your life and your choice. Nobody can force you to do something you don't want to do.'

We were at Brunton Park when these conversations took place, and eventually I had to go into the boardroom, on my own, to give my decision some final consideration. I closed the door behind me and collected my thoughts. I don't know how long had passed when I came back out and said I was still undecided. Dad told me to go back in and settle on a choice, once and for all.

The second time I nudged the boardroom door open, I told both Dad and Knighton that I had opted for Palace.

'Are you sure?'

'Yeah.'

The reasons were plain enough in the end. I had been made to feel at home by Noades, compared with the board-and-school-dinners feel of Man United – plus my ego demanded that I had to play. I didn't want to feel distant from the real action, or the adulation. I felt I could get that much quicker at Palace, and if it turned out to be a stepping stone to even greater heights further down the line, so be it. Maybe, I reasoned, I would go to Man United when I could be more confident of going straight into the team. If I was that good, surely they would come back for me later.

'Right,' Dad said. 'You're going to have to ring Alex Ferguson and give him your decision.'

'Really? Do I need to?'

'Yes – it's the right thing to do.'

So back into the boardroom I went. With my stomach flipping, I made the call. I really didn't want to do it, but managed to tell myself that this was the last hurdle before my new life in the Premier League could begin.

That gave me enough courage to pick up the phone and say no to Alex Ferguson.

If he was disappointed, he masked it pretty well. He asked what my reasons were, and whether I felt I'd win as much with Palace as I would with Man United, but when I explained it was about more than that, he appeared to understand.

'It's a shame, son, but if that's your decision, I wish you all the very best. I hope you do well for them. Maybe our paths will cross again in the future.'

I felt the last trace of weight lift from my shoulders as I came back out. I didn't feel like I'd knocked back Manchester United for good. I honestly thought I was making the best step for my career. I didn't want to be at the back of the queue again. Even at one of the biggest clubs in the world, there would be no adoring crowds at reserve grounds, no ten out of tens in the paper if I had to work my way up from the bottom again. Provided I performed, the opportunities were more immediate at Palace.

FIVE

GLAD ALL OVER

Things happened in such a blur. The conversation with Ferguson, the train back to London, then training with Palace the next day. My adrenaline was pumping, but I didn't feel any pressure from the step up. I wasn't aware of a culture shock. My confidence was high and after a couple of sessions with the Palace players, it was all go.

It also helped that, to begin with, I had an unusual arrangement when it came to accommodation. For my first few months, I would live with Ron and Novello. I don't know how many new signings get to lodge with the chairman these days, but I was privately thrilled. Ron had made me feel so welcome when I had visited with Knighton that I imagined his place as a home from home.

Their house was situated on a nice, private road in Purley, south of Croydon. There were some huge residences on that street and Ron's was by no means out of place. There was a swimming pool and a games room, and when I was greeted by Ron, Novello and their two sons – one my age, the other a little older – it felt like

I was moving in with a host family rather than being out on a limb in a city I didn't know. Really, what more could a twenty-year-old from rural Cumbria ask for? I was comfortable straight away, and wasn't staying in a hotel, bored out of my mind.

The team spirit at Palace was at odds with how they were doing in the Premier League. There was a serious risk of relegation, but people seemed fairly upbeat, even when I watched them lose 3–0 to Wimbledon in my first week at the club.

I played in a friendly at Wimbledon's old ground, Plough Lane, which Palace were temporarily using for their reserve games, and felt I did okay. Then there was a second-string match at QPR, and in no time I was being pushed towards the first team.

That was fine by me. I was nervous – but that was different to having doubts. I wasn't down on myself, as I had been when I felt far from the first team at Carlisle. The more important the fixture, the less fear I felt, because I knew I must have made the grade in order to be selected.

Even at my peak I always had to deal with butterflies on the morning of a game. My body was sensing the pressure to perform, and only when I got on to the pitch and touched the ball did this feeling disappear. It had been with me ever since cup finals for Denton Holme. It also had the effect of killing my appetite.

I was never a big breakfast person, and this wasn't a time when sports scientists measured your every calorie and nutrient. I felt I could have played football for the rest of my life without having had anything to eat beforehand.

My routine was simple. I would skip breakfast, play, then have a snack after full time, followed by a big dinner later. If ever someone threw a banana my way, or recommended a couple of Jaffa Cakes, I handed them back.

It was only when I signed for Palace that I learned that Premier League clubs did things slightly differently. The medical staff made up protein drinks and insisted that I drank them. I sipped away at them, barely disguising my disgust.

Maybe I would have appreciated them more had I felt a serious need to improve my diet. The truth was that I was in good shape and eating well. The reason? Novello's cooking, which was sensational. A restaurant would have been proud of the juicy steaks she laid on.

The dinner table was also interesting because of the conversation. Palace, it turned out, were the subject of a takeover bid from Mark Goldberg, a millionaire computer businessman, who had a ten per cent stake in the club but now wanted overall control. The media reports said he was preparing a £30million offer.

His plans were ambitious. It was an open secret that he wanted Terry Venables to come in as manager, which must have put Steve Coppell, the current boss, on tenterhooks. Goldberg had prepared two five-year plans – one that would take effect if we stayed up, and one he would put into practice if we went down. The big picture was a redeveloped stadium with top-class facilities, fit for the European nights that were Palace's destiny.

On the golf course, and over dinner, Ron opened up about Goldberg's approach.

'I don't want to sell it, Matt, honestly I don't,' he said. 'But he's offering stupid money. It would be silly of me not to.'

There were several remarkable aspects of Goldberg's offer, but the most significant seemed to be that there was no deal in place to buy Selhurst Park or the training ground at Mitcham. Instead, all he would be getting was the team – the players. Ron would retain the stadium and rent it to the new regime. My temporary landlord may have been Palace through and through, but it did seem a ridiculously good deal. How could he turn that down?

I made my debut as a half-time substitute against Coventry at Selhurst Park. We lost 3–0, but it was a meaningful afternoon for me. My first touch as a Premier League player mattered. As the ball came to me, I killed it, and Cruyff-turned between two Coventry men. Later I was named man of the match, which gave me further confidence. It was an introduction I could live with.

Another sub appearance against Chelsea followed, in a 6–2 defeat. Things clearly weren't going brilliantly for the team, but I loved these early tastes – even as the disruption at the club picked up pace, I saw little point in worrying as long as it didn't affect me directly.

A couple of days after the Chelsea game, Coppell was relieved of his duties. To be exact, he was 'moved upstairs' to be director of football. Goldberg had apparently been involved in the decision, and while he had now told the world of his plan to hire Venables, that was going to take time to pull off. In the meantime, control of the team passed to Attilio Lombardo, Palace's Italian wing legend, our bald eagle. Regardless of the decisions being made over my head, I just wanted to be on that stage.

Selhurst Park was great. The fans were positive and created a fortress feel even when results went against us. They played 'Glad All Over' and I was struck by the attitude of our undaunted supporters. It was in line with mine, and we aligned perfectly on a March day in Birmingham.

It was my third game, I came off the bench again, and again we lost – this time to Aston Villa. The difference was that I gave the fans reason to cheer me. There was a scramble for possession a few yards into the Villa half, I got to the loose ball and shielded it from an opponent. Simon Rodger took it forward until he was tackled, and after that it was like the fast-forward button got another push. I beat one man, chopped my way past a couple more and then feinted, before smashing it past Mark Bosnich from twenty-five yards. It was a consolation goal in a 3–1 defeat, but the Palace fans behind the goal celebrated it like a last-minute winner.

I felt glad that I had scored so early into my time at Palace. It seemed to get people on my side and I fed off the positive things they started saying. There were some big names in that team, like Lombardo and his compatriot, Michele Padovano, but if I could score a goal like that, against one of the Premier League's best goalkeepers, surely I deserved to be on the same pitch as them? I *must* be good enough.

Four days later, we went to Newcastle. This was a big one for me – close to home, a team I had a fondness for, and the knowledge my family and half of Wetheral would be watching from the Leazes End. Even better: I was picked to start.

The build-up wasn't conventional. Apparently there is a tradition at Italian clubs where players and staff toast a new manager with a glass of champagne over dinner. The night before the match, we honoured this ritual by raising our glasses to Attilio, and the mood was lighter than you would have expected from a team staring down the barrel of relegation. In Italy they presumably put the champagne away after one glass. But this was England. Some players whispered to bar staff to slip them some more bottles and put them on Palace's bill, while others had extra booze sent up to their rooms.

Much of this took place openly. I was still in the bar with a group of teammates as midnight passed, and it must have been around two when we looked at our watches and decided it was probably best to call it a night.

As we got to our feet and started walking unsteadily to the stairs, I saw Andy Linighan, our veteran defender. He was sitting at a table behind a cluster of empty glasses. His comfortable posture gave the impression he was going to be there for a while yet.

'Andy,' I smiled. 'I think it might be time to go to bed, mate.'

He gave me a look of weary disdain.

'Son,' he said, 'I'm thirty-five years of age. Nobody tells me when to go to bed.'

We left him to it.

It may not have seemed the best preparation for a game, and certainly no sports scientist would have recommended it. But something in that impromptu session worked. Maybe it was just what the team needed.

I've never suffered from hangovers and I felt fresh as I walked out and looked up at St James' Park's massive stands. I started the game at full speed and we took an early lead. Then, when Shay Given parried a Tomas Brolin shot at the Leazes End, I pounced at close range to score.

You can't imagine how that felt – especially when we held on for a 2–1 victory. The next day, I was named Star Man in *The Sun*, who called me 'a real discovery'. *The Independent* said I had been 'a revelation'. It had the same effect as getting ten out of ten for Carlisle at Wycombe. I felt like the man.

Linighan? Unused sub.

It wasn't long after this that England called. I was named in the Under-21 squad to face Switzerland in Aarau, which came as a surprise, because I had no idea I was being scouted. I didn't make it into the team, but I found myself around some highly regarded players like Jamie Redknapp, Emile Heskey and Nicky Barmby. It was another reason to feel like I belonged at the top.

I felt unbeatable; but Palace weren't. Sadly, the Newcastle win was a rarity. The Goldberg situation was making the club unstable and among the squad things weren't much better. Lombardo was a sound guy, and probably the biggest name at the club. He liked a laugh but was also very professional. His problem was that he hardly spoke any English and, as a result, he was accompanied by this small guy everywhere he went – his translator and a bit of a gofer.

The squad was also padded out – and I use the word advisedly – by Brolin. The Sweden legend wasn't exactly in the best shape of his life when he came to Palace. He had made his name at the 1994 World Cup with some big goals and that twirling celebration of his, but now he seemed to be living off those old days. His performances were poor, he was clearly overweight, often turned up late for training, and the smell of alcohol sometimes followed him. His profile, which probably appealed to Goldberg, was making promises his body couldn't keep.

Others struggled to live up to their names. Padovano was on his last legs, nothing like the force he had been in Italy. Then there was Saša Ćurčić.

Saša had signed from Aston Villa a couple of months after my move. He was a naturally gifted player, but also what you might call a bit of a character. I had forgotten that our paths had briefly crossed in that Bolton friendly at Carlisle. While I was enjoying my moment, his night had gone differently. There was a brawl in the penalty area that resulted in Saša being sent off. That, I should have realised, was a hint at the fire in him. He was unorthodox in every way. On the pitch he could be brilliant, but erratic. This made him a good fit for that era at Palace. It wasn't a settled place, but I tried not to let that bother me much. I was gaining great experience and showing off whenever I got a chance. We were eventually relegated, but I can't say I was crestfallen. It was a blow for everyone, but we all thought it was going to be a temporary dip. Goldberg was poised to throw money at everything, Venables would be coming in, so what was there to worry about? We would be back in the Premier League in a year, and on the sort of ride others could only dream about.

Towards the end of that season I was called up again by the Under-21s and this time made my debut against Sweden. An ankle injury ruled me out of the Toulon Tournament in the summer, but that didn't matter as much as the knowledge I was in the thoughts of the decision makers at international level. Everything was going well for me. My snowball ego was getting bigger all the time.

In the spring, I had been back to Carlisle to watch my mate Charles Shepherd win a Lonsdale Belt in a big boxing bout at the city's Sands Centre. He then returned the favour by coming down to watch me play in Palace's last game of the season. Afterwards, the plan was to head back north for a few weeks – but this was delayed when, in London, a motorcycle clipped my car, scraping its side. The rider pulled up, made out like he was shaken up, and gave me his number. When I called it that night, there was no answer. Charming.

I ended up having to pay for the damage myself. I took my car into a garage in Croydon, and while the repairs were carried out, I was loaned a replacement: a purple Nissan Micra. It wasn't the most obvious look for a newly fledged Premier League striker or a champion boxer, but that was how we rolled in the summer of '98. We made a snap decision to head to Cornwall for a couple of days, but neither of us did any research into how long it would take to drive from south London to the far south-west.

It was a warm day as we chugged along in the purple box on wheels, me driving and Charlie nodding off in the passenger seat. We paused for a breather and then swapped places, and it was my turn to drift off to sleep when I felt a bump-bump-bump-bump-bump . . .

I came to with a start to see that we had veered across the road and introduced the Micra to the central reservation. This had also brought Charlie to his senses, as he had woken from his own slumber to bring the car to a safe halt.

We laughed nervously as we stopped to inspect the car. The bumper was damaged, but little else. 'I'd better drive from here,' I said.

Thankfully, that summer ended better than it had started. Although I'd only played a handful of games, I was named Palace's young player of the season by a couple of supporters' groups. Ron was still chairman, because the takeover hadn't yet been finalised, but Goldberg was on the scene and telling anyone who would listen that he wanted to sort me out with a new, long-term contract.

I called Tony Woodcock. He still wasn't the most proactive of agents – I felt I was telling him how to do his job half the time – but for this task he actually flew over from Germany, accompanied by his boss.

We met and discussed how we would approach negotiations. We agreed on what I imagined to be a standard line: aim reasonably high but, as things go on, make it clear that there is a number below which we won't agree to a deal.

Even if Woodcock came out of the room with the lowest amount we had discussed, I'd be quids in. If we got everything we were going to ask for – a solid wage, decent bonuses and a contract lasting three or four years – then happy days.

Woodcock went into battle with Goldberg and, when he reappeared half an hour later, beckoned me towards his Mercedes. We sped off to a nearby hotel for a debrief. Over coffee, he explained how challenging the discussions had been.

'Matt,' he said, 'they've agreed to everything.'

Not just that – they'd offered even more. What else would Matt like? Would he be willing to sign for six years? How about an appearance fee? A goal bonus? A loyalty bonus? A bonus bonus?

As Tony recounted the discussion, it was clear we weren't just pushing at an open door – we'd been offered the keys to the mansion. We went back in and signed the deal. It was worth a basic twelve grand a week, rising each year, with bonuses and clauses that had the potential to seriously stack up.

I had started on three grand when I joined Palace. This had been a life-changing afternoon, and it had come easily. But it was never the money that fired me. It was a nice position to be in, so soon after getting modest amounts at Carlisle, and I could now afford the BMW Z4 I'd had my eye on. For me, though, the new contract meant that I must have made it. If Palace were throwing everything at me, it was because I'd proved myself among the best players in the country. I already knew that the next time I went on the pitch, there would be even fewer obstacles in my path. It was only a question of how much I could achieve.

It helped that I was in some good company as I set off on the next leg of the journey. I was exploring a new world in London and broadening my outlook because of some of the players I now knew.

Hermann Hreiðarsson was one of the best. He was an excellent defender and also became a close friend. He came to Wetheral a few times, and also invited me to his homeland over the summer. He came from the Westman Islands, off the south coast of Iceland, and was keen to show me its thermal lakes, cliffs and natural spas. That sounded like an adventure worth having, so I booked a flight and arranged for Hermann to collect me at the airport.

After proceeding through customs, I collected my cases, came out of the airport's front gates and breathed the fresh air. As I prepared to set off and look for Hermann, I saw three men walking towards me. Before I could get my bearings, they sped up in my direction and grabbed my arms. One pulled a hood over my head and the others forced my hands behind my back, roughly tying them together. They dragged me a few paces until I heard the doors of what sounded like a van being unlocked and opened. I was thrown in, and the vehicle then zoomed off, destination unknown.

I was inside this strange nightmare as I bumped along in

the dark. I lost all sense of how much time had passed but, eventually, the doors slid open and I was hauled back outside. I was frogmarched into a building which seemed, from the echoes, to be the size of a warehouse.

I heard the sound of chair legs being scraped across the floor. 'Sit down.'

I sat listening to several men arguing loudly in, I could only presume, Icelandic.

When the shouting subsided, I sensed something splashing next to my chair. A liquid was being poured around me, but I didn't have the time to figure out exactly what it was because, finally, my hood was whipped off – and there in front of me, roaring with laughter, was Hermann.

There's a lot to be said for the Icelandic sense of humour, I suppose.

The rest of the trip passed by a little more enjoyably, but with further hazards. After exploring part of the island in a dinghy, with whales nearby, there was the great Icelandic art of puffin hunting. There were hordes of them on the cliffs and the technique involved lying down and stealthily sneaking up to one of the poor birds to catch it in a net.

'Then you just grab it!' Hermann had roared in explanation. I crawled all over a rock trying to catch one of these bloody puffins and eventually managed to swipe at one with my net – it turned around and took a massive chunk out of my hand with its beak. As blood trickled down my wrist and the puffin waddled off, I figured it was probably best to leave it to the experts.

Another night, we went to a restaurant, where Hermann translated the menu. He assured me our options included sheep's brains and eyeballs. 'You have to eat this if you come to Iceland,' he said, with a big grin.

Again, I hope he was joking.

Back home, things were surreal in a different way. The Venables era was almost with us. It was finally confirmed that the former England manager would be arriving at Palace in June. The newspapers suggested he had been made a ridiculous offer to leave his previous job with the Australian national team. Given how my own contract talks had panned out, I can't imagine El Tel had to drive too hard a bargain.

I was twenty, having the time of my life and looking forward to making the most of it. If a big-talking man in a suit is making all this a little easier for you, so be it. You don't waste time checking if the foundations are solid. You certainly don't give a second's thought to the idea it might all come back and bite that big-talking man a great deal harder than that puffin had gone for my hand.

SIX

LEAVING THE CIRCUS

I couldn't wait to work with Terry Venables. It was only two years since he had taken England to the brink of glory at Euro '96 and he was known as a great man-manager. Even at a dysfunctional club like Palace, it felt like he would have the players' respect from the start. If anyone was wavering, day one of pre-season under the new boss quickly clarified things.

At Carlisle, I had been used to a traditional July. Roughly translated, the schedule was as follows. Morning: Run your bollocks off. Afternoon: Run your bollocks off. It was one long grind, running until you were sick. When the footballs finally appeared, some time toward the end of the month, it felt like Christmas morning.

Under Venables, it was different. There was fitness work, but not at the same intensity. On the first Monday the balls were already out, and at the end of the session, he got us all together.

'Okay lads, we're at Crystal Palace running track tomorrow.'

We looked at each other, bracing ourselves for a day of toil. The following morning, we gathered at the track and went through our warm-up stretches. Then we were put into groups, and waited for the hell to unfold.

This is what happened.

1) 400m at jogging pace.

2) 400m sprint.

3) 200m sprint.

4) 100m sprint.

The final group of lads dipped over the finish line as the rest of us wondered what else would be in store in the afternoon.

'Right lads, that's us. Off tomorrow, see you Thursday.'

Now *that's* a pre-season! No wonder players loved El Tel.

The Venables era began in earnest with the Intertoto Cup, a bizarre summer tournament that offered clubs a route into the UEFA Cup if they hadn't qualified the normal ways. Venables wanted nothing to do with it. In his view, the risk of injuries before the league season started outweighed the slim passageway to European competition. He didn't even take the team for the first leg of our tie with the Turkish club Samsunspor, leaving his assistant Terry Fenwick in charge. We lost 2–0 at home and then, with Venables reluctantly taking the reins for the return leg, we were finished off by the same scoreline. The fact our team coach was pelted with rocks by Turkish fans probably didn't improve his opinion of the competition.

It wasn't a promising start, but that tournament had never been our objective. We were being geared for an all-out attack on the First Division. There had been an international recruitment drive as Goldberg, whose takeover was now complete, brought in players from far and wide. There was an Israeli left-back, David Amsalem, the Australian winger Nicky Rizzo from Liverpool, a French defender called Valerian Ismael and the Chinese pair, Sun Jihai and Fan Zhiyi.

It was all quite exciting – until you realised many of them weren't all that great. Sun and Fan came with enormous profiles and attracted a great deal of curiosity as they were unveiled by Venables. They were like Beckhams of the Far East – it was reported that their debut against Bury was watched by five hundred million people on television. Great for marketing, but that did not mean they were necessarily an immediate fit at Palace.

Venables, on the other hand, seemed perfect for me. He was known as a good tactician, but he also seemed to identify that complicated team-talks and detailed instructions weren't necessarily going to get the best from me. While most of the squad were involved in shape sessions the day before a match, he started to excuse me from them. This, Venables said, was because I'd always disrupt things by getting the ball and dribbling around people.

'Go and practise your free kicks, or play some head tennis,' he said. 'Go on, off you go.'

I loved that. It meant I didn't have to overthink things or be analytical about systems and structures, defending corners and the like. If management is about getting the best out of individuals and knowing what makes each person tick, Venables nailed that. He realised I was at my best when I could go on to the pitch and basically do as I pleased.

Our opening league game against Bolton was on a sweltering hot day and Selhurst Park heaved with anticipation. Palace had laid on a calypso band and also, in case things felt too exotic, Chas and Dave. It felt that the script was written for me when I scored our opening goal. It was probably a sign of things to come, though, when Bolton ripped it up, scoring a late equaliser which meant we had to settle for a 2–2 draw.

We had a team that should have challenged, but we stuttered out of the blocks. After all the build-up, and the spending, it must have been a let-down to the supporters. Inside the club, we also wondered when the new faces in the dressing room would start to click.

The Chinese lads were nice guys, though they tended to keep themselves to themselves. Hermann was a solid bloke and Matt Svensson was a good addition, someone who worked hard for the team, instead of a Brolin figure, living on past glories. There was also a decent bunch of English lads, like Linighan, Rodger, Dean Austin and Jamie Smith.

Expectations were high and when we met them, it was only fleeting, just long enough to give the fans a frustrating glimpse at what the team was capable of. There is a game you can watch on YouTube that, in isolation, might deceive you into thinking Palace were a cut above the rest that season. It is a 5–1 win against Norwich from October 1998. I score twice, and my celebrations tell you everything about my state of mind during this period. After the ball finds the net I sprint away unstoppably, and the word that comes to mind when I watch it now is euphoria. It's footage of a young player riding a wave, starting to realise how far he could go.

Around this time, I ended my arrangement with Tony Woodcock. Things had gone back to normal – me ringing him up to tell him about opportunities, rather than the other way round – and I needed someone a bit more proactive. I certainly found such a person.

Simon Fuller, who had managed the Spice Girls when they hit the big time, was in the process of setting up his own sports agency. He had Liverpool's Steve McManaman on board, and word must have got around that I was available, because an invitation soon came my way for an opening night for what Fuller thought was going to be his next big thing in music: another manufactured pop group full of shiny young things called S Club 7.

After the performance, Simon introduced himself and invited me to dinner at The Ivy. There, he asked if I would consider signing with his agency, called 19. He showed me his offices, and gave the impression of being a very big hitter. He sold it to me and I bought in.

I thought Fuller was going to be managing me personally, but I only met him a couple more times. Instead I was assigned to another member of his team, Kate Buxton.

Immediately, doors began to open to a world that I scarcely knew existed. She whisked me to concerts, after-show parties and London's most fashionable nightclubs. I was young and naïve and never thought to say no to any of Kate's suggestions. After watching the Lighthouse Family, I was led backstage and invited to meet them. I had no idea what to say. I shook hands and mumbled how pleased I had been to watch them play.

As part of these adventures, I was sometimes shepherded into a warehouse after a show. Young men and women came around with canapés and champagne. Once, I sat down on a comfy chair to find that a little silver tray had been placed on the table in front of me. On the tray was a small mound of white powder. It was all very casual, the most normal thing in the world. Many of the people at these parties made the most of it, and nobody looked twice.

I couldn't do it. I never dreamed of doing it. Being around it made me uncomfortable and I was far too scared to try something like that. When I invited my brothers and sister down to stay, they saw this scene for themselves. We'd end up having a few drinks and then going home.

You could see how that sort of caper could become alluring. It was literally on a plate if you wanted it, and these rooms were full of beautiful, glamorous people. In Carlisle I'd been used to nights out at clubs like the Pagoda and Legends – renowned in their own right, but maybe *not quite* central London – but now I was in the glamorous end of the capital, cutting past the lines and into the Super VIP zone.

I can't say it was completely without its attractions. Many lads of twenty-one would have paid good money to breathe the same hot nightclub air as Kate Moss, the S Club 7 girls and Kylie Minogue, especially if some of them happened to take a little more interest in footballers from Wetheral than you might have expected. But it felt surreal to me, and I felt out of place. I never wanted the clichéd life of the young footballer on the town, taking a different girl home every night. I still had a strong connection to home and the way I'd been raised. I was looking for something more.

The Premier League was six years old and Sky Sports had turned on the money tap – cash was flooding into the game. This included commercial opportunities and my new agent pointed me towards a lot of promotions and endorsements I found a bit unsettling. My confidence came on the football pitch, where I knew I could excel. Modelling underwear? Not so much. I was offered a lot of money to be the new face of Brylcreem, but I wasn't interested in that, or the television campaign for the mobile network Orange, who also tried to recruit me.

The further I got from football, the more I felt like running out of the room. I hated talking to lifestyle magazine journalists, but if football was the subject, it was a different story. Articles that talked up my ability and potential were fuel for my ego. One in *FourFourTwo* magazine described me as the best striker outside the top flight, ahead of highly rated players like Kevin Phillips and Robbie Keane. More stories appeared in the papers, linking me with bigger clubs. A buzz about my performances grew, despite Palace's mediocre results. And even if some of the stories weren't true, I thrived on them, like I thrived on the roar of the crowd.

The Goldberg vision had started to seem like a mirage. In September 1998, Hermann was enticed away from Palace by Brentford, two divisions below us in the bottom tier of English football. If that didn't exactly reassure supporters, it raised further eyebrows that the new manager at Brentford – as well as the chairman – was none other than Ron Noades. He had taken over the west London club after selling to Goldberg and was clearly keen to make a splash. Taking Hermann – for a fee of £750,000 – certainly had that effect. It felt like a mistake for Palace to part with a player of his standing and character, and there were more to come.

After the Norwich game, Goldberg had suggested in the press that I 'might not be fitting into our style of play at the moment', which seemed bizarre. There was speculation that the real motivation was balancing the books. Goldberg's dream came at a price he couldn't meet.

The new owner was realising you can't run a football club as if you're playing a computer game, spending money like it didn't matter. On the surface, it appeared he had the resources to back his ambition – he was always very generous. On one occasion, the other Palace players urged me to ask the owner if he could help with a team night out. 'You're his favourite,' they said. I don't know if that was true, but I called him anyway.

'Hi Mark. We're having our players' do in London, and we wondered if it would be possible to borrow one of your limousines so we can go in together?' Goldberg had a car business, and occasionally blended in at Palace by turning up to games in a white stretch limo.

'No problem, Matt. Are you sure one will be enough? How many do you want?'

'Well, there'll be about twelve of us – would a couple be all right?'

'Yeah, 'course.'

At training, I told the lads the mission had been a success.

'Nice one!'

'Told you you were his favourite!'

Then, in the changing room, I got another call from Goldberg.

'Just about those limousines – how many bottles of champagne would you like in each of them? Three? Four?'

'Oh. I think two will probably be enough.'

He met us in Soho, marched to the bar and kept the drinks flowing.

At some stage, though, the money must have dried up, and that winter it became obvious that I was up for sale.

I hadn't scored a glut of goals, but there was still no doubt in my mind about how I was performing. I knew it wasn't my fault that we weren't achieving as much as planned. I was playing relatively well in a team that wasn't. It might have been a selfish way of seeing things, but I was getting plenty of personal recognition, and that kept my spirits up.

It became common knowledge that I was on the market, as stories started emerging about the unravelling of Goldberg's empire. The *Evening Standard* back page had me going to a different club each day. Arsenal were linked, then Chelsea, then Man United, then Aston Villa, then Southampton.

Then Newcastle. One night, after dinner with Kate, we got in a taxi, heading for another party. She was a little the worse for wear as she reached for her mobile phone and jabbed in a number. The conversation was loud enough for me to hear who was on the other end: Freddy Shepherd, the Newcastle chairman.

He also sounded fairly well lubricated. After a few minutes, Kate leaned over and passed me the phone.

'Hello?'

'Here, Matty, man, don't fucking sign for Chelsea. Come and fucking sign for Newcastle, son.'

I was wondering what to say.

'Come on, now. You supported Newcastle as a kid, didn't you? Listen, we want you here. We'll look after you, of course we will. I'll get Ruud to ring you tomorrow.'

True to his word, Ruud Gullit, the Newcastle manager, called me the following day. He was a touch more sober in his approach but made it clear that he wanted me at St James' Park, if I'd consider it.

I would have walked to Newcastle to sign for them. It turned out, though, there was more than one team in the race who wore black and white stripes.

The following week I was left out of our league game at Bolton. There were reports afterwards that I had refused to play, but that was rubbish. I'd never have done that. I was invincible now, wasn't I? The bills were piling up on Goldberg's mat. Perhaps it suited the club that I didn't get injured. I couldn't know for sure.

A couple of days after the Bolton game, Goldberg finally came out and admitted publicly that I had to be sold. This was the final straw for Venables, who had grown increasingly frustrated by how tight things were becoming. Too many decisions were being made over his head and, even if he was on a ridiculous contract himself, he couldn't put up with any more of it. He resigned.

Coppell came back downstairs to take temporary charge. On the morning of our next game, against Stockport, he called me, sounding serious.

'Janny, I need to let you know that you're not going to be involved today because we've accepted an offer for you.'

Bloody hell. Okay . . .

'Come to the ground and we'll have a proper chat about it.'

I don't know why I didn't ask more on that call, but I did what Coppell suggested and met him at Selhurst Park.

It was then that he divulged who had made the bid.

'It's Juventus.'

Steve explained that the offer had come in the previous day, and I was due to go out to Turin for discussions.

I felt a rush of adrenaline. Juventus were huge, off the scale. They had reached the last three Champions League finals. Their squad at the time included Pippo Inzaghi, Alessandro Del Piero, Zinedine Zidane, Didier Deschamps, Edgar Davids, Paolo Montero. And they wanted me.

When I met up with Hermann and his wife that night for a few drinks, none of us could get our heads around it. The whole thing became more bizarre the longer we thought about it.

'Juventus, mate – seriously!'

'I know! Can't believe it!'

The *Football Italia* highlights show was at the peak of its popularity on Channel 4 at the time. We clinked our glasses and started roaring its signature sound to each other.

'Gooooooooooolazoooooo!'

I didn't get long to entertain the fantasy of fighting for Zidane's No.10 shirt. A couple of mornings later, things went in a different direction again.

Newcastle's approach was now official, and Arsenal and Chelsea had also registered their interest, but the next call I got from Palace told me that a different club had taken pole position. It was now possible that I would not be going to St James' Park or the Stadio delle Alpi, but Ewood Park, Blackburn.

Palace's need was more desperate than anyone had realised. While Juventus, like most clubs involved in a transfer deal, wanted to structure their payments over a period of time, eventually amounting to £5 million, Blackburn Rovers had offered a larger up-front payment, but a smaller fee in total. Cash up front was exactly what Palace needed – to the extent that, if I didn't go to Blackburn, the club would be at risk of going under. That's what they told me, anyway. I felt like I was in a whirlwind. This was my career, yet I found it difficult to control the situation, or to work out who to heed. Kate was pointing me in one direction, the club were pushing Blackburn and I didn't stop to question whether any of the people in my circle had reasons other than my best interests at the heart of their advice. Looking back, I really didn't question much at all.

I sat down and thought about Blackburn. There were reasons for me to go there. Brian Kidd had just taken over as manager from Roy Hodgson, and I had enjoyed his training sessions and his friendly manner during my week at Man United, a couple of years earlier. They'd won the Premier League four years before and, with Jack Walker still pumping the money in, the club felt like a big enough deal.

In these hectic few weeks I had gone from being Palace's star player to the prized asset to be sold. Being at the centre of it all was both exciting and exhausting. Newcastle, in the end, couldn't do the deal they wanted, because they were eager to offload players as part of the agreement. They already felt my asking price was too steep, and a player-exchange element was no good to cash-strapped Palace.

Coppell had also been speaking to Dad about the situation. My father's view was that I would be better off staying in England, as I was still learning my game, but it made sense to keep all my options open. As Blackburn's interest came to a head, Kate told me that it would be unwise to get my dad further involved until it was all sorted.

In hindsight, I should have challenged that. Kate, though, was in charge of my affairs and very convincing in what she said. I was too green to interrogate her advice. The upshot was that Palace needed me out, Blackburn seemed to suit various parties on a financial level, and there was enough in the Kidd connection for me to think it was as good a place as any for the next stage of my career.

The fee crept up to £4.1 million and the deal was done. It was a crazy, frantic conclusion to a mad time at Selhurst Park. I loved Palace – the players, the people, the club – and I wish it had been a more stable place. I could hardly believe my time there was over, only a year after I had made my big decision to pick them over Man United. Unfortunately, the club had become a basket case, and it made sense to get away from that chaos.

A couple of days later I was at Ewood Park, posing in the blue and white halves with a football in one hand and a Blackburn scarf over my shoulder.

SEVEN

INVINCIBLE

Nothing could stop me. The confidence, the ego, that feeling of invincibility, it all came with me from Palace to Blackburn. I made my debut against Spurs at Ewood Park and one moment illustrated all of this perfectly.

In the forty-third minute, I lost possession near the Spurs box, but their attempted break faltered and the ball was sent looping back towards me. I cushioned it, and felt Sol Campbell, the Tottenham defender, pull me slightly as I balanced with my back to goal. I saw the picture in a split second. There was a route to goal, but only if I was prepared to take a risk. I flicked the ball into the air and volleyed it immediately on the spin from twenty yards. It flew low past Ian Walker, so unexpected a shot that the goalkeeper didn't move his feet.

It didn't matter that it was my first game for a new club, with thousands of new eyes on me. It didn't matter that Campbell was an England defender and regarded as one of the best around. I would have tried that against anyone. The only difference in doing it on a stage like that was the sensation was amplified. The rush was stronger, more addictive. And as my snowball ego hit a new top speed, scoring a goal like that on my debut removed at the roots any new doubts I had about whether I could make this move a success.

I found that I preferred playing in the Premier League, because you got a little more time on the ball. Although Blackburn were struggling, I was still surrounded by quality players, or a core of them at least. If you had Tim Sherwood, Chris Sutton, Jason Wilcox and Tim Flowers around you, things surely couldn't be so bad?

Blackburn were a family club, underpinned by Jack Walker's wealth and devotion. He had ploughed millions into Ewood Park and had shed tears when they became champions in 1995. As the weeks went by, I began to see just how much he cared.

He came into the dressing room, win or lose, to greet the team and wish us well. It was clear to everyone that this was a lifelong love for him. Jack had an aura, but also a homespun air. He would often lighten the tension on a matchday by reaching into his pocket and performing a coin trick for the players. He was born in Blackburn and lived for Blackburn Rovers.

I lived for the buzz. Another England Under-21 call came in February, to face France at Southampton. I came on at half-time, scored a goal that was wrongly disallowed for offside, set up an equaliser for Lee Bowyer and then won the free kick that led to Matthew Upson's winner. I remember a rapid young player in that French team – Thierry Henry, I think he was called – but afterwards I was more interested in what the head coach, Peter Taylor, said to me in the team hotel.

'Janny, you changed the game. I should have started you.'

I was interviewed by *Match of the Day* magazine around this time and, while I'm not sure how they persuaded me to pose with my shirt off, they did tap into exactly how I was feeling.

'My aim,' I told them, 'is to go as high as I can. The bigger the stage, the bigger the buzz.'

The same, alas, did not apply to the team. As the campaign went on, the pressure increased with each game and every poor result was a weight around our necks. It was, it became obvious, an ageing and transitional squad, whose best young players were yet to fulfil their potential. I suffered a knee injury which kept me out of a handful of fixtures and, by the time I returned, things had become even more tense.

The confidence that we would pull away from trouble had been replaced by something more foreboding, and that awful sense that your fate is slipping out of your hands. I'd experienced this at Palace, when the possible became the inevitable, and it was difficult to watch what the struggle was doing to Jack, who even came on the pitch at one stage, talking into a microphone, trying to rally the supporters.

I don't remember the fans seriously turning on us, even as we won one game in fourteen. I'm sure they were unsettled by where it was heading, but any serious flak seemed to pass me by. Maybe they absolved me because I'd only just arrived. Either way, as we tumbled, we could certainly have done with a kinder game than Manchester United at home to save our skins.

Against the team I could have joined, who were on the brink of winning the treble, we needed a victory in order to take our fight to the last day. We had to confront Giggs, Beckham, Schmeichel, Yorke and Cole. Kidd had to outsmart Ferguson.

We were probably resigned to our fate. We gave it our all, in an urgent game with a few feisty challenges, and stayed in it to the end. I missed a late chance, they hit the post, there were a few more scrapes in both boxes, but the outcome was a goalless draw and a future of playing Walsall, Stockport and the like in the second tier.

The cameras found Jack in the crowd as tears fell down his

face. That hurt, but it also gave us resolve. We would put it right. This time next year, and all that.

Leaving London for East Lancashire was certainly a contrast. After joining Blackburn, I'd moved into the Dunkenhalgh Hotel, an old country manor in Clayton-le-Moors. It was luxurious, and I wanted for nothing, but after a couple of weeks the novelty started to wear off. After training, I would go back to my hotel in the sticks and, other than the odd game of golf, there wasn't a great deal to do.

I accept this won't attract much sympathy, but the truth is I got a bit bored. I don't like being on my own for long spells, and every other week I would head back down to London for nights out with Hermann and other friends. Alternatively, I'd get in my car and drive back to Carlisle or Wetheral. While things were fine on the pitch, I felt a little bit isolated, and in need of a closer circle of people, some companionship.

Left alone for too long, a bored footballer with too much time and money on his hands can be a dangerous animal. Through Kate, I had bought a new Porsche Carrera. It cost an absolute fortune, yet when Jay, my brother-in-law, picked it up from the showroom he found it already had a few hundred miles on the clock, which was odd. Anyway – a Porsche is still a Porsche, a new toy to test.

When the boredom was chewing me up, I often invited one of my best friends from back home, Giles Vasey, to come down to Blackburn, watch my game, and then head out for something to eat. One of his trips seemed to be taking longer than usual, although my impatience was no doubt making the time drag.

By the time he arrived, I was all over him.

'Two and a half hours? It doesn't take that long from Carlisle to here. I'll bet you twenty quid I can do it in an hour and ten minutes.'

When it was next my turn to head north, I set about earning that twenty quid. I'd just turned off the motorway roundabout for Carlisle when I called Giles on the hands-free.

Fifty-eight minutes had gone.

'Get your money out, I'm nearly there!'

'No way!'

As I ended the call, I saw flashing lights in my rear-view. The police pulled me over and immediately twigged who I was.

'Do you know how fast you were going, Mr Jansen?'

'Erm . . . probably a bit *too* fast?'

'You could say that. We've clocked you at an average speed of 126mph for the past eight miles.'

'Oh. Shit.'

The policeman said they'd also got me at 102mph and would put me through at that. I already had six points and could expect the same for doing over a hundred. I went to court, where the judge bluntly dismissed my solicitor's argument and banned me for six months. I could hardly complain at my punishment. Sometimes a feeling of invincibility can be a dangerous thing.

Jay replaced Kate as my agent. There had been a few issues that had left me feeling uncomfortable and I decided it was best if we went our separate ways. It took a bit of legal work to get out of certain contracts, but it was worth it, because I wanted to be represented by someone I was more at ease with.

Jay had just finished his degree at Edinburgh University, where he had met my sister Clare. He'd been training to be a clinical psychologist but had reached a point where he wasn't sure that a career in that field was for him. We got on well and I had confided certain things to him, and it didn't feel unusual when he suggested he could look after my affairs. He may not have had a background in the industry, but he was smart, and I felt I could trust him.

After my driving ban, I moved to a rented place closer to Blackburn's training ground at Brockhall Village. Jay and Clare moved down to live with me, and he also drove me around for the six months until I could get behind the wheel again.

Eventually, I felt the need to live somewhere a bit more exciting and started looking at property in Manchester city centre. I found a block of nice apartments which had two connected penthouses at the top of the building. I bought one and became part-owner of the other – where Jay and Clare moved in.

They provided company for me, but a footballer's life still offers lots of free time, so I looked for other ways to lift the tedium. I invested in a grand piano and took lessons, which I found hard going. I didn't want to spend hours poring over scales and theory and classical sonatas. I just wanted to be able to sit down and rattle off a few Elton John numbers. I managed to learn 'Song for Guy' all the way through and later, if there was a piano in the lobby of a team hotel, I sometimes impressed the lads by knocking out a couple of verses.

When they asked me to play a bit more, though, I'd shit myself. I wasn't proficient enough to be able to show off. I liked the idea of being able to sit at the keys and command the room, but I didn't want people crowding around and watching me if I knew I wasn't that good.

That applied to anything that I did. When I went back home, I never felt that people looked at me differently just because I was earning a nice bit of money now. I didn't feel I'd changed and maybe this was why aspects of the new football world felt uncomfortable. I maintain to this day that I dyed my hair blond before Beckham got the idea, but he could have the rest. He reached for the spotlight and was happy to be so marketable. You got the impression he could have gone through a hundred different photoshoots every day. As with football, he worked extremely hard at that side of his life.

I felt the opposite. Any time I put myself out there, I was always on edge, waiting for something that might go wrong.

In August, I spoke to *More*, a magazine that supposedly highlighted football's most eligible bachelors. The resulting article made public my affection for the *Friends* star Courteney Cox, and also my seduction technique ('I can only make beans on toast and pot noodles, so I buy a takeaway, pile up some dirty pans and serve it up so it looks like I've cooked it').

It was cringeworthy and made me shrink away from doing that kind of interview again. If I didn't believe I could do something well, I couldn't stop myself from hating it.

The new season in the First Division began indifferently for Blackburn. We started with a goalless draw against Port Vale which reaffirmed how far we'd fallen, and pressure built quickly on Kidd. A gastric virus wiped me out for a month and a winless run had us mired in mid-table. The football was different – fast and physical – and we hadn't adapted well.

Training could be excruciating. Brian's philosophy was that the fittest football team would win the most games, which is fair enough – but you have to get the balance right. Apparently, at Man United, Ferguson would sometimes come outside, interrupt one of his hard sessions and declare that the players had done enough. I recognised this in some of the work we faced twenty-four hours before a game. Friday is often the day to take the pace off, make the focus more tactical and technical, and ensure something is left in the tank. But there were times when Brian pushed us so hard it felt like pre-season. After a while, some of the lads started commenting on the fact we were conceding goals late in games. It might have been a cop-out to blame all of that on being jaded from Brian's Friday sessions – and you can understand why a struggling manager would want to work a struggling team intensively – but it wasn't producing results.

Everyone liked and respected Brian, which made his plight tough to witness. At Man United he had been the good cop to Fergie's bad, and at Blackburn you rarely found players getting cross with him, even when he left them out of the team. Some people outside the club wondered if he was too nice to be a manager, but I doubt it was that simple. Football had become fickle where managers were concerned and results over a short spell could be fatal. Brian had been given a decent amount of money to spend but hadn't been able to turn the team around. He probably wished he'd been managing in an earlier era, when bosses were given more time to ride out a difficult start. A bit like his old mentor at Old Trafford.

Brian was fired after eleven months as manager. He got the bullet a few days after a miserable home defeat by QPR, and Tony Parkes was appointed caretaker. Parkes was another Blackburn Rovers institution, someone who would steady the ship when the waters got choppy. He was also, in the dressing room, regarded as the eyes and ears of the regime. His first game in charge was against Ipswich. When the squad was announced, my name was nowhere to be seen. I made it back in for the following game, against Fulham, but only as an unused sub, and things didn't improve from there. I didn't get on to the pitch in Parkes' first eight matches.

I was surprised and pissed off. It seemed that he preferred to use senior players and not, I felt, for the right reasons. As I sat out those eight games, I told myself that Parkes wasn't tough enough to leave out the strong characters and the big voices. He built his team around experienced figures like Nathan Blake, Ashley Ward and Egil Østenstad.

He didn't speak to me about it much, and it wasn't in my nature to kick up a fuss. That probably encouraged him to carry on that course. I didn't cause him any problems, even though I felt he was crazy to put others in my place.

Something in my attitude had changed, however. If this had happened at Carlisle, before my ten out of ten against Wycombe, I would have turned in on myself. I would have searched for all the things I was doing wrong and started to doubt whether I was good enough after all.

Not anymore. My ego now shut down any idea that I was out of the side on merit. Even when some people said that I'd lost my place because Tony preferred a more direct style of play, I thought that was bollocks. I'd always been decent in the air and would win my share of flick-ons. Surely everyone knew by now that I loved competing with the big brutes and getting one over on them.

Instead of tormenting myself, I felt a fire burn.

Okay, Tony. You're weak. I'll go somewhere I'm wanted. Then I'll prove you wrong.

The anxious kid, tentatively climbing the ladder, was a distant memory. In the reserves, I resolved to catch somebody's eye. Rumours started and at one game for the second string I was informed that Rangers had come to watch. I scored two and set one up, but nothing happened.

Parkes, meanwhile, was making the right noises about my future, telling the press I was still 'an integral part of the club'. He wanted me to stay and get us back into the Premier League.

Why aren't you picking me, then?

My appearances remained sporadic, but then fate played a friendly hand. In fairness to Parkes, results did pick up over the winter and there was a time when it looked like we might reach the play-offs. That prospect, though, fizzled out in March, and at that point the club abandoned their plan to let Tony see things through to the end of the season. Instead, they brought the future forward and appointed Graeme Souness as manager.

Souness had been working as a television pundit since leaving Benfica and had made it clear he was eager for a new challenge.

Blackburn was certainly that, but we were still a big deal in a winnable division. The potential was obvious – if someone could reverse the drift. Souness was a big name with an illustrious career behind him and a reputation as a taskmaster.

A player always has his own selfish thoughts when a new manager comes in. If you're in the side every week, you wonder if he'll fancy you the way the old boss did. If you're out of favour, maybe the new guy will put you back where you belong.

From the outset, Souness made it clear that no player would be leaving the club until he had assessed everyone. Then, almost immediately, he started playing me.

When things go in your favour, it can colour your opinion, but I also warmed to the way Souness worked. As well as giving me the fair crack I felt I deserved, his image as a fearsome character seemed to be a bit of a caricature. He didn't mince words if he had something to say, but if he took to you, he was great.

It's not as if he had a hopeless squad to sort out, either. Team spirit was never a problem and the dressing room wasn't full of slackers. Kidd had brought in some good players and good people, and maybe it just needed a leader, an authority figure, to get things going again.

I loved Souness' training, too. It was markedly different to Brian's, especially on Fridays, because all we did was play five-a-sides.

'This is how we won European Cups at Liverpool,' said Souness, who usually joined in.

I completely agreed with him. Get your tactics nailed and your phases of play drilled. But if you're playing at that level, you should know how to mark someone. If something needs to be analysed, do it on a TV screen. On the grass, there should be greater emphasis on mastery of the ball. Small-sided games promote that. You are constantly using the ball, doing things that are relevant to the game. It keeps you fit and sharp, there is a competitive edge, and you couldn't argue with Souness when he said it had worked at his other clubs.

Those five-a-sides fostered a lively atmosphere. In a few short weeks, Souness had lightened spirits, and there was the sense of a clean slate even as that season was fading out. I was also very much back in favour.

On the penultimate weekend, we went to Selhurst Park. I opened the scoring but didn't celebrate out of respect for my old club, who were fighting for survival in all sorts of ways. Palace turned it around to win 2–1 and the standing ovation I received from their supporters afterwards only reaffirmed my feelings for the place.

Then it was Manchester City at Ewood. This was a big day, because Joe Royle's team needed a result to get into the Premier League. Our ground was awash with sky-blue shirts and, although the game was a sell-out, I'm sure some Blackburn fans had flogged their tickets to City fans. Others gathered on the embankment overlooking the ground, and it was one of the most intimidating atmospheres I can remember at a home game.

It's a strange position to be in, with nothing to play for while the opposition are going for everything. We had Souness to impress, though, and I opened the scoring. The City fans weren't quiet for long, however, as they came back to win 4–1, the mother of all pitch invasions greeting their promotion.

I'd assumed the fact I'd played well personally was going to be lost in the chaos. I was named man of the match but City had won and were going up and that was the day's only story.

Back in the dressing room, with the noise raging outside, Souness cornered me. 'You were top class today, son,' he said, then turned and walked away. This reassured me as the summer break loomed. I was surely in his plans.

Not everyone was happy, though. I hadn't realised that day how close I'd been to someone else's plans, but some time later

Dad recounted the tale. At Newcastle, the Gullit era had been short and not very sweet, and in his place had swept the great Sir Bobby Robson. St James' Park had regained its voice – and Robson had his eye on me. Of all people, a certain Mick Wadsworth was his assistant, and after the City game Mick had called Dad.

He was not in the brightest of moods. He wanted to know what on earth I'd been doing, playing like that? Didn't I want to sign for Newcastle?

He then put Robson on the phone to my father.

'I don't know what you're playing at,' he said. 'We were going to sign the lad, but now he's just put another million on his head. Why didn't he ease off?'

Dad responded by asking Robson how he would have felt if one of his own players had hidden for ninety minutes to try to ease his way to another club.

This did not pacify the great man, and the discussion was brief.

'Well, good day, Mr Jansen. We won't be signing him.'

I wasn't party to the conversations, but Dad was right in what he had said. I would never have deliberately played below my best. My attitude, had I known about it, would have been: if he really wants me, he'll come for me. I'm worth what I'm worth. Also, the show-off in me would never have allowed me to hide. Souness had put me back on the stage and I wanted to milk every moment.

EIGHT

UTOPIA

When you aren't in the team, the spotlight moves on quickly. I learned this during my short time in the wilderness under Parkes, as England selected a couple of Under-21 squads that didn't include my name. My reprieve from Souness came too late for me to win back my place for the Under-21 European Championships in Slovakia in the summer of 2000.

Instead, I booked a holiday to South Carolina and worked on my golf swing. Then my phone buzzed. Michael Bridges, the Leeds striker, had withdrawn with an injury, and I was to be his replacement.

There's never a bad time to be involved with England, but I wasn't exactly celebrating on the plane back to Europe. Would this be worth disrupting my holiday? I knew I was making up the numbers and I wasn't convinced I was going to join a happy camp. Peter Taylor, who'd raved about me after the France game, had been removed as head coach despite a one hundred per cent record in qualifying. The change was overseen by the FA's technical director, Howard Wilkinson. Taylor's replacement? Howard Wilkinson.

There are some managers who gain an unfair reputation, but the nickname Sergeant Wilko was thought to be a good fit. He'd enjoyed major success, notably at Leeds, but his dour, disciplinarian image didn't seem to fit with a group of young, potent players.

I arrived at our hotel and was introduced to the squad. Then it was out for training. After a few routine drills, Wilkinson set up some passing sessions. It was straightforward enough, except for the large speakers at pitchside, which were connected to the headset worn by the coach. Wherever you were on the pitch, Wilkinson came over loud and clear. The theory was sound – it saved Wilkinson from yelling for two hours straight. But there were drawbacks, particularly when the head coach forgot about the equipment he was using, or neglected to find the off switch. Every muttered thought was broadcast for the group.

'Oh, he's fucking given it away again.'

'That was fucking hopeless.'

'Fucking hell!'

Wilkinson was standing close to one of the other coaches, having what he thought was a private conversation. Every tut and sigh came through the speakers. We just shook our heads. It was laughable.

The camp was boring and regimented. I found it hard to relate to the head coach and many of the other players felt the same. There was little freedom. It was back to your room, out for training, back to your room, down for dinner, be there at this time, leave at that time, don't think about going there and definitely don't do that. Everywhere you turned there were boundaries and when you are away in a group for two weeks, the urge to break through them is overwhelming.

We started our campaign with a 2–0 defeat by Italy, who had future World Cup winners Rino Gattuso, Andrea Pirlo and

Cristiano Zanetti in their line-up. I came on for Carl Cort in that game.

We had a couple of days before our next game and a plan to escape the barracks was hatched. Nothing wild or reckless was on our minds – just a little freedom. A handful of players came out, while a member of the backroom staff, who wasn't a big fan of the Wilkinson regime, sorted us out with some Slovakian currency. We found a bar a few hundred yards from the hotel and sat down with a couple of beers. Seth Johnson, Lee Hendrie and I were the last to leave. It's not as if we staggered back to the hotel, or had caused any trouble while we were out. The following day, though, word of our little adventure had reached Wilkinson. After training, the three of us were summoned to meet him. This gave us just enough time to settle on a plan, which was to deny everything. How would he prove it?

When the time came, we sat outside Wilkinson's room and were then beckoned in, one by one. Seth went first, and came out a few minutes later, saying nothing. Lee was next. It was like waiting for a court hearing, when you're wondering if the prosecution barrister is going to be on his game. Eventually I was asked inside.

I found Wilkinson stony-faced and in no mood for leniency. He asked where I'd been the previous night. I replied that I'd been for a walk. He asked whether I'd been drinking at this particular bar. I feigned a frown and said no, not at all.

'Well, I'm sorry, but those other two have told me that you were.'

They had cracked under interrogation and left me high and dry. My reputation sank further at a team meeting later that day, when Wilkinson thanked Seth and Lee for owning up and then expressed his disappointment that I hadn't done the same.

The tournament fizzled out for England. I didn't get on the pitch for our next two matches, a 6–0 win against Turkey and a 2–0 loss to Slovakia that saw us knocked out. We were hardly national treasures in the first place, and when the story inevitably made the papers, the tabloids were all over the idea of a few bad-boy footballers tearing it up on international duty. It didn't seem to matter that all we'd done was have a few quiet beers. The FA took a dim view and gave Seth, Lee and me a three-month ban from international football.

Looking back, I can't pretend in any way that I wasn't at fault. I'd had a good season, I was a young lad, and I was bored, but I have to accept responsibility for what happened. If memory serves, I overslept and was late for training that morning too, so ultimately it was down to me. At the same time, there's no denying that it was still a difficult trip and it became a toxic environment to be part of. I should have stayed in South Carolina, but the damage was done. Now I had to face Souness when I got back to Blackburn.

On the first day of pre-season, he caught my eye.

'I see you got yourself into a spot of bother,' he said.

He smiled and winked.

To my great relief, Souness laughed off the whole thing. In public, he made the right noises – we'll deal with it internally, disciplinary measures will be looked at – but in private he couldn't have been less bothered by it. I was fortunate, I suppose, that our manager was the leader of the great Liverpool teams of the 1980s, whose fondness of a night out was legendary.

I was glad to be back in the fold, away from Sergeant Wilko's boot camp and somewhere I felt appreciated. It was Souness' first pre-season and he made it clear that we shouldn't be aiming for anything less than promotion in the coming season. I looked around the squad and found no reason to disagree. There was experience in Garry Flitcroft and Craig Short, a couple of canny new additions in John Curtis and Craig Hignett, and a couple of young players with a dash of magic in Damien Duff and David Dunn.

The build-up to the campaign enabled Souness to lay down his principles. He wanted us to play, but also to press. He would demand maximum commitment at all times, explaining that this had always been his way as a player. We were to get in the opposition's faces and play our football once we had earned the right.

That was fine by me. I always worked my bollocks off. Souness seemed to like me both as a person and a player. He had a habit of describing me as 'son-in-law material' and made it clear that I should express myself on the pitch. He was also, unlike Wilkinson, happy for the squad to socialise, provided we came up with the goods.

We won our opener at Ewood Park, 2–0 against my old club, Palace. The following week, the club and the town came together in mourning for a loss that would galvanise Blackburn and its football team for the season ahead. Jack Walker had been battling cancer for some time, receiving treatment at his home in Jersey, but the announcement that he had died still hit everybody hard. There was a huge turnout at his funeral. At Ewood Park, there was an immediate sense of responsibility. We had to honour his memory.

In our first home game after his passing, we faced Norwich City on a scorching East Lancashire day. Each player laid a red rose in the centre circle before kick-off, and they played 'Time to Say Goodbye'. People were crying in the stands and there was a pressure to perform that was quite different to the norm.

We held a 2–1 lead until the final ten minutes, when I controlled the ball outside the box and smashed it into the top corner. Norwich pulled one back, but the 3–2 victory was an appropriate tribute to Jack.

Souness signed Mark Hughes on a free transfer from Everton in October 2000 to add some steel to our team. Hughes was thirty-six, also the Wales national team manager by now. You felt his presence as he rolled up for training. Then you had to suspend your disbelief as you watched him train – because he was hopeless. In two-touch, he took four touches before losing the ball. He spent more time attempting overhead kicks and volleys than anything else. By any measure, he was shocking. But when Saturday came, he was right on the money. While his pace had gone, he loved a tackle, and in a physical division it was obvious why Souness felt he could do a job. He became a great foil for the younger, creative players in the team. He waged war with defenders while the rest of us buzzed around him. This helped me hit a decent flow of goalscoring in the autumn and, with Dunn and Duff growing in confidence and class, we parked ourselves in the promotion race.

Fulham, who had spent a fortune, were the division's big-hitters, but Souness had found a formula that seemed to work. It also helped that we had three young players – Dunn, Duff and me – whose time seemed to be coming. We knew we had the manager's trust and we thrived on each other's positivity. This also led to more public attention, which of course had its pitfalls. I didn't mind the headlines and the hero worship, but I still hated getting dragged into the extra-curricular stuff. On one occasion, I travelled with Jay to London for a radio interview, where Terry Butcher was in the studio. I stumbled over my first answer and a dark cloud remained over my head for the duration. I stalked out of the studio, fuming.

'Why do you make me do all this stuff?' I barked at Jay. 'I'm never doing this crap again.'

Jay tried to assure me that the interview had sounded fine, and that nobody listening would have given my tiny stumble a moment's thought. But I wasn't hearing it. I zeroed in on the negative and let it take hold. Because talking into a microphone didn't come naturally, I was over-critical of myself. I had no confidence that I could nail it, and the first slip had confirmed my worst suspicions.

When I was invited to present trophies at a junior football club's awards ceremony in Blackburn, I turned up late and left as early as possible. Afterwards, some parents wrote to the club to complain that my 'bouncer' – Jay – had ushered me away so soon. I didn't mean any disrespect – I just didn't feel comfortable.

The dressing room was a happier place. I roomed with Keith Gillespie, the Northern Irish winger known as Besty, who had joined Blackburn a few weeks before me. Keith was a nice lad who loved a bet and persuaded a number of us to get involved with a syndicate that shared ownership of a horse. We committed to the necessary stable fees and awaited news of the animal's transformation into the new Red Rum. Months passed. Nothing. Eventually, Besty called.

'Janny, Janny, it's running in Ireland today. Oh, mate, it's looking so good. Get some money on it.'

I placed a decent bet and thought little more of it, until I realised that several hours had gone by and there had been no word from Keith. I called him and he sounded very downcast.

'Oh Janny, you're not going to believe this. It was pissing it, absolutely pissing it, about ten lengths clear, then it fell at the last hurdle and broke its leg. It's had to be put down, mate.'

'Shit!'

'Now, I know what you're going to ask, and no, unfortunately it wasn't insured. But there's some good news. We've found another horse, and it's even better than that one.'

Fortunately, our other social escapades were more successful. As a squad we played golf together, went paintballing together, had a few beers together, and all with Souness' consent. This can't be underestimated in football. Enjoying each other's company gets you a long way. You pull for each other that little bit extra.

It was also refreshing that we were at the right end of the table. Until now, I'd gone from one struggling side to another. It had been a learning experience, but finally I had the prospect of being in a winning team.

Through February we established ourselves as contenders and I had started scoring goals for fun. One of our biggest wins, 4–1 at Bolton, was watched by the new England manager, Sven-Göran Eriksson. The papers said he had come to watch Dunn and me.

Really? Was he going to take notice of players in the second tier? I suppose it had happened for Steve Bull in 1990. But not very often since.

I scored twice and revelled in the attention. Maybe Bratislava was in the past after all.

In late March, Souness announced he was taking us all to Dubai. An international break had opened a window of opportunity for some warm-weather training and Souness felt it would refresh our minds for the run-in. He also recognised that packing a large group of lads off to Dubai didn't have to be like a school trip.

'Listen,' he said, as we prepared to board our flight. 'You can do whatever you want out there, as long as you're ready for an hour's training every day, at six p.m. Enjoy yourselves, but don't be stupid with it.'

It was as close to a week's partying as you're ever going to get at the sharp end of the season. We got pissed on the plane and were mainly left to our own devices once we reached Dubai. We went to the races, sank a few more beers, and spent the next day sobering up before the evening's training session. We repeated the same cycle for six days. It was a proper bonding trip, and also some escapism at a time when the season was reaching its business end. It was perfect timing from Souness – not that everyone appreciated this.

Our first game when we got back was the derby against Burnley. This is always a must-win game for Blackburn. The respective supporters genuinely hate each other and, from the Burnley end, there was a bit of negative press about our week in the sun – look at these prima donnas, lounging around Dubai before the biggest game of the season.

We'd lost just once in sixteen games before then, and it was sweet on several levels when we smashed them 5–0. I grabbed a couple of goals in the second half as we turned a fierce rivalry into a formality. The stands at Ewood were rocking and our Dubai trip didn't come in for much stick after that.

A couple of weeks later, Fulham got the better of us at Ewood. That took a little shine off the fact I had just hit the twenty-goal mark for the first time in my career, but it proved a minor blip. A couple of draws at Stockport and Wolves were consolidated by a home win against Huddersfield, and then we went to Grimsby and had a big 4–1 victory in the pissing rain.

Eyal Berkovic, who had joined us on loan from Celtic a couple of months earlier, shone that night. He was very good technically and was great at picking a pass. That night made us feel we were well and truly on course. Souness treated us to fish and chips on the way home – and then we dispatched Portsmouth at Ewood.

I was named in the PFA team of the year with Dunn, Duff and Henning Berg. The way I was now feeling, I would have been disgusted if I hadn't made the cut.

Victory against Pompey was the perfect build-up to our next game, at Preston, where victory would take us back up to the Premier League. Fail to win, and we would have another chance at Gillingham on the final day. But we knew how sweet it would be to start the party with a game to spare. We booked a private VIP room in a nightclub in Blackburn called Utopia.

Preston was another local derby, although not quite as heated as that with Burnley. It was another full house on another wet night. Just as Man City had dominated Ewood a year earlier, it now felt like there were as many Blackburn fans in Preston's ground. We had an early goal disallowed, and found it tough to break the home team down, but eventually it came, seventy-two minutes in. Short climbed powerfully to meet a Hignett corner and I got myself into an area where, if the ball came my way, I couldn't really miss. The ball bounced off the turf and reared high into the air. I jumped and put away the easy header, feeling a little nudge in my back as the ball found the net.

I raced away and ripped off my shirt, as players eventually crowded round me. The result was one of the only bookings of my career, and when, adrenaline surging, I later made a rash challenge, I was relieved not to see the referee reaching for his pocket again.

There are inevitably some nervy moments in the closing stages of a game like that, but I can't remember much of what happened. The reports say Preston's Jon Macken hit the post in the last minute, but all I really recall is how it felt when the whistle went: a massive release.

Preston were in the process of building a new stand at Deepdale and, because one of the walls was low down, it couldn't contain some of our fans, who spilled on to the pitch. Flitty, our captain, had also removed his shirt by now, and on his white vest he had scrawled the words: JACK THIS IS 4 YOU. Flitty later chastised me for nicking his goal – it was he, standing behind me, waiting to nod it in, who had brushed my back.

As the celebrations continued on the pitch, the lads were jumping around, singing: 'Utopia! Utopia!'

We were due in for training at midday the next day, but that wasn't going to hold back the party. In the nightclub, fans and players mingled in heady spirits. It made for an extremely relaxed final week of the season and, when we went to Gillingham the following weekend, nobody bothered to stop us from staying on the piss.

A few players were rested for the game, which was probably for the best, while Souness skipped the trip as he went on an overseas scouting mission. We shredded the socks and tie belonging to one of his right-hand men, Phil Boersma, and left a few others in need of spare kit before they could sit in the dugout.

Somehow we came away from Kent with a draw. I had finished the campaign with twenty-four goals and was starting to think more confidently about what might be on the horizon. A couple of weeks after that great night at Deepdale, I gave a few interviews and no longer pretended to disguise my ambition. 'Now we've been promoted to the Premier League,' I said, 'I hope I will get a few more chances to impress Mr Eriksson.'

NINE

ARE YOU NOT ENTERTAINED?

Promotion brought a new contract which, although the most lucrative of my life, wasn't the result of combative and complex negotiations. It wasn't quite Goldberg offering more than I had dared ask for at Palace, but it was certainly a smoother process than getting a few hundred quid out of Michael Knighton at Carlisle. I suppose my bargaining position was pretty good. I was the club's player of the year and leading goalscorer, I was moving into the last couple of years of my current contract and the papers were once again full of reports linking me with other clubs.

The club approached me, not the other way around, and there didn't seem any sense in angling for a move. I was the happiest I'd been in my career. I wanted to stay, provided the terms were okay. Blackburn wanted me to sign for another five years, but I was happier with four. After two years I might be in a position to renegotiate and go up another level again. One way or another I'd have pots of money in the bank.

It's not as if the good times are going to end any time soon, right? I'm invincible.

I was on a golfing holiday in Spain with a friend that summer when Jay concluded negotiations. I called him from Puerto Banus and he confirmed that it had all been agreed. It hadn't taken long and neither side had played hardball.

The figures written down in my new deal reflected my growing worth. I was elevated to a basic wage of £20,193 per week, rising to £23,077 by 2004, also increasing by £1,000 after fifteen appearances, another £1,000 after thirty-five, another £1,000 after fifty, and with a bonus structure that could further enhance things. There was also a new release clause, on a rising scale. Come 2002, it would cost an admiring club £10 million to prise me away from Ewood. The following summer, the price would be £13 million. In 2004, I would cost £15 million. These sums were topped up by a lucrative deal with Adidas that included a £1 million bonus should I ever play for England. I was now in a very comfortable financial position.

My earning power also allowed me to help my family with certain things, like bills and holidays, and I enjoyed being able to do it. Personally, however, the money was not a great motivator. I saw it as a consequence of success and little more. There was no glory or adulation to be had through a sturdy bank balance alone.

I wanted to be a star in the Premier League. I cracked open a bottle of champagne in Puerto Banus to toast Jay's work and recharged ahead of the new campaign. I'd never been more excited about starting pre-season. We were back in the big league; I was on top of my game and ready to show the country what I could do. If Mr Eriksson was watching too, so much the better.

A Souness pre-season was tougher than the Venables model. It was unscientific and tough – old-school. *Lots* of running. After that first blast of fitness work, we went to Austria and Germany, and then Italy, for a series of friendlies. As ever, he trusted us to have the occasional night out, but the emphasis was on hard work.

That wasn't a problem for us. We were a well-bonded group before and the fact we'd achieved success drew us even closer together. There was great anticipation within the squad about what the next adventure would bring, and nobody was about to jeopardise that.

There was also great anticipation amongst supporters about what the club would do in the transfer market. It was felt we had a talented squad that could hold its own, but the gap between the top two tiers had grown as the Premier League mushroomed. One or two wise additions are always needed any time you move up a level. Nobody wanted to see all our good work put to waste, and the best way of guarding against this was to add to our goalscoring threat. A new striker always gets people talking. And there was plenty of talking where Ciccio Grabbi was concerned.

He was a new name to me and many of the other lads when he came in for £7.2 million. It turned out he had scored a hatful for Ternana in Italy's Serie B, and Phil Boersma in particular was almost drooling when he told us all what to expect.

'He's a world-beater, this lad.'

Then he arrived – and the world remained unbeaten. He was a nice enough guy, but not quite the goal-machine that was going to fire us up the Premier League. We assumed Souness and his staff had done their research, and so we resolved not to judge him too early, but £7.2 million was a lot of money for someone who, on first impressions, barely seemed to be worth seventy grand.

We started in attack together for the first few games of the season and we didn't hit it off as a partnership. The team dug out a few points, but at times it was like playing up front on my own. There was no real understanding and the more he struggled, the more it seemed to affect his work rate. His number often went up when substitutions were being made. I suppose he must have lost a bit of belief along the way. Mainly, though, he wasn't up to it.

It took me five anxious games of the new season before I scored my first goal, against Ipswich. Ciccio did eventually open his account against Everton, but it didn't take long before Souness tried other options alongside me, like Hughes. Other times I did play as a lone striker.

That first goal back in the Premier League eased a little of the tension. A few weeks later, I scored again as we took West Ham to the cleaners at Ewood. They had a decent side – Michael Carrick, Paolo Di Canio, Freddy Kanoute – but we murdered them 7–1. If there had been lingering questions about our ability to make the step up, that game in October provided a definitive answer. We looked like a Premier League team. It also helped that some of Souness' other signings were of better calibre than the floundering Grabbi.

Tugay Kerimoğlu, for instance. He came in from Rangers and was a class act. He couldn't speak much English and didn't show much inclination to learn, and he had zero pace – but none of that mattered. He didn't need to run, or speak fluent East Lancastrian for that matter, because, as the saying goes, the first two yards were in his head. From midfield, he could pick a pass better than anyone at the club, a creator who was ideal for a forward like me.

He was also a chain-smoker, who comfortably got through more than twenty a day. Once, at half-time, Souness was pacing around the dressing room, waiting to give his team-talk.

'Where's Tugay?' he asked.

Across the room, puffs of smoke started spiralling from a toilet cubicle, like dry ice on a concert stage.

He would invariably turn up before a game stinking of smoke. After the first forty-five minutes he would light up again. But, as sure as one cigarette followed the last, he would put in a performance.

There could be a lesson here. While Tugay's smoking could have been used against him if he wasn't producing, everyone knew he was a class act. I'm sure there were some people who frowned on it, but when you saw him on the pitch, pulling strings, there wasn't much to complain about. In this respect, Tugay was a throwback to a time when players lived how they chose and weren't weighed down by Prozone stats or PowerPoint presentations from the analytics team.

You might not recommend the lifestyle Georgie Best or Paul Gascoigne ended up leading, but they could turn up to a stadium the day after sinking a few pints and still be the best player on the pitch. They wouldn't have been better players for filling their heads with numbers. They wouldn't have been more intuitive performers if they'd been forced to live like monks.

A player knows his own body better than anyone else. If the odd crafty cigarette hadn't slowed Johann Cruyff, Gianluca Vialli, Zinedine Zidane or Socrates, then it made no sense to force Tugay to stub out his Benson & Hedges. Souness wisely left him alone, and his quality helped us consolidate a reasonable start.

We had a decent defence, and a good goalkeeper in Brad Friedel. Midfield was solid, with Tugay and Hughes, who dropped back into that position when it was recognised that it suited the combination of his ageing legs and enduring love of a tackle. Berg provided calming experience at the back, and Flitty was a forceful leader. Dunn and Duff had taken to the big stage as everyone had hoped they would.

Many of the right pieces were in place. It was obvious, though, what we were missing. Souness' first attempt to fix our problem up front was to bring in Dean Saunders to work with the forwards. Saunders, who had just retired, would sharpen us up and pass on some of his knowledge. In reality, though, it didn't have much effect. Saunders was a naturally funny character, great for spirit and banter, but more often than not he just joined in with the rest of us. The sessions weren't noticeably different and I started to wonder if there had been other reasons for his arrival. One or two players on the fringe of the team had started moaning about Souness, his assistant Alan Murray, and Boersma. When you're not in the side, it can be easy to find fault with those responsible. Yet it seemed to me like the manager and his coaches were, with this latest idea, trying to give the impression they were doing something different. Perhaps they thought Saunders, who was close to Souness, would help dampen down a little unrest. Maybe the manager had told the board he was bringing in a striker coach to ignite the struggling Grabbi.

At no point, though, did Dean feel like the solution to our problems. The answer was far more obvious. When it eventually came, the difference was dramatic.

Eriksson and his assistant, Tord Grip, started paying Blackburn more attention as the season went on. A newspaper article suggested I could be in line for a call-up. Pundits even speculated whether I might be able to solve the legendary left-sided problem, which had been a national bugbear ever since Ryan Giggs opted for Wales.

I could dream about a call-up, but they'd be nothing more than dreams if I didn't continue to deliver for Blackburn, and that's where my focus remained as we started to build a run in the League Cup. Playing in that tournament, in the quarter-final against Arsenal, something changed for me. A special opportunity was suddenly in front of me and I grabbed it, and it felt like I would never let go.

Arsene Wenger held one or two of his stars back from that competition, a policy that had worked for him in the past. But we still had Martin Keown, Giovanni van Bronckhorst, Edu, Sylvain Wiltord and Kanu to deal with. Anyway, I'm convinced that Arsenal could have put their full galaxy of stars out that night and we'd have beaten them. It felt like we had cracked a secret code. Souness started Hughes up front and the way he sparred with Keown allowed me to run off him and cause some havoc. On the right, Gillespie was on fire; Tugay was the conductor in midfield, and it resulted in a complete team performance.

I can remember the crowd singing 'Are you Burnley in disguise?' to the Arsenal players – and I can remember each of my three goals. The last was the best: a counter-attack that started in our own box, before we passed it around Arsenal and Duffer was set free down the left. He played it slightly behind me, but it wasn't difficult to adjust and slot it home with my left foot.

I ran away with three fingers raised and, after the 4–0 victory, got all the lads to sign the ball. My first hat-trick. And surely not my last. It was an untouchable night.

Even an injury sustained in our next game didn't take the shine off things. I landed badly against Newcastle and my ankle ballooned. I left the ground on crutches, but eleven days later I was coming off the bench against Sunderland. I was back to full speed – and just in time to get to know our latest signing, and the long-awaited solution to our trouble at No.9.

Souness had first tried for Robbie Fowler, but he had opted for Leeds when leaving Liverpool. At the same time, the relentless goalscoring of Ruud van Nistelrooy had edged Andy Cole to the margins of the Manchester United squad and Souness saw a chance. 'We're a team that normally creates a lot of chances, but we just haven't been putting the ball in the net,' said the manager as he welcomed his £8 million man. Cole had made a career doing just that.

We started together in a defeat by Spurs that came at the back end of a poor run in the league. Souness then rested me for our Worthington Cup semi-final first leg against Sheffield Wednesday as I had a hernia which was starting to make itself known. From the bench at Hillsborough, I saw Cole get his first goal for the club as we left with a 2–1 lead. Four days later, I was back in the side as we put Charlton away 4–1. It was a massive win that kept us away from the relegation battle. I clicked with Cole immediately. We got a goal each and seemed to complement each other in style, because we could do both sides of the forward's game – either one of us could drop short to receive possession or run in behind. Our link-up play was too much for Charlton. So this is what it felt like to be in tune with someone in a Premier League attack.

I was excited to be around Cole. He was quiet and reserved but had a sharp sense of humour once you got to know him. He had an image as a sulker, but that wasn't fair. It would be more accurate to say he wouldn't let you into his world until he had sussed you out.

His arrival, in January, was proof of the club's ambition. Souness had taken command of the problem which had held us back and it was a signing that worked on more than one level. He was only thirty and still guaranteed goals in the Premier League, and a player of his experience, success and ability also helped the rest of us think bigger.

We both scored in the second leg of the semi against Sheffield Wednesday and that was enough to seal our place in the League Cup final – Blackburn's first major cup final for forty-two years.

Graeme Souness: My abiding memory of Matt Jansen? I'm sitting in the dugout as manager of Blackburn Rovers, and Matt has the ball. He keeps going with it, and I'm thinking, 'What are you doing? Pass it, man, pass it!'

I'm about to get out of my seat to give him a verbal volley – but when I do stand up, I find myself applauding because, instead of passing, he's turned an opponent on a sixpence and slotted the ball into the net.

That was Matt. He was unpredictable, which is a quality all successful strikers must have. He had that ability to do something magical when you least expected it.

I didn't know Matt before I took charge at Ewood Park. I'd been working in Portugal and had seen relatively little of him. I quickly realised, though, that he was one of a group of young players at Blackburn who had ability and potential. There was Damien Duff, David Dunn, Damien Johnson and Matt. As a manager, you're excited to have players like that. You see it as your job to help them progress as quickly as possible, which those four did.

He was very easy to manage. You can't get it right with every player you work with, but I had the impression that he came from a really solid family. He wasn't an ounce of trouble. There were times he would get disappointed, and drop his head a wee bit, but that would last five minutes and then he would be back. On the training ground and on the pitch, he wanted to learn and succeed.

The word I would use to describe him in games is *mercurial*. There were times he would be frustrating, when he spent too long on the ball and overdid things, but he had ridiculous talent, and I felt he was destined to have a super career. He also had an athletic physique, with strong legs and calves – and he was brave. A good striker must be courageous and this applied more so when Matt played as he faced some big lumps who could dish it out a bit more than they are allowed to now.

Something else that marked Matt as a player was his instinct. It's a very hard thing to coach in a striker: when to stand still, when to move in the box, when to anticipate, when to get in front of someone, when to pull to the far post. It can improve with experience, but the best players have that ability to see pictures instantly and react accordingly.

Take Matt's goals out of our promotion season, in 2000/01, and we don't go up – simple as that. We had a good side, and everyone played a part, but goals change games. That ability to nick a goal, even if you're not playing well, can suddenly put a spring in your step. Matt was responsible for plenty of that, and he proved he could handle the step up to the Premier League.

Whilst on this path, he benefited from some excellent teammates. When I consider my own career, I know I learned more from the players I played with day-in, day-out, through watching them and picking up their good habits, rather than from a coach saying anything in particular. I'm sure it was the same with Matt. At Blackburn we were lucky to have some very good senior pros – such as Craig Short and Garry Flitcroft – while in that first season back in the top flight I brought in Andy Cole to play alongside Matt. Andy wasn't the best trainer, but in terms of his movement in the attacking third, and his ability to be in the right place at the right time, he was excellent to learn from.

We soon encountered Arsenal again, this time in the league. Wenger had polished up more of his big guns for this one and in a feisty start at Ewood, Dennis Bergkamp and Henry gave them a two-goal lead. We then swept back and I scored twice before half-time. It was a proper game, played at serious pace, and throughout I had Martin Keown all over me like a rash.

He was one of the best at the dark arts, but, as ever, that just got my juices flowing. Climbing up the leagues had put me against any number of characters who felt they knew how to take you into uncomfortable places. Some were smarter than others. Roy Keane certainly liked to put it about, and usually got his way. Ugo Ehiogu was a mountain of a defender who did all he could to stop you getting around him.

Another side that comes to mind, from the tier below, is Sheffield United. They were a very physical team with an unpleasant edge, led by the player who typified all that: Keith Curle. His style was to lay on an afternoon of annoying, old-school rubbish. Standing on your toes, pushing you at random.

If the ball was at the other end of the pitch, he would take his chance to put his shoulder into you.

I'm sure it worked for him with many players. He didn't play hundreds of games in the top flight by being an angel. Me? I just thought, 'What a knob'. It made me want to go back up against him and score.

Keown was rough and a bit dirty, but I felt I was giving him the run around that day. After my goals I was flying and there was one point, late in the second half, when I was tracking Henry. He opened that long, graceful stride – but he couldn't get away from me. This was Thierry Henry, the kind of player that seemed as quick as Usain Bolt, and yet I was keeping pace with him. What was that about? Adrenaline? Belief? I stayed at his shoulder and shielded him into the corner. I'd love to have seen my Prozone stats from that night. I'd never felt energy like it.

By that point, Dennis Bergkamp had floored us with what turned out to be the winner. I'd felt, though, that I'd won my personal battle with Keown. The game had also ended painfully for him because, midway through the second half, he'd come in to tackle me but ended up in a heap. He'd suffered a hairline fracture of the tibia in his right leg, and he would be out for at least six weeks. It would cost him the chance to play in a series of England friendlies as the national team prepared for a big summer in Japan and South Korea. He was thirty-five, but still deemed to be in contention for the World Cup. One article gravely noted that 'Keown's World Cup hopes were now in the balance'.

Despite further speculation, I was overlooked by Eriksson for England's next game, against Holland. Bolton's Michael Ricketts was the next cab off the rank, while Darius Vassell scored on his debut. In any case, I had more pressing things to deal with. Blackburn weren't out of the woods as far as relegation was concerned. And we also had the small matter of a cup final on the horizon. Tottenham, at the Millennium Stadium, Cardiff.

That Spurs side had some serious players: Gus Poyet, Steffen Freund, Ledley King, Christian Ziege, Teddy Sheringham, Les Ferdinand, and with Glenn Hoddle as manager. The bookies leaned heavily their way, especially as we were weakened by the loss of Short, Flitcroft and Tugay, all suspended. Lucas Neill was also cup-tied. It was a lot of experience and quality to be without for one of the biggest games of your life. Souness, though, used this to our advantage. The night before the game, we got together in the Vale of Glamorgan, which had a reputation as the lucky cup final hotel. He then named the team and gave a brief talk.

'Listen,' he said. 'Spurs are massive favourites. Nobody expects us to win. You shouldn't have any fear whatsoever. Just go out there and enjoy yourselves. Make the most of the occasion.'

That was all we needed. Once again Souness had relaxed us when the pressure might have weighed heavily on us. When we saw the stadium the next day, and walked the pitch, nobody seemed nervous. 'Wow,' I thought. 'Pretty good, this.'

They closed the roof for the game, which ramped up the atmosphere even more. There were more than seventy thousand people in the stadium. If anyone was going to feel the pressure, it was surely the overwhelming favourites – especially when we felt our way into the opening stages reasonably well. We weren't going to be rolled over, and didn't I have a decent memory or two against Spurs?

It took twenty-five minutes for things to fall into place. I relied on my spring to beat Ben Thatcher to a header, and it broke for Besty, thirty yards out. He controlled it with his chest and took on the shot, but scuffed it to the left. I had broken into space and it came my way via Thatcher's shin. I slid into the shot and drove it through the legs of Neil Sullivan, the Spurs goalkeeper.

I turned and ran in the direction of the bench. There was something I had to do.

Russell Crowe's film *Gladiator* was popular, and as a squad we had watched it in the build-up to the final. In one scene, Crowe's character Maximus cuts down several enemies in the gladiator pit, decapitating the last man before hurling his sword into the crowd.

'Are you not entertained?' he bellows. 'ARE YOU NOT ENTERTAINED?'

Craig Short had turned from the screen at that moment and looked at me, grinning. 'Janny, if you score, you have to do that.'

You don't score in a cup final every day. So, as I ran with my arms outstretched, staying in my stride as teammates grabbed at me, I looked for Shorty.

'Are you not entertained?' I mouthed. He wore a huge smile.

So did I. The noise from our thirty thousand fans was unreal and it filled us with belief. I knew straight away that it was a moment I'd never forget. Even when Ziege equalised before half-time, we resisted the onslaught that many had expected. Spurs missed some good chances after that, while Brad Friedel was inspired in goal. Then, in the second half, we pounced again. King failed to clear a long ball from Berg and, as he nodded it down, I saw the glimmer of light that I needed. I nipped around his blind side and helped it on to Cole, who beat Sullivan with a clever finish.

It was sweet for Cole, who had been infamously dismissed by Hoddle in his time as England coach as someone who needed too many chances before scoring. If the person you are talking about enjoys proving people wrong, comments like that can come back to bite you. Cole certainly had a bit of that in him.

We held Tottenham off from there, and what a feeling it was when the final whistle cut through the clamour. It all came at once: the sense of achievement, the adrenaline rush, the knowledge I had done something that would never leave me. Don't we all have childhood dreams like this – sitting on the coach to the cup final, approaching the stadium through a sea of fans, scoring, then setting up the winner and lifting the trophy? I had lived it with Blackburn and it felt better than I had ever imagined.

We went back to our hotel to celebrate with a few drinks and then a few more. Some of the lads went home, but I was in no mood to stop. Jay sorted us out with another hotel for the night, and while most of my family headed back up north, we went out in Cardiff for an evening I can barely recall, and rolled in at a time I certainly can't remember.

Garry Flitcroft: I was injured when Matt joined us at Blackburn, but when I came back and played with him, it was easy to see what a good footballer he was. He had speed, skill and a real ability to jump. I always joke that, in the gym, Matt and Robbie Savage (who joined us a few years later) were the weakest in terms of lifting weights – but Matt's leg strength was frightening. His thighs and calves were massive, and while he wasn't the tallest of strikers, he had the sort of spring which shocked even some of the top centre-halves he came up against. His finishing was also excellent – we used to have a running joke after training about how many goals he scored that day, in five-a-sides or shooting practice. If you set him up, you knew he'd bang it in.

On the pitch he was a bundle of energy and he'd run his heart out for you. From midfield, I could knock the ball into the channels and he'd chase hard, or I could knock it into his feet and he'd twist, turn and keep hold of it. I suppose he was a bit greedy sometimes, but you have to be like that as a striker.

The night we got promotion at Preston stays with me. After he scored and ran off to celebrate, I was the first to reach him to give him a cuddle. I'll never forget his face: that aggression, that passion. It was a big, big moment for us. I also never fail to remind him that he took that goal off my head, and as a result got all the glory on the night out, instead of me!

Off the field he was a fun guy, hard-working and generous. He would help you as much as he could. I don't remember him falling out with anybody or raising his voice. He never missed any of the nights out that I organised as captain. On those evenings he'd always be among the last to leave.

Although he had great ability as a player, he wasn't a big-head. That's probably why the lads accepted him. When you get a new signing there can be some jealousy but there was none of that with Matt. He fitted in well to our group, which had a good mixture of experienced players like me, Craig Hignett and Craig Short, and young kids with real energy like David Dunn and Damien Duff. Our team spirit was excellent and Graeme Souness gave us all a bit of leeway. In return, we gave him everything we had.

We progressed well in the Premier League and Matt played a key part both in that and our League Cup run. The club had high hopes for him, and I know John Williams, the chief executive, thought a lot of him. Blackburn was a big club, but I felt it inevitable that he would eventually move on to one of the top teams in the country, and play for England.

A few months earlier, in Ayia Napa, Lucy Corner had glanced at a big screen in a bar where she had been enjoying a drink with a friend.

'Oh my God,' she said. 'That's the guy who lives in our block of flats.'

I'd seen Lucy a few times in passing, but our paths had never properly crossed. After the final, I must have had extra confidence because I got Jay to ask if she wanted to come to a concert with me. I had a box at the Manchester Evening News Arena, and Bryan Adams was playing that weekend. A couple of the other Blackburn players were coming with their girlfriends, and I asked if Lucy would like to join the party.

She didn't seem sure at first, but later got back to me and asked if she could bring a friend. 'That's fine,' I said, secretly worrying that her friend would be her boyfriend. Thankfully, her friend was a girl, and we spoke properly for the first time that night. She explained that she was studying languages at Manchester University and her finals were around the corner. She seemed really clued-up, really smart. It just felt like we clicked. We went on a couple of dates and I felt relaxed in her company. She seemed to feel the same.

I hadn't had a steady girlfriend since I'd been at Carlisle. I'd been on dates but hadn't found anybody. At twenty-four, though, I had a clearer sense than before that something was absent from my life. I wondered if Lucy might be that missing piece.

It felt real and right. I was happy, more complete, my snowball ego had never been bigger and my feeling of invincibility was now total.

There was England, too.

The future held no fear whatsoever. Why would it?

TEN

BORIS

Lucy: Meeting a footballer wasn't exactly top of my list of life ambitions. My heart was set on travelling, seeing the world. I was at university, studying Italian and Spanish, and had spent the third year of a four-year course overseas: nine months in Sicily, and part of the summer in South America and Mexico. I loved it so much that I wanted to go back to Italy to live as soon as I graduated. The weather was better, the food was better, it was much more laid-back. There was just something magical about being abroad.

I'm an only child, and always felt quite independent. I went to a boarding school where, in the holidays, they encouraged you to travel, be an au pair, that sort of thing. My parents felt I was too young for a gap year immediately after school, and that's one of the reasons I did a language degree – so I would get that year abroad in the middle of it. When I returned to England for the final year of my degree, I spent most of my time daydreaming about the day I could get back on the plane. Academically, I'd run out of steam.

Whilst I was at university, my father had bought a flat in Manchester – for me to live in, but also as a bit of an investment. We were told that someone from *Coronation Street* had bought one of the others, and a footballer as well. That was no biggie for me, because my knowledge of the sport was pretty slim, to say the least. I hadn't been brought up in a footballing family, we never went to watch Grimsby, our local team, and my father wasn't the sort of man who went down the pub at weekends to watch the game. I knew Manchester was a massive football city, but I would have struggled to identify any player that wasn't a real household name.

At the end of my third year a friend had asked if I wanted to go on holiday. We got a last-minute deal to Ayia Napa and fell into a standard routine: beach all day, come in, go to bed, then get up at midnight and head back out once all the English tourists have stopped puking in the streets. One day we were walking past a big, open sports bar and there was a game on. It was August, early in the season, and Blackburn were playing. I squinted at the screen and recognised one of the players.

'Oh my God, that's him – he lives in my block!'

In our flats you seldom bumped into anyone. There were only twenty-nine of them, and it could be a bit of a ghost town. So while I had noticed Matt, I didn't know the first thing about him.

'Oh – he's really fit,' I said. It then became a bit of a running joke between me and my friend for the next few months. I kept buying *The Sun*, and Matt seemed to be Dream Team Star Man every week. This guy in my flat, who I'd never heard of, was quite good!

I became more aware of him, often seeing him out of the window, heading off to work, but I'm not sure we would have met had it not been for my father. He encouraged me to go to the management meetings in the apartment block, and it was there that we met Jay. One day in January, my father cheekily asked Jay if he could get us tickets to see Blackburn play Manchester United. A few days later Matt came to drop off the tickets, and that's when we met.

We went to the game, a lot of Matt's family were there, and afterwards Jay invited me up to the flat, where a lot of them were gathering. My parents had driven home by that stage, and I wasn't all that comfortable with the idea of just rocking up, knocking on the door and going into a flat full of Matt's family. I barely knew him. So I went out with my friends instead and thought nothing of it.

A month or so later, Jay knocked on my door. Matt had a box at the MEN Arena for Bryan Adams, he said, and would I like to go with him?

I didn't have the heart to say that I was more into clubs like Holy City Zoo and the student scene than an old rocker like Bryan Adams.

'Oh. That's really kind,' I said.

When Jay left, I called an old schoolfriend, who was a huge Bryan Adams fan. 'You have to come up to this concert – this footballer has invited me to go. I don't even like Bryan Adams! This is so embarrassing, please come.'

Thankfully, she agreed. It was a Saturday, and Blackburn were playing Bolton away. They drew 1–1 and Matt scored – not that I had a clue at the time. My friend Pippa and I had been shopping all afternoon and were dressed pretty casually when there was a knock on the door, and there was Matt, in a suit.

Matt, Jay and Clare took us to the Stock restaurant in Manchester, where we met some of the other Blackburn players and their partners. Pippa and I felt like fish out of water, especially when the conversation of many of the footballers turned to money – who had bought what for how much. It wasn't very endearing, but Matt seemed a little different. He was reluctant to throw his own wealth into the discussion, and also appeared quite shy.

As the night went on, I found it easy to talk to him. One of his teammates, Nils-Eric Johansson, was also good fun. They were more balanced and low-key than you expect stereotypical footballers to be. And Bryan Adams, to my surprise, was amazing.

Because Matt was quite normal and down-to-earth, we hit it off very easily. I think that's why it progressed so quickly. There wasn't any pressure to go on dates. It was a more easy-going relationship. Typically, Matt would ring me after training and ask if I wanted to go for a coffee, or a drink. Footballers have a lot of time on their hands, so it was either go out with me, play on the PlayStation, or bet on the horses. A no-brainer!

So, when I should have been studying, I was often in a restaurant with Matt. Other times, we camped out in his flat on his two big La-Z-Boy chairs, and watched films for hours. I was no longer exclusively focused on my studies, so I was more than happy with that.

Surprisingly, for a bloke, Matt was quite up front very early on about the sort of relationship he wanted. He said he was keen to settle down. Knowing him as well as I do now, that was a most un-Matt thing, because he's not the most decisive person. But he was very clear, and if I wasn't up for that, he didn't want to waste his time. He might not have put it so bluntly, but that was the message.

I was a bit flummoxed. I was twenty-two, and settling down wasn't part of my grand plan. I was going to trot off to Italy, live the life and get married no sooner than thirty. I told myself that I would have to be sure about this, because, while I'd barely bumped into him before, you could bet your life that if we got together and it all went wrong, I'd stumble across him every day in the apartment block. It had the potential to be awkward and horrible if it didn't work out.

But it just felt right, even as I got a glimpse into the strange world he inhabited. In the players' lounges, people dressed like they were going to the Oscars, as I turned up in my jeans and T-shirt. It seemed like people were out to perform all the time, which wasn't me at all.

Because it was so alien, it probably didn't hit me immediately what a star Matt was in that world. He didn't play up to it, so, to me, he was a completely different person.

I also felt uncomfortable calling him Matt, because his dad had the same name. Football people also called him Matt, or Matty, or Janny. I didn't know what to call him.

Who was he to me?

The answer came quite randomly. Matt also called himself different things, maybe for similar reasons, and one of those was 'Jonsen', which I suppose was a slight variation on Jansen. This then morphed just as randomly into 'Johnson'. Come on Johnson, he would say to himself, when trying to get himself going on the pitch, or in some task at home.

For a while, then, I called him Johnson, but not long afterwards, it changed again, because of a certain political figure of that name who was becoming increasingly well known. As a result, Johnson morphed into Boris, and that was my title for Matt from there on. It may seem completely weird, but it just stuck. Boris and I were an item.

ELEVEN

ON THE BRINK

Graeme Souness: Matt's rise was meteoric and, given the type of player he was, it was inevitable he would be given his chance by England. We didn't have the highest profile at Blackburn, but we played good football and Matt was an emerging young player who was scoring goals. Why wouldn't the national team take notice? He was unfortunate with the illness that cost him his first cap, but the fact he came so close to going to the World Cup underlined what England thought of him.

He was only going to get better, and I'm certain he would have had an England career. Would he have been a regular? We can never answer that. I'm convinced he would have played for his country several times, and the rest would have been up to Matt and his development.

Sven-Göran Eriksson: When Tord Grip and I watched Matt play for Blackburn several times, we very much liked what we saw. He was quick, he could play the last pass, he scored goals, he had an excellent left foot and he was technically very, very good. He could dribble and he could beat people.

When we talked about him, we agreed that he could play in different positions: in the number ten position, or to the left. That made him very interesting for us. When you can dribble past people, and you are clever, you have something special and we thought Matt had that.

I would guess that it was a surprise for some people when he was picked for that friendly game against Paraguay, but we felt, 'Why not?' He had played a very good season for Blackburn, and we would never have picked him for England so close to the World Cup had we not been so impressed with him. He was absolutely in our minds for that tournament. People talked very well about him as a man, and in training he was also very good. It was easy to have him in the squad.

I'm certain that he would have played against Paraguay, whether from the start or during the game, to see if he would remain in our plans for the tournament. It was a real pity that he got sick; a pity for everybody, and especially for Matt, that he did not have that great opportunity.

When selecting your final World Cup squad, you have to take a decision and, of course, you will never know one hundred per cent what is right and what is wrong. When it came to deciding between Matt and Martin Keown we were talking about player number twenty-one, twenty-two or twenty-three in a squad of twenty-three, so you are probably not talking about a player who will start the first game in the World Cup.

In the end it was unlucky for Matt that we had not seen him with the other players in that friendly. Who knows? If he had played that game, he might have been in the squad.

I do not recall that Tord and I argued about it – it was a decision we took together, and our feeling was to go for the more secure player. We had known Martin Keown for a long time and that settled our decision. We felt Matt was a good player but, because he had never played for England, we could not be sure.

It is hard to say what could have happened had we taken him to the tournament in Japan and South Korea. We did very well there until we lost to Brazil in the quarter-final. They were better than us and there's not much more to say than that. Maybe Matt would have done something, maybe not. None of us can know about that.

Our feeling, though, was that he would play for England in the future. That was my thought, Tord's thought, and the thoughts of the English coaches as well. We felt he deserved that chance.

After England, after the call-up that was and the World Cup summons that wasn't, there was another enquiry from Manchester United. It hadn't gone very far by the time I decided to go away with Lucy for a short break.

I was comfortable with that. I was loving my time at Blackburn – the team, the support, the club, I felt fantastic – and was in no rush to pursue anything. If they were serious, it would work out, and until then it was time to relax.

When it had looked like I might be going to the World Cup, Lucy's dad, Barry, had asked the university if, under the circumstances, she would be able to postpone her finals so that she could accompany me to the pre-tournament gathering in Dubai and then to Japan and South Korea. They had agreed but, now that was no longer on the agenda, she was able to finish her exams before we got ready for Rome.

Life was good. I was so happy.

Lucy: It makes me cringe to think of my father approaching the university and saying, 'Her boyfriend might be going to the World Cup, and she will obviously be going with him, so can she do her exams when she comes back?' But that's what happened.

It was such a bizarre time. Amongst all the planning and preparation, Matt was measured for his England suit, in case he made the final cut. We also got an invitation to David Beckham's garden party, which was due to take place shortly before the squad flew out to Dubai.

I didn't want to go. I still wasn't at ease in that world. Looking back, I can't believe I passed the opportunity up. But I was still young, still focused on my own priorities.

Of course Matt was upset when he was left out of the squad but he was more upset by the gastroenteritis that kept him out of the Paraguay game. We both were. When he came back from hospital, he walked into my flat – and it was like looking into a mirror, because I was just as bad.

Matt was green and pale and miserable, and so was I. The difference was, when the club doctor came around to fix him up with a drip, I didn't get anything! You soon learn your place in the pecking order when you're with a footballer.

He took the World Cup announcement on the chin. He said Sven had been really good with him, and I suppose at twenty-four it was fair to assume he'd get another chance. He seemed to move on quickly. 'Okay, I'm not going to the World Cup, but we've got the whole summer to ourselves, so let's get some holidays booked.'

He was still bright and happy.

He waited until I'd finished my exams and was then bursting to go away. I'd wanted to stay a while, so I could celebrate the end of my degree with my friends, but he whisked me away. He said he'd always wanted to go to Italy, and he probably knew I couldn't resist the place. When he suggested a city break, Rome seemed the obvious destination. I don't suppose I put up a huge fight.

So we flew, Boris and I, from Manchester on the Friday, with the intention to come back on the Monday. The following weekend, we would be off to Canada for his brother Jo's wedding.

Our hotel was really nice, near the Spanish Steps, in a lovely area of Rome. It was smoggy and warm; a bit clammy, but not too hot.

There was so much to see, but everything in Rome is quite spread out. That's the reason the scooter idea came about. You don't see a decent car in Italy because they're all bashed up – they're crazy drivers! So, we thought, let's be really cool and Italian, and get one of those *motorini*. It was the best way of seeing the city. We took in loads of the sights and just basked in it all.

The champagne thing was hysterical. It was this really crappy café next door to the Pantheon, and I thought Matt would kill me for ordering the Cristal, but I found it quite funny. A waiter came out with a tablecloth, flowers, a candle, and everybody in the place was looking at me. Then the bottle came. One sip, and . . . agh, it was like cough medicine! Sweeter than anything, and thick in your throat. I thought I'd be sick if I drank any more.

'You're such an idiot,' Matt said. We gave the bottle to this other couple and got the hell out of there.

It was embarrassing, but not in a bad way. It was our first holiday together and we found everything amusing. Nothing really mattered. We were in our own little bubble.

There's a great feeling of relief for a footballer when the season finishes, and Matt seemed really happy with his lot. He kept saying we could stay on longer if I wanted. But I didn't want to be that person who got into a new relationship and immediately ditched all her friends. They were all in Manchester, partying, and I didn't want them to think I'd turned my back on them. The fact my boyfriend was a footballer might have given them some misconceptions. Getting home was in the back of my mind. At the same time, what could be nicer than chilling in Rome?

The night before we were due to fly home, I was itching to head out of the hotel for a last little look around. Matt was a little tired.

'Don't be so boring,' I said.

We found the scooter and set off. My helmet can't have been on properly, because somehow it came off and, by the time we pulled over, it was nowhere to be seen. The police by the roadside told us we couldn't continue without wearing one, but were happy enough for us to go back up to the hotel, as we suggested.

Matt was like, 'Here, have my helmet,' but he was driving, so it made sense to keep his on. He started the bike and turned it in the direction of the hotel, eventually coming towards that crossroads, with cars sticking out everywhere.

When both sets of lights are flashing amber at a crossroads in Italy, you edge towards them and judge whether you should go. At home, flashing amber at an empty pedestrian crossing means proceed with caution, but really you're good to go.

I'm not sure Matt realised this subtle difference, but I didn't tell him to watch out, because I assumed it would be okay. I wouldn't say we were crawling, but we weren't flying. Cruising, I suppose. You couldn't see a thing around the corners so, as best we could, we saw that nothing was coming, and moved forward.

The hotel was a couple of hundred yards away. We were so close. Sickeningly close.

TWELVE

COMA

Through the haze, a few short memories. The man in the next bed looks like he's auditioning for a part in a Mr Bean film. Everything is in plaster – his arms up here, his legs up there. He starts coughing and sneezing. I flinch. Don't give me your germs!

Then, the catheter. That was painful.

Then, the wheelchair on the cobbles.

Then, the plane. Hello, Ole Gunnar.

Nothing else.

Lucy: I was lying on the floor. I pushed myself up straight away, and felt a pain in my knee and ankle as I got to my feet. Otherwise, I felt fine.

I knew what had happened. I'd seen the taxi, but it had all come together in a flash, and we'd been pitched from the bike before I'd been able to process anything.

I looked up and saw Matt, face down, a few metres away from me.

He was moving, but only in a juddering way. His helmet had

come off and it looked like he was out cold. I hurried over to him and saw that he had a really bad cut on his face, around his right eye, the eyelid included.

I suppose this is when I went into some sort of autopilot. I reached down and took hold of his limp arm. 'Squeeze my hand if you're all right,' I said.

He squeezed.

Other things rushed into my mind.

'Can you feel your legs? Can you feel your legs?'

I don't remember if he squeezed at that point. But it seemed that he could hear me, even though he wasn't saying anything.

Rome was busy, and lots of people had stopped around us. Because I could speak the language, I was able to ask someone to call an ambulance. One was on its way, I was told.

Matt wasn't moving and all I could do was stay with him and wait.

I always felt I was quite good in a crisis and now, instead of going to pieces, something inside me was able to deal practically with what was going on. There was probably a bit of shock involved, too.

The next thing I did, though, can probably be put down to the fact that many people have weird reactions after an accident. When I stood up, I noticed I was barefoot. I had been wearing a smart dress for dinner and some strappy shoes, which Matt had bought me from Prada. I couldn't see the shoes. I walked around the little crowd of bystanders. 'Have you seen my Prada shoes? Have you seen them?'

Eventually I found them, all scuffed and wrecked. Matt was in the same position, lying on the cobbles in his suit, and I kept waiting, until eventually a police car arrived. The officers approached the taxi driver, who had stopped after the collision, and took some details from him, before allowing him to drive off.

I was relieved that the ambulance wasn't far behind. Matt was quickly lifted into it and they took him away. For reasons that weren't made particularly clear, I wasn't allowed to go with him. Instead, I was asked to get in the police car.

The car was all plastic in the back, with no upholstery, no door handles and no windows. As the doors closed, I had a burst of hysterical, panicked claustrophobia. I'm in the back of a police car, I haven't done anything wrong, I can't get out, my boyfriend is not talking and he's gone off in an ambulance.

What's going on?!

It was the first time that my mind went haywire, but I calmed as the policemen explained they were taking me back to the hotel, and that I would need to retrieve our passports.

It was, obviously, a short journey. I went into the Hotel Eden and explained to the staff what had happened. They opened the safe and gave me the passports. I then went back to our room, changed into some tracksuit bottoms, a T-shirt and some flipflops, and then I rang Jay.

Rome was an hour ahead of the UK, but it was still going to be much later than you would normally expect a call from abroad – or anywhere, for that matter. Jay had two small children, and I knew he'd be asleep, but he was the one I needed to call. He wasn't only Matt's agent, they were friends, and he would be able to relay the news to Matt's parents.

Jay: My phone kept ringing and ringing. It was nearly 2.00 a.m. in Manchester.

I knew it was Matt, because I had a particular Darth Vader ringtone for him. It was quite funny, but not necessarily at that time of the morning. I remembered that he was in Rome, with his girlfriend, and I had a strong suspicion what would be at the other end of the line the moment I picked up: Matt, drunk, pouring out his feelings. 'Oh, I love you man, you're my best mate,' – that sort of thing. That's lovely, but maybe not at 2.00 a.m.

Clare, who'd also been woken by the phone, told me to ignore it. But each time the Dark Lord stopped, he started again a few seconds later. The phone was downstairs. On and on and on it went.

I stirred a little more and remembered something else. 'You know,' I said, peeling back the covers, 'I think he's hired those mopeds today.'

Knowing that Matt doesn't do anything by halves, I had a picture of him renting the biggest, most powerful and expensive bikes in Rome. I stood up, yawned, went downstairs, found the phone, went for a pee and, standing over the toilet, dialled Matt's number back.

It wasn't Matt who answered, but a man with an Italian accent. He said he was a surgeon. 'You need to come over as soon as possible, because your friend is very ill.'

Oh my God. What the hell?

I was now wide awake. The house phone then started to ring. I picked it up and spoke to Lucy.

'There's been an accident. Matt's in hospital. I don't quite know what's happened, but can you please come out straight away?'

My second son, Elliott, had been born days ago, and had been very poorly with jaundice, needing regular blood transfusions. I was jaded and worried, but I knew I had to spring into action.

Lucy: I burst into tears when Jay answered the phone, but then tried to compose myself and tell him what had happened. He seemed quite calm and rational, and tried to reassure me. He said he would make arrangements to fly out as soon as possible.

After the call ended, other thoughts rushed through my mind. Would we have to pay for the scooter? Where on earth is the hospital? And how am I supposed to get there?

From left to right, Matt's brother Jo being held by his sister Clare, while his brother Danny looks off camera and Matt smiles at Jo.

Matt aged 12, then an Austin Friars school pupil, showing off his skills in the build-up to the Italia '90 'Soccaball' competition final, June 1990. *News & Star*

Matt, second right, with other competitors, poses with George Best
at the 'Soccaball' skills final in Manchester, 1990.

Matt aged 13, far left, with (left to right) Andrew Hewitt, Wain Lawson, Steven Holt
and Gavin Armstrong, Carlisle six-a-side soccer winners, August 1991. *News & Star*

Matt signs a new professional contract with Carlisle United in the boardroom at Brunton Park. From left, Matt's father Mat, Matt, Michael Knighton, Mervyn Day, February 1996. *News & Star*

Matt making his league debut for Carlisle as a substitute against Mansfield in Division Three, Brunton Park, October 1996. *News & Star*

Matt, second right, with (l-r) Warren Aspinall, Lee Peacock and Stephane Pounewatchy, pictured after a 0-0 draw at Stockport in the Auto-Windscreens Shield northern final second leg, which secured a place in the Wembley final for Carlisle, March 1997. *News & Star*

Matt in action for Crystal Palace against Oxford at Selhurst Park in August 1998. *Getty Images*

Matt stands for the anthem before the European Championship Under-21 qualifier against Bulgaria at Upton Park in October 1998. *Getty Images*

Blackburn's latest signing holds up his new shirt. *Reuters*

Matt in action for England Under-21 during the 2000 European Championships group match against Italy at the Slovan Stadium in Bratislava, Slovakia. Italy won 2–0. *Getty Images*

Matt celebrates scoring for Blackburn against Preston North End at Deepdale in May 2001, helping seal Blackburn's promotion back to the Premier League. *Getty Images*

A battle on the field which would become a battle for the final spot in England's 2002 World Cup squad: Matt in action against Arsenal's Martin Keown at Highbury, January 2002. *Reuters*

Matt gets between Ledley King and Ben Thatcher to shoot past Neil Sullivan to score Blackburn's first goal against Spurs in the League Cup final at the Millennium Stadium in Cardiff, February 2002. *Reuters*

Matt and Michael Owen take a breather during England training at the Racecourse Ground, Wrexham, April 2002. *Getty Images*

Matt signs autographs for Japanese fans at the England team hotel near Chester in April 2002 before England play Paraguay at Anfield. *Reuters*

The front page of the *News & Star*, Carlisle, reporting the news of Matt's illness which cost him his England debut against Paraguay, April 2002.

JANSEN: Scored last night

Uncapped Jansen the surprise in Sven's 23

EXCLUSIVE

By MARTIN LIPTON and JOHN CROSS

MATT JANSEN is today poised to become the first uncapped member of an England World Cup squad in more than 30 years.

The versatile Blackburn forward will be unveiled as Sven Goran Eriksson's shock selection in his final 23 after a late change of mind by the England coach, who watched Jansen score in Blackburn's 4-3 defeat by Liverpool last night.

But Eriksson suffered a blow when he discovered Nicky Butt injured a knee in training on Monday.

The Manchester United midfielder will be out for two weeks with ligament damage, but will still be named by Eriksson today.

The deadline for announcing squads is May 21, and should Butt fail to recover he is likely to be replaced by Michael Carrick, who will be with the under-21 squad.

That will mean heartbreak for Danny Murphy, whose bid to **TURN TO PAGE 58**

An article in the *Mirror*, predicting Matt's inclusion in the England squad for the 2002 World Cup.

Left and below: Matt and Lucy on the scooter they were riding when they had the accident in Rome, May 2002.

Matt and Lucy talk in the garden during Matt's initial period of post-accident recovery at Lucy's parents' house in Claxby, Lincolnshire, June 2002.

Lucy and Matt at Market Rasen races, on Matt's first proper outing since he had recovered from the accident, June 2002.

Matt, nearly a year into his comeback, scores a stunning goal
against Liverpool at Ewood Park, September 2003. *Reuters*

Matt beats Manchester United's Mikael Silvestre at Old Trafford, November 2003. *Reuters*

Graeme Souness sends Matt on against Leeds United at Ewood Park in April 2004. *Reuters*

Matt returns to Ewood Park in January 2006, this time playing for Bolton. *Reuters*

Matt, a free agent, pictured back at Carlisle United
for pre-season training in summer 2007. *News & Star*

In action for Chorley against Preston
North End in a pre-season friendly, July
2010. *Reuters*

Matt, then assistant manager, and the Chorley players celebrate winning
the Evo-Stik Premier Division title, April 2014. *Josh Vosper*

Matt, manager of Chorley, poses with the Vanarama National League
North Manager of the Month award for September 2016. *Josh Vosper*

Matt with his youngest son Freddie, May 2018. *Josh Vosper*

Matt was manager of Chorley for three years before resigning in June 2018. *Josh Vosper*

I had no money on me because Matt had all our cash in the suit he was wearing. I arranged a taxi and told the driver everything that had happened. I was quite breathless as I told him in my clearest Italian about the police putting me in the car with no door handles, and the fact I had no money because my boyfriend was in hospital, and . . .

I didn't need to explain much more. He took me straight to the hospital. I think he felt sorry for me.

The entrance, to the rear of the building, was very dark and dingy, with the walls tiled like an old butcher's shop where you'd see meat hanging from hooks. As I walked up a ramp and then moved through the reception area, it was very quiet and seemed low on staff, presumably because it was so late at night.

I quickly found his ward. It was a really basic, crappy room, with six beds set out in two rows of three. I saw that Matt was in the middle bed of one of the threes.

He was on his back and strapped up to some sort of machine. As I got closer to him, I noticed they had stitched the cut above his eye, and there were tubes here and there. But what really shocked me, to the point that the memory still upsets me now, is that he was also shaking, as though he was having a small fit.

Seeing him like that was very difficult to bear. He was normally so strong, so fit, so successful, such a presence. Now he was broken and helpless.

I looked up and took in the room. Either side of Matt were two older men, who at first glance didn't seem to have a great deal wrong with them. I also noticed that all of Matt's things had been placed in a box, along with his lovely suit, which was ruined.

I wasn't sure what to do, where to sit or where to go. I took a few deep breaths and tried to rationalise the situation, but that just led me into a state of denial. I started telling myself that what had happened wasn't really bad, was it?

I snapped back into crisis management mode and tried to find someone to speak to. There was a woman at a desk in the waiting area. I started asking her questions.

'Where's the doctor? How are Matt's legs? He's a footballer, it's very important.'

I noticed another man hanging around the reception area. He looked quite greasy and I saw that he was carrying a notepad and pen. He walked towards me and muttered an introduction, before launching into a load of questions.

Maybe that's how some journalists worked out there. Perhaps he waited around the A&E department to catch a juicy story. He must have overheard me talking to the receptionist, because he kept asking about 'Matt' and could I explain more about him being a footballer? When I realised what he was after, I recoiled, and answered 'no' to all his questions. Eventually he left.

The rest of the night passed in a fog, but some things are still vivid. Back in the ward, I saw there was a cheap and tatty-looking wheelie-bed near to Matt. I was exhausted, so I climbed on to it with the idea of getting a few hours' sleep. Then I felt something . . .

The old guy from the next bed had leaned across and grabbed my bum.

At that point I nearly lost my senses.

This has to be a piss-take, I thought. How could it possibly get any worse? My boyfriend is lying here in an awful state, I don't know what's going to happen, and now I've got this old perv trying to grope me. It was like some sort of hideous nightmare. I got up off the bed, because there was no way I was going to risk lying there all night, but I couldn't tell you where I went or what I did after that.

I knew, though, that Jay would soon be on his way.

Jay: The room was truly awful. It had basic, concrete floors, paint was peeling off the walls and there was no air conditioning, so it stank.

Hospital staff were bustling in and out of the ward, bringing food for the other patients, but Matt was still unconscious. I wasn't sure what to expect but for someone who had been in a serious accident, he didn't look battered and bruised. I noticed a grazed knee and a scab on his head. Otherwise, you would never have known the extent of his injuries.

The doctors eventually took Lucy and me aside and explained his condition. The brain, they said, is enclosed in fluid inside the skull. When you are propelled forward and strike a stationary object, it results in your brain moving backwards in that fluid. It's a kind of cushion, and any damage depends on the nature and force of the collision.

In Matt's case, his accident had resulted in loads of little dots appearing on his brain. The doctor said they were multiple, tiny haemorrhages. He also said that things could have been much worse.

Had he suffered a full-on, larger brain haemorrhage, he would have died.

Lucy: By the time Jay got there, Matt had stopped moving and shaking. He was just flat out, in a coma. As time went by, and the doctors started telling us a little more, we realised we had to occupy ourselves somehow. I'd been checked out myself – a few cuts and bruises, but otherwise fine – and so we went back to the Hotel Eden for something to eat.

We ordered room service, picked at the food without any great appetite, and returned to the hospital. We remained in this routine for a couple of days, feeling very sombre.

I was also tense because it still wasn't clear if or when Matt would be out of the woods. You can't help but fear the worst when you hear the words 'brain injury' and I had this pent-up feeling that he might wake up as someone completely different.

The medical people eventually called us back in. They told Jay and me that his brain had been scanned again, and the blood had come out, which was good news. They said the words we wanted to hear: that he was going to be okay, also repeating their opinion that, if he hadn't been wearing a helmet, he probably wouldn't have survived.

The tension must have just burst out of me at that point, because I started crying and, for a while, I couldn't stop. I cried because I knew he would eventually be waking up as Matt.

Jay: Next, I went to look at the crash site. I could completely see what had happened. They had basically clipped the back of the taxi, and the moped had jolted like a horse. Matt and Lucy had somersaulted a considerable distance; probably twenty or thirty feet. The miracle was that Lucy only had a few scratches. Matt must have landed first and broken her fall as he collided with the cobbled street.

I went to find the place they'd hired the moped. The bike was in bits. Absolutely destroyed.

Matt was in a coma for the best part of four days. In that time, I had the British Embassy on the phone, because he was a high-profile British citizen. They were okay, if a little stuck-up, and because they had taken possession of his valuables, I had to go and collect them – a bracelet, his Rolex watch and some Euros.

Blackburn Rovers were also in touch. Graeme Souness sounded furious. 'What the fucking hell was he doing on a moped?'

'Graeme,' I said, 'I wasn't with him, and there's no way I would have let him . . .'

John Williams, the Blackburn chief executive, was calmer. Everyone was eager to know Matt was all right, and the club also offered PR assistance if I felt it was needed. They were concerned, as was I, that the taxi driver might make some sort of claim. As Matt's agent, I worried that, if the guy found out he was a Premier League footballer, he might go to the papers. Thankfully that never happened. We never saw or heard from him.

Graeme Souness: He was extremely unlucky with the cards that fate dealt him that summer. When I first heard about his accident in Rome, my first response was to ask Phil Batty, our club doctor, if Matt was okay. My second feeling was one of anger, because Phil had given the players a letter at the end of the season which had made certain stipulations about their summer break: there must be no waterskiing, for instance, no equestrian pursuits, and no motorbikes.

I was, though, more concerned than annoyed. I wanted to know that he was going to be okay. Football is no longer the most important thing when faced with a situation as serious as that. What matters is the boy's health and welfare, and it was predominantly the job of our medical team, as well as the Blackburn chief executive John Williams, to handle that side of things.

Lucy: Matt hadn't budged for three days, but there was a moment when the person in the next bed sneezed, and Matt lifted his hand. He has always had a thing about germs – he can't stand it when someone on a plane coughs near him – and that was his first movement.

From there, he slowly started waking up.

Initially, he was quite woozy and confused. He recognised Jay and me, and mumbled a few words, but it was a very gradual process. He didn't exactly sit up and start chatting straight away. There was still a lot of sleeping, and when I saw that he was trying to figure out exactly what was happening, he looked so vulnerable, almost helpless.

Jay: He drifted in and out of consciousness, but when he was awake, he was very thirsty and hungry. He was saying things like, 'I love you, man . . . thank God you're here . . . where am I? . . . Do my mum and dad know?'

It was very emotional. I was relieved, at first, that he recognised me, and I asked him what he remembered. He said about hiring the bike, but that's all he could recall.

There was one occasion that I managed to bring him round with a jolt. He had a catheter in, and as I moved around the bed, I accidentally knocked it. He was certainly awake then.

Lucy: A while after he came round, the medical staff came to his bed and started asking him questions.

'Do you know what month we are in?'

'June.'

That was promising. Having gone to Rome at the end of May, the medics weren't sure if he would have registered the change of month.

'Can you name the British Prime Minister?'

'Tony Blair.'

He was croaking as he gave the answers, but it seemed like he was coping. In the meantime, Jay set about getting him moved from that horrible ward. He got Matt transferred to a specialist brain injury unit, which was another world: clean, modern, large windows and, unlike the backstreet A&E place, out of the city centre, surrounded by garden areas with benches, and with a river running past.

Jay: It had been very surreal, going back and forward from a lovely five-star hotel to that grim hospital ward, so it was a relief when he was moved to the second facility. It was world class.

I know Lucy was glad I was there, but I can't overstate how great she was throughout the whole situation. She was much calmer and more level-headed than she probably remembers. The fact she spoke Italian, and was able to translate everything we were told, was also an enormous help. It would have been much more difficult without that.

Garry Flitcroft: The club doctor Phil Batty and our physio Dave Fevre first told me what had happened. I was in the treatment room at Blackburn and when they explained Matt had had an accident I was shell-shocked, and worried for him. The rest of the lads were also devastated. I wouldn't say we were kept informed in great detail from there, but Phil and Dave were able to tell us certain things and reassure us that his condition was improving.

Lucy: I suppose, because Jay had taken such good charge of the situation, I didn't think too much about it at the time. But as I look back now, I struggle with the fact my parents weren't on the first plane to Rome the minute they knew what had happened.

I'm an only child, and they were always protective of me to a fault. For example: at seventeen, after I passed my driving test, my father, Barry, took the radio out of the car for six months so that I could get used to the noise of the engine, judge when to change gear and, above all, ensure I'd be concentrating on my driving without being distracted by the music. A seventeen-year-old without a car stereo – I was traumatised!

Jay, though, wanted to handle everything with care, because of who Matt was, and because of Blackburn Rovers. I imagine he told my parents that it was best if they didn't come straight to Italy and, knowing my mother and father, they probably didn't want to rock the boat or risk getting in the way. They had only met Matt once, and I guess they weren't familiar with everything that comes with being a top-flight footballer.

I did speak to them, though, as soon as I could. It must have been difficult for them. It must have been strange.

Barry, Lucy's dad: My first reaction was one of shock, but hearing that Lucy was fine, I was able to settle somewhat. Early the following morning I spoke with Matt's mother and father, and it was agreed that Jay would go over. He would co-ordinate things from there, and there was no need for me to go to Rome.

I had a bit of telephone contact with Lucy and was anxious to find out what had happened. Lucy described how, when the emergency services had arrived, nobody could speak English, so she had ended up barking out instructions in Italian. That had put her in a position where she could drive things and ask questions about what was happening to Matt. When Jay got there, it took a bit of the pressure off her, and that was reassuring, because she did suffer from shock and needed an opportunity to get herself together.

Initially, though, she appeared to be running on adrenaline and was very much in control. For most of the time that we spoke she came across as being very cool and collected, determined to make sure everything was okay – and this was very much her nature.

Lucy: Matt's parents were on the phone to Jay, who then said they wanted to speak to me. They thanked me for being there, for staying with Matt and not immediately coming home.

It was nice of them to say, although I have to confess I found the idea that I would ever have just packed my things and gone completely strange. 'Right, that's me off, see you later, Matt.' I don't think so.

Eventually, he was discharged. The doctors said he would need lots of rest and recuperation at home, and not to expect him to rush back to normal, but he was going to be fine.

We went back to the hotel for one final night, ordered more meals on room service, and called some of Matt's relatives. Although he was able to talk to people, he was still a bit wobbly, and came out with a lot of gobbledegook. It was also obvious he wasn't really with it. When Jay called Danny, he passed the phone to Matt, who started asking his brother how his job was going 'on the telephones'.

Jay leaned over to Matt. 'Mate, he hasn't had that job for two years.'

Jay: We probably tried to get him home too soon, because moving him from place to place turned out to be far from straightforward.

It was as though he was drunk all the time, since he found it hard to walk in a straight line. He was also slurring his words and, all things considered, that probably isn't the best condition to be in when trying to get through airport security.

I had a medical letter in my pocket confirming he was fit for travel. Fortunately I didn't have to use it, but the whole experience of guiding him from the airport entrance and on to the plane was difficult. There was one point, when he wobbled towards the metal detector security area, when I wasn't sure we were going to make it. But we did, and I was glad when we were finally on board and Matt was in his seat.

We hadn't been on the aircraft for long when I saw a recognisable face. Ole Gunnar Solskjaer, the Manchester United striker, was on the same flight. He came up to greet us.

'All right Matt, how are you doing?' he said.

But Matt couldn't really process it. He slurred some sort of greeting in reply, but Ole must have wondered what on earth was going on. We had contained the news of the accident pretty well, and Ole wouldn't have known about it. It was just one more surreal moment in a quite extraordinary situation.

Lucy: It was a British Airways flight, which had a few Club Class seats in the front. We were on one side and Ole Gunnar

Solskjaer and his wife were on the other. There was some sort of greeting between them, but it was brief. We were just focused on propping Matt up, getting him through the flight and getting him home.

We weren't kidding ourselves that he was okay, but we wanted him home as soon as possible.

THIRTEEN

NOT RIGHT

Barry: To begin with, they came back to Manchester. Matt's parents drove down from Cumbria and collected them at the airport. I was in Lucy's flat, and looked down to see Matt get out of the car, being held up as though he might otherwise topple over. There was nothing in his eyes or his expression. He looked completely out of it.

It was difficult to watch Matt attempting to eat his food. It was like a small boy getting to grips with the experience for the first time. Half the food was going in, but the rest was falling down his face. Lucy was almost having to feed him. It was all so distressing.

Because he had been detained in Italy for a week and then allowed to return, I presumed that, by now, he would be okay. I was quite shocked when I saw the state he was in.

Within twenty-four hours or so, Matt's parents were having to shoot off to Canada for his brother's wedding. There was clearly no way Matt could go with them, and nor could he go home to Cumbria, while he was obviously in no condition to be left on his own. We decided that Matt and Lucy would come to Claxby and stay with us, at least while his own family were abroad.

I took the view that he would want to be with his parents as soon as they came back, but for Matt, that made no difference. I don't think he knew where he was or who he was with at that stage.

However, while he was very well known in the Manchester–Blackburn area, he could be anonymous in the Lincolnshire countryside. It would, I hoped, allow him to recover in relative peace.

Lucy: Matt's flat was quite dangerous for someone in his condition. The bed was up on a mezzanine level, with stairs, and given how he was moving, that was fraught with danger. It seemed a much safer idea for him to come to my parents' house. It was a much easier place to look after him than in a block of city-centre flats.

It was, I suppose, the sort of situation that thrusts everybody together. I don't think our parents had even met by that point, so they encountered each other for the first time through their children being involved in this bad accident. The following day, Matt's family got up early to go to the airport, so my parents – who didn't know Matt very well at all – were now basically in charge of someone at their weakest and most vulnerable.

None of us had any experience of being in that situation, and we just had to take things one day at a time. Aside from Matt's welfare, I knew I also needed love and support from my parents and so I was very happy that we all went back to Claxby.

Barry: Matt had been to Claxby before but he was barely aware of what was going on. He was still barely aware of who he was.

Lucy: To begin with, he basically slept for nineteen or twenty hours at a time. He was very much out for the count and none of us had any idea when he would get up, or how he would be.

It turned out, in the short periods he was awake, that he was in a very strange state of mind. He developed a craving for full-fat milky coffees and as many cookies as he could lay his hands on. After eating about twelve of them, he would then go back to bed for hours.

In these early stages he was like a baby in many ways: wake up, feed, back to sleep. My mum, Judith, spent much of the time in tears, because she was quite a sensitive person and couldn't cope with seeing him like that. My father and I were trying our best to be practical, but we knew it was a very unnatural situation. Had Matt and I been living together for four or five years it might have felt a little easier, but we had only been a couple for a matter of weeks.

Further things started happening when he was awake. There was one time when he suddenly appeared downstairs, wearing only his underpants, and started some really random conversation with my parents. It wasn't embarrassing, as such, but it was very far from normal, and we all knew it.

Barry: When he was up, he was like an infant that you had to keep an eye on. Any time he wasn't in the room, we were on tenterhooks. 'Where's Matt?'

We had an outdoor swimming pool, and we had to be on regular alert in case he wandered off down there. He'd been in the pool before, so he knew it existed, and we were conscious of that. He did once stroll off in the direction of the pool, and we had to go haring off to grab him.

It was a big house, an old Victorian rectory, so all the time we had to be aware. Over the next couple of days he became steadier on his feet, so we grew less concerned about him crashing into walls or falling down stairs. But we still had to take the utmost care.

As he spent more time awake, I thought of things that could occupy Matt and introduce some sort of normality. We didn't have Sky Sports, so I subscribed for Matt's benefit. We thought it would be good for his recovery, something familiar to him. He spent hours gazing at the TV as Sky Sports News went around in its constant loop.

It was a slow process, but after about four days there was suddenly a huge change. I got up one morning and found the kitchen in an incredible mess. It looked like we'd been burgled, with the intruders having helped themselves to the contents of our food cupboards.

Later, when Lucy and Matt got up, I learned what had happened. Lucy explained that, in the middle of the night, Matt had clicked back into a degree of lucidity and had started to ask lots of questions: 'Where am I? What's happened?' So they had got out of bed, come downstairs and sat together for hours, eating toast and talking.

I took that to be a major turning point. It was as though a switch had been flicked and he had gone from being a child to an adult again.

Lucy: When we weren't watching a lot of Sky Sports News – just like we do now! – we often sat outside on two big sunbeds, chilling out. It was summer, the weather was pretty good, and my parents had a big garden.

Matt just lay about, really. The weather was nice, the environment was relaxing, and it seemed as though he was steadily improving and becoming himself again.

I couldn't help myself from chewing things over, though. *What's going on? Why has this happened?*

I was also concerned about Matt returning to football. If it had been an obvious injury, it would have been fairly clear when he would be okay again and ready for training. His problems were less visible and much less clear, and I suppose none of us really knew that the difficulties were just starting.

The memories come back sporadically. There is much that simply isn't there.

How I was when I first got home? My family coming to see me in Manchester? Lucy driving me to Claxby, and me being like a child, food pouring out of my mouth as I ate with my hands? Nothing.

Nor do I remember how I was when I reached Barry and Judith's home: the constant sleeping, the complete loss of inhibitions or sense of right and wrong, the burping and farting, walking into Barry's study at 7.00 a.m. wearing only my boxers to begin a conversation with the parents of somebody I had only been dating for two or three months.

Everything I've been told about that time suggests I'd regressed to a primitive state of mind, with my body just taking over. It did what it felt was needed, and my brain wasn't in control.

I do have a memory of sitting in Barry's front room watching Sky Sports News going round and round and round and round. One of the stories that kept coming back on the bulletins was about me and my accident. I didn't understand why that was on.

The World Cup was under way and apparently I watched several games, but I don't remember that. I do have a memory of Barry sitting on a seat outside his garage, and now I know that he was watching me in case I took a risky walk towards the pool.

I don't remember the episode when I apparently snapped back into consciousness and left the kitchen like a bombsite.

Lucy took me to Blackburn one day. I can remember walking around the training ground, with a chap with a dog. Then she drove me back.

Lucy: At home, we would try to respond any time he engaged with one of us. We were eager to try to answer his questions, and it felt like he was building up a bit of a pattern in his mind.

Also, the better he seemed to get, the more he wanted to get out and do things. We knew that at some stage he would need to be reintroduced to the outside world, so my father had the idea of taking him to the races at Market Rasen. Matt was into horse racing, and it felt like a low-maintenance, low-key thing for him to do, out in the fresh air and somewhere he wouldn't be recognised.

That was the theory, anyway.

Barry: I knew that Matt and Lucy had been to one or two race meetings and, while I had no interest in horse racing, I knew there was a meeting at Market Rasen, which was only three miles away, the following Saturday, so we agreed to go. It would be away from the public gaze and hopefully something he could enjoy. We paid to get into the enclosure and the day was proceeding quite normally until, suddenly, a group of about a dozen blokes recognised Matt and started to make a beeline for him.

It turned out to be a coachload of Burnley supporters.

As they approached Matt, I wondered if my worst nightmare was going to unfold, given the fierce competition between Burnley and Blackburn Rovers fans, but they were very courteous towards him. They clearly knew all about his accident and spoke to him in a very respectful and sympathetic manner.

In a way it was good, because, as well as asking for autographs, they were talking directly to Matt, which meant he had to engage with them. Some of them asked questions about the accident, and Matt tried his best to say some coherent things in response. I interjected now and again, attempting to fill the gaps, but after ten minutes or so I detected that Matt was tiring and made an excuse that we had to go somewhere.

From a therapeutic point of view, it was quite helpful. It was the first time Matt had spoken to anyone outside the family since he had got back from Italy. It just so happened that it was a group of Burnley fans! It helped, I felt, to remind him who he was, and that he was a footballer. I made sure he didn't overdo it, but all in all it appeared to be another little step forward.

Lucy: I remember going with him to the training ground at Blackburn. Hardly anyone was in. There was Kathryn, who worked in the office, and Phil Batty, the club doctor, but not many others. I remember them being quite shocked at how bad he was.

Then we went to see a neurosurgeon in Liverpool, who was really good, really nice. Matt had to be evaluated and there were lots of tests.

Jay: One of my concerns had been to make sure things were as low-key as possible in terms of how the story was reported. The only time it was out of control was very early on, when a billboard for the *News & Star* in Carlisle said POLICE TO QUIZ MATT JANSEN. I called the editor: 'You've done this to sell your newspapers – it's outrageous!'

The headline made out that Matt was under some kind of suspicion, rather than the more boring truth: that the police interview everybody after an accident.

Otherwise, it was a case of trying to guide Matt through the initial stages of his recovery. We went to see a neurosurgeon, a private specialist that Blackburn Rovers had arranged. In the middle of the interview, Matt started laughing uncontrollably. 'What's wrong?' the neurosurgeon asked.

'Can you get me some cookies?' Matt giggled.

He was on another planet. He was craving sugar, but the word 'cookies' was the only way he could get this message out.

The neurosurgeon later asked me for some time on my own. He was as explicit as doctors get in saying that it was highly unlikely that he would play football again.

That was quite dramatic news to deal with. I didn't say anything to Matt, partly because he was still away with the fairies and wouldn't have remembered it anyway, but I did mention it to his dad and my wife.

Then, though, the verdict changed dramatically. A couple of weeks later the doctors said he was now making a really good recovery, and the prognosis was better than had been feared.

Otherwise, he was at Claxby, making slow progress. Barry and Judith were amazing in how they looked after him, and I always had full confidence that he was in good care.

There was an insurance policy to which the club contributed a phenomenal amount of money, but because he had been on a moped, we couldn't claim on that.

Quite soon after coming back to England, I did some tests at the Liverpool John Moores University brain unit. They were basic problem-solving tests, the sort you would give to six-year-olds. I was crap in the first ones, but apparently scored miles better when I returned a few days later. I kept getting sent back for these tests, and the progress of my results indicated I was getting better and better.

Lucy took me to and from Brockhall, where Phil Batty and I went on really slow walks around the perimeter of the training ground, just chatting. He was, I suppose, getting a measure of how I was.

I was also assessed by Tim Pigott, consultant neurosurgeon at the Grosvenor Nuffield Hospital in Cheshire, and Dr Eric Ghadiali, a consultant neuropsychologist. The letters they exchanged show how my immediate recovery was assessed. Initially, the correspondence shows, it was felt that I would be out of football for at least six months. There was also 'an outside chance' that I 'might not play football again'. I'm not sure I registered this at the time.

The medical documents also reveal the physical extent of what had happened in Italy. A CT scan from the hospital in Rome had shown several 'small punctuate haematoma within the dominant frontal lobe of the brain'. The accident had resulted in 'post-traumatic amnesia of three days' and the medics found that I remained 'muddled, tired and confused'. You can say that again.

Looking at the letters, the prognosis seemed to improve as June turned into July, but that I remained 'fatigued', 'slightly irritable' and had 'some difficulties in keeping track of events'. There were also 'some mild impairments in cognitive functioning', such as 'a slight loss of intellectual abilities, particularly affecting processing speed'.

Dr Ghadiali, in a letter dated 16 July, recommended further neuropsychological assessment, and made another point clear: 'He is not suitable for returning to training in the normal way at this stage.'

Barry: Once Matt realised more clearly what had happened, he resolved to get back playing as soon as he possibly could and appeared to progress on a fairly steady path back to normality.

Phil Batty at Blackburn was heavily involved in his recovery, liaising with the neurosurgeons and making referrals. Footballers at that level get the best of treatments and in that respect there was little I could add.

Through all of this, it was beneficial that the press were a week or so behind the story. Part of Jay's brief was damage limitation, and he succeeded in keeping the media at bay. As such, Matt was reported as arriving home when in fact he had already been back for some time. Today, with social media, that would probably be impossible.

Eventually he reached a stage where he was fit and able to return to his own flat. I was just pleased to have been able to help. I'd taken a career break in 2002 which turned into full-time retirement, so

I found myself in a position to offer what I could, as much for Lucy as for Matt. Lucy was still relatively young and, although her recovery was much simpler, there had still been the shock to deal with and she had needed to be back with her mum and dad.

When Matt left Claxby, you could have looked at him and concluded there was nothing really wrong anymore.

Lucy: Any other plans I had for that summer had obviously gone on the shelf. There was no way I was going to leave Matt's side. We were still within the first six months of a new relationship, but I felt like I was his rock, his go-to person.

There were lots of tests, lots of evaluations. Someone had to decide when he could head a ball. Could he ever head a ball?

In physical terms, I made what appeared to be a pretty spectacular recovery. By the time I went back home to Manchester I felt largely okay. At a glance, the recommended six-month period without football would have appeared over-cautious in my case.

At Blackburn, Souness was fine with me and welcomed me back into the fold. Phil Batty had been caring throughout this period and he formed a plan to ease me back into some sort of training. I don't suppose anyone at the club had a guidebook to tell them exactly how you rehab a player who has been in a coma.

At Brockhall, I began what was basically a mini pre-season with the physio, Dave Fevre, who I had first encountered during my trial at Manchester United. Dave explained that the first steps would be focused on balance, finding my feet, as well as some time in the gym and a bit of running with the other players who were returning from injury.

I was there on 17 July, a day after I had been advised not to train 'in the normal way', but it was far from full-throttle to begin with. Dave's drills were simple. In one, he passed the ball and invited me to take him on before shooting for the bottom corner of an open net. In another, he fired the ball into my feet, testing my control. Before the accident, I was razor sharp at things like this.

Dave fizzed the ball to me, and it spun off my foot and rolled a couple of yards. I groped to bring it back under control.

Well, that wasn't right.

This happened a few more times. Instead of killing and cushioning the ball, my close control was haphazard.

I found, as these drills went on, that I had to process each part of the task, instead of doing it all instinctively, as it had always been. Everything had slowed down. It felt very awkward. The best comparison I can make is this: on an average day, I might leave the house, get into my car, switch on the ignition, drive out of the gate and head to the golf course, and by the time I am pulling up in the car park, I haven't given a moment's thought to how I got there. It's a routine sequence of events that happens quite naturally, without breaking down each phase.

Now I've got the keys.

Now I'm putting them in the ignition.

Now I'm putting it into reverse.

And so on.

When Dave sent the ball towards me, that's exactly how my brain now wanted to figure the process out, step by step:

Put your foot to the side.

Control the ball.

Take it that way.

Do a scissors and change direction.

Now shoot.

It wasn't subconscious anymore and, the more mistakes I made, the more stressed I felt. Dave, and others watching, assured me there was nothing wrong and that it was going to take time to feel myself again. But those little errors accumulated and took up residence in my head.

I looked up at Dave. 'I'm not right here.'

Garry Flitcroft: When he came back to the club, I could tell that he wasn't himself. I have a vivid memory of running out to train one day and going past Matt, who was doing some of his early rehab away from the main group of players. The doctor was just throwing a ball into Matt's hands, but his co-ordination wasn't there. He kept missing the ball.

Hold on a minute, I thought. What has this accident actually done to him? When I remember that scene, it makes me think he did remarkably well just to get back playing again.

As my training gradually increased, it was deemed fine for me to start heading the ball again. This allowed me to take part in games of head tennis in the gym. This was an instinctive and fun skill for me – some of my matches with Tugay had been epic, and he was eager to take me on again. It didn't take long before he clipped the ball towards my right foot. I waved my leg hopelessly towards it and lost the point. Back it came, moments later, and the same happened. I just couldn't get the ball back. Some of the lads watching were pissing themselves laughing. My attempts to use my right foot must have looked like I was having some sort of fit. Tugay won the game hands down and the smile I painted on was thin.

These tiny failures chipped at my confidence. I began to feel like a golfer with the yips. The thought process I now required for every touch of a football was completely alien to me, and I couldn't shift the uneasy sense from my mind.

I can't do it. I'm not right. I'm not right.

Nobody saw or heard these thoughts very much to begin with, because I was having a difficult enough job working them out for myself. Superficially, I was back in the fold and increasingly able to take part in fuller training. But the little errors persisted. It wasn't yet feeling natural, and I found that each mistake nurtured a thought I had never felt before on a training pitch: *I'm not sure I want the ball here. I'll mess it up.*

Out on the grass, a game of keep-ball was starting, with everyone in a circle and two in the middle.

'You can join in with this, Janny,' someone said.

A minute in, I went into the centre and inevitably gave the ball away. It arrived at Craig Short's feet. I ran towards him as he booted it. The ball smacked me clean in the face and my nose went *splat.*

I fell to my haunches and everyone crowded around me. My eyes were streaming and there was blood pouring down my face. I glanced up and Shorty looked horrified.

It was obvious that people were worried about my head taking such a strong blow, but no harm was done (other than to my nose) and I carried on with few ill-effects. Later, Phil Batty said it was probably the best thing that could have happened. If I could take a blow without any repercussions, that was a real positive, and I must be on the right track.

By September, Dr Ghadiali reckoned that I had made a 'complete recovery from a neuropsychological function point of view'. Fitness testing also showed I was in good enough shape, and after the rigours of my mini pre-season the club allowed me a couple of weeks off.

This came as more of a relief than I had expected. We went on safari at the Kruger National Park in South Africa, and then to Mauritius, where we were joined by Jay and Clare.

I loved every minute of it. I was spending time in a couple of wonderful places, but I was also happy to be away from the training ground, trying to control a ball, or beat someone, or think of the right pass, or . . .

That wasn't me.

When I returned to Blackburn, the next step was to get back

playing again. A reserve game against Everton was looming and I was pencilled in to start.

I was shitting myself.

I told Phil, the doc, that I felt apprehensive about it. He tried to reassure me, but I was terrified as the day approached.

The game was at Halton Stadium, Widnes, with a few hundred people watching. I didn't want the ball, because I knew how I had been messing things up in training, and as the match began this feeling became self-fulfilling. I was still thinking about every tiny movement and when the ball came to me, I had already resigned myself to the fact I might make a little mistake. Sure enough, that's what happened. For the best part of seventy minutes, I had a beast.

Then I got the ball and bent it into the stanchion from thirty yards.

Whoa. What was that?

The reaction from the other players was as you would expect for a goal like that.

'Fucking hell, Janny! What a goal!'

But I had no idea how I'd done it. It felt strange and unnatural. The sense I had was that it had happened to me, rather than having been in control of my own actions. It certainly wasn't the old show-off returning. However it had looked, it hadn't reassured me one bit. I came off the pitch convinced that the yips hadn't gone anywhere.

Later that night, they showed the goal on Sky Sports News. As the footage played, and I whipped the ball past the Everton keeper, the narrative was plain and simple: Matt Jansen is back.

No! I wanted to scream at the TV. No he's not! Not yet!

FOURTEEN

FEAR

Just as time seemed to speed up when I was rising, things slowed down as I struggled to reconnect to the way I had played before the accident. The days went past in a crawl and on repeat: the same mistakes, the same worries, the same feeling that things weren't right. At training, I waited for the moment when it would all click back into place. At home, I felt the first traces of anxiety.

It didn't cross my mind that I might have tried to return too quickly. I didn't appreciate that my head was, to use a comparison Barry often makes, like a snow globe which had received a good shake and then needed time for all the little white flakes to settle again. They were still floating around the globe when I attempted my comeback, so my goal against Everton did nothing to reassure me. It actually made things worse, because something that had once been my fuel, confirmation of everything I felt positive about, had felt so alien to me. It didn't matter how many people were convinced that I was on the way back if I wasn't one of them.

One day ate into another and to begin with, I kept all these doubts and fears to myself. I would go to training, make the usual stumbles, recognise that I didn't want the ball anymore, and then go home and spend the rest of the day with a cloud over my head.

I'm still shit. I don't know what's wrong with me.

People at the club told me to be patient and it would come. But it wasn't coming.

'Just relax, Matt. Give it time.'

Inside, the words strained to escape: *I'm trying to fucking relax. It's not fucking working!*

Everything was said with the best of intentions, but nobody knew how I felt. What I really wanted was for someone to rationalise it, to tell me I had a blood clot on my brain, or that I was damaged in some other way. Someone, please, explain everything. Give it a name, give me some proof. Give me a reason why things aren't working.

Nobody did, or could. That made things worse.

Shortly after the Everton game, I was prescribed a course of antidepressants. The idea was that they would blur the edges and allow me to get through training and games without worrying about every step, whilst also keeping me in a calmer frame of mind at home. They didn't work.

As I made my first-team comeback, I was still living on fear. I came off the bench to replace our new signing, Dwight Yorke, in the second half against Newcastle at Ewood. The reports say I got a standing ovation from the Rovers supporters and we stuffed them 5–2. I don't remember any of that. All I remember is how scared I was.

Those reports also include an interview I gave to the *Independent on Sunday*. 'I ran down the touchline, and that's when it really hit me,' I told the reporter. 'Oh, God, I'm coming back on to a football pitch – it was terrifying.'

The interview continued as I rolled out the usual clichés. Relief my first touch was okay, delighted at the crowd's reception, pleased to be back, blah, blah, blah . . .

Lies. Only one word was completely authentic. By admitting that the thought of playing football was 'terrifying', I was giving the world a hint at the truth.

It wasn't enough to change anything. A couple of substitute appearances followed, along with a couple of reserve games and a low-key outing against Walsall in the League Cup. Souness was keen to get me back to full power and I don't suppose he appreciated that, while I was desperate for exactly the same thing, I couldn't bear the idea that people would see a lesser version of me on the pitch. This was my conflict now: I wanted to play and I didn't want to play. I wanted to show off, and I couldn't bear to be on the stage while I wasn't myself.

A new snowball. And boy, did it grow.

I continued to see the neurosurgeons and did my best to explain my feelings. They listened intently, but weren't able to tell me I was brain-damaged or provide the kind of explanation I was desperately seeking. At home, I struggled for sleep, and eventually decided to ditch the antidepressants. The chemicals weren't working. Then I started feeling worse, so I started taking them again, washed down with a few beers. Then I ditched them again. Then I felt worse again. I was looking in vain for a magic solution which would stop me lurching from one extreme to the other, yearning to play but then feeling relieved when Souness left me on the bench, or out of the squad completely.

Then January came, and a trip to Aston Villa in the FA Cup. It was almost exactly six months after the neurosurgeon had suggested I might not play for that length of time. My physical recovery had been so swift that I had been fast-tracked. And now I was starting at Villa, when the initial prognosis had been that I would only now be returning to training. Somehow, this appeared to be seen only in positive terms. Another step on the road back for Matt.

On the morning of the match, I went for a walk with Phil Batty.

'Phil, I still don't feel right,' I said.

As ever, he tried to reassure me, but the fear attacked me again in the tunnel before kick-off. Then, in the sixteenth minute, the ball broke behind the Villa defence and I drilled it past the keeper. Just like the goal against Everton, it didn't feel normal, and when we reached half-time at 1–1 I was glad of the respite. As I came off the pitch, I remembered Dad and Lucy were behind the goal, so I looked for them. I quickly saw Dad near the front of the stand. As I neared the tunnel, he came across to greet me.

'Am I doing all right, Dad?' I asked him.

'All right? Are you taking the piss?'

He was wearing a big smile and proceeded to tell me how well I'd been playing. It was like he was talking about somebody else.

Early in the second half, Yorke, who had been booed throughout by the home fans who once sang his name here, put us back in front. On the hour mark I found space to score a free header. It put us on the way to a 4–1 win, and afterwards I saw Dad again in the car park.

I asked him again how I'd played. Once again, he beamed. 'You'll do for me, son.'

It was nice of him to say so. But why wasn't I feeling the same?

In the papers the next day, I was the universal choice as man of the match. There were also quotes from Souness, who said that, for the first time in months, 'Matt will be going home with a clear head and a big grin on his face.'

The headlines reflected all of this, but I frowned when I saw them. I knew they were fiction.

The truth? I'd gone home from Birmingham thinking one cold thought: *Shit. After this I'm going to be starting again next week.*

Garry Flitcroft: In the period when Matt got back into the team, I noticed that he was quiet and a bit downbeat. It seemed like his confidence had been knocked – and this was significant, because Matt had always been a confidence player. It was as though he no longer believed he could do some of the things that had come so naturally beforehand. I think it was hard for the other players to see him like that as well, and I remember one occasion when I sat down with Matt and tried to give him some encouragement. I said that I'd been out for fourteen months with a bad knee injury, and some people had said I was finished, but I proved them wrong. I hoped that would help him see that he could get there eventually. Yet as much as people tried to pick him up, I think he just kept going home at night and telling himself that he couldn't get back to his old self.

My pessimistic attitude was a new experience for Lucy, and it must have tested her patience in those strange early days. She saw me at home when others didn't, witnessed me trying to make sense of my doubts and confusion. I knew that she had stood by me and supported me after the accident. More than ever, I recognised that she was the final piece of my jigsaw and, that winter, I asked her to marry me.

In a few short months we had been through more than some couples experience in a lifetime. It felt right, just as it did when she said yes. In that aspect of life, at least, I was still very happy.

Lucy: Fighting his way back was a long, hard slog. That was something Matt hadn't really had to do before. He had never been one of those players that had to drill everything time and again until it sunk in. He played off the cuff, and that made him what he was.

This had the effect of making it doubly difficult when he had to grit his teeth and battle to get it all back. It was an uphill struggle and there were days when it seemed too much for him. Clearly it wasn't happening as quickly as he had wanted or expected, and that really troubled him.

Injured footballers are a nightmare. They are constantly looking over their shoulders. This possibly made Matt feel he needed to get back into it as quickly as he could. I think he also felt a little guilt, that Blackburn had been absolutely fine with him, in spite of the fact he had got on a scooter on his holidays.

When he found he couldn't hit his old heights straight away, it only made things worse. At home he started asking more questions about the accident – 'What was I like, what did I do, where did I go?' Because I could remember everything that had happened in Rome, I didn't particularly enjoy reliving it over and over again. But he was desperate to fill the gaps, desperate to find some answers, so I tried my best.

Matt has always been a very impatient person. I remember a time when, after having a hernia operation in Austria, he was advised to stay in bed for two days. Instead, he discharged himself early and called me from the airport, asking if I could pick him up.

He thinks he's the bionic man. On a box of tablets it might say, 'Take two pills three times a day', but he will disregard that, convinced his body will react differently. Instead, he'll take six in one go.

I suppose this idea that he is a bit different from the norm played some part in how he approached his comeback. If someone had told him he should be taking a certain amount of time before playing football again, part of his character will have wanted to take that on and beat it and be known as the person who recovered from his predicament the quickest. So, even as he felt there was something fundamentally wrong with him, even as he was sleeping fitfully and wondering when he was going to get it all back, he decided he should be throwing himself into things at Blackburn. Nobody was particularly persuading him otherwise and unfortunately things didn't get much better.

The Villa game was only my second start since the accident. I was then left on the bench for our trip to Man United in the Carling Cup. I had conflicting thoughts about that.

1) I've just scored two goals and been man of the match. Why have I not kept my place? Did I not play that well after all? What's going on?

2) Thank fuck for that. I can't make any mistakes if I'm not playing.

In the first team, Yorke was resuming his old Manchester United double-act with Cole. Jay had a row with Souness about signing Yorke that summer, feeling that another big-name striker competing for my place was the last thing I needed at a time when I was fragile. I can't say I shared the same irritation.

Among a cluster of further substitute appearances, I played a reserve game against Bolton that was watched by a tiny crowd. My ego hated performing in front of a handful of people, but also appreciated the fact there weren't thousands there to see me mess up. I did get another start, against Sunderland in the FA Cup, but Souness whipped me off at half-time. Apparently, before doing so, he had been conflicted himself, telling Phil Batty that he was worried it might 'destroy' me. It was another knock to my confidence, but also a mighty relief, because it meant I could pull my tracksuit back on after forty-five minutes and watch the rest of the game from the bench.

Sven-Göran Eriksson: When we heard about his accident,

everyone in the England squad was very sad. It sounded like something very bad and of course we were concerned for him. As time passed, everybody thought that he would come back as a football player and carry on with his career. I saw him in some games after that, but he was not the player we had seen before. You would look at him and think, 'He needs more time'. He was there, he was playing, but he was not as sharp as he had been before the accident.

With England, Tord and I always followed players we had picked, or had talked about picking. Not always in person, but we had scouts looking at them – let's say thirty-five to forty players, maybe more. We regularly got a report on every player that was in our thoughts and Matt was absolutely followed up in this respect.

I remember some of those reports. 'No,' they said. 'He's not back to what he was.'

It is difficult for me to say what happened as a result of the accident but of course it is very, very sad that his career at the top level finished much too early.

At some stage in my unsatisfactory comeback, decision makers at Blackburn got together to discuss my situation, and a new plan emerged. A loan move, where I could get some regular starts. That's what I needed to restore the old magic.

There were rules against being loaned to another Premier League club, so I had to drop a division. In February, I went to Coventry.

I was advised it would help me in the long run, and Blackburn's eagerness to get me some games was reflected in the fact they didn't demand much from Coventry in terms of wage contribution. I wasn't exactly doing somersaults, though, at the idea of playing in the league below, less than a year after getting picked for England. The truth is I didn't want to be there any more than I wanted to play at any other ground. I had to give it a go, but I was in the wrong frame of mind from the start.

Gary McAllister, who was player-manager at Coventry and presumably got the deal done because of his relationship with Souness, collected me from my hotel for my first morning session. He was bright and friendly but he was up against it in different ways. Coventry were in financial trouble, trying to offload some experienced players and big earners like Dean Holdsworth and Julian Joachim. They were also struggling in the wrong half of the table, instead of fighting to get back into the big league. Certain players were training on their own, the word was that McAllister's hands were tied regarding other signings, and in hindsight they had more than enough problems without adding mine to the mix.

I started in a defeat against Bradford to no great effect. Then we went to Grimsby, where I'd had such a great night with Blackburn a couple of years earlier. Leading at half-time, we were then awarded a penalty when Joachim was fouled in the box. John Eustace, the Coventry captain, approached me.

'Do you want to take it, Janny?'

I felt a rush of panic.

'No, no,' I said, laughing nervously. 'You're the regular taker, mate. You have it.'

I'd not taken many penalties in my career – David Dunn was the regular taker at Blackburn – but, at the same time, I would never have turned one down. Now, though, I knew I didn't want the pressure. Eustace had tried to help me, but I swerved it. I breathed out hard as he placed the ball and made it 2–0. Then I went back to my demons: wanting the ball, not wanting it, waiting for the magic to come back, wondering when it would all happen, straining for the moment and sitting disconsolately in the dressing room after another ninety minutes when it hadn't returned.

It soon became obvious that I'd merely relocated my problems to a different part of the country. After the second game, I didn't want to play the third. After the third, I didn't want to play the fourth. On it went. I was awarded man of the match in one game but there was no convincing me – I still felt shit and scared.

McAllister left me out of a couple of games and told Jay I wasn't quite doing it in training. Jay threatened to end the loan early, feeling it was pointless if I wasn't going to be playing. I got back into the side and stuck it out until the end of the season. I arrived back at Blackburn no closer to the player or the person I'd been before the accident than when I had joined Coventry.

There was one more game in the Premier League season. If we won at Tottenham, it would mean qualification for the UEFA Cup. I was on the bench and watched as we rose to the occasion, building a 4–0 lead before Souness put me on for the closing stages. I crept out of my bib and slapped hands with Hignett. The away fans were in happy voice, but my fifteen minutes crawled by.

'How long's left, ref?'

'Another seven minutes.'

That long?

I should have been excited to be involved in such a big game. Instead, I was desperate for it to be over before it had started. I wanted to get out of White Hart Lane, get home, collapse into the summer break and leave the stress and torment behind for a few more weeks.

A few weeks of denial, that is. That summer I walked into an entirely new problem: I started to forget about the torture of the previous months and, as May slipped into June, I deceived myself into thinking that my problems were over. The truth was, I had merely put them into storage.

Away from football for the summer, I wasn't going home

anxious from a bad day's training. I wasn't standing under the dressing room showers asking myself why I wasn't feeling the same. I wasn't tossing and turning in bed quite so much. I was probably a better person to be around. I conned myself that I was okay, and that next season, after a bit of rest, things would be fine.

I also kept myself in good shape, running and going to the gym, but that stuff always came easily. If anything, I became a bit obsessive and compulsive about it after the accident, because it took my mind off the issues when a ball was involved.

That continued as pre-season rolled around. I was at the front of the running – which always looked good – and as fit as anyone could have hoped.

We went to America for a pre-season tour, and that also seemed to convince Souness that I'd returned a different player. It was a fairly relaxed trip, with a bit of golf, a couple of nights on the piss and a game against DC United in Washington that passed without any problems.

I actually did okay in the friendly, but it was low-key, with barely any Rovers fans there.

No pressure.

Souness later said my form had been one of the highlights of our pre-season, and he put me in the starting line-up for our first few games of the new Premier League campaign. I scored in our second match, against Bolton, but I didn't feel like I was there yet. I felt thousands of eyes on me, wondering who this lesser version of Matt Jansen was, and the vicious circle resumed. By September, I was really struggling again and it made no difference to me at all when, against Liverpool at Ewood, I scored a goal that, to anyone else, must have appeared extraordinary.

Eight minutes had gone when the ball fell to me twenty-five yards from goal. Jamie Carragher, one of the country's most determined defenders, was closing in from the right. Approaching the D, I dinked the ball over his head, then wrongfooted him again as I shifted it back inside before smashing it home left-footed.

The ground went bananas and I ran off to celebrate. But I didn't feel excited, or joyful. My expression was strained because I was closer to anger than jubilation.

What the fuck's wrong with me? How did I do that? Why can't I keep doing that?

Once again, I had no idea how it had happened. This time it was worse, because this was on the big stage, and the passing of nearly a year hadn't made things any different.

It was a goal born of fear. I'd felt completely out of control.

From there, I went in and out of the side for a couple of months: dropped when I shouldn't have been, playing when I had no right to be anywhere near the side. These were my own thoughts – I had no idea what Souness or anyone else was seeing.

I had no idea if or when it would all come back to me. I'd tried all sorts – going on loan, antidepressants, running myself silly, the occasional prayer – and nothing had worked. I became depressed again and progressively found that the only thing I could rely on to give me any sort of relief was a beer. I got into the habit, whether at home or with a couple of the lads, of knocking a couple back. It took my mind off the problems and helped me hide away. The temptation to hole up in the apartment with Lucy, switch on the telly and have a few drinks became overwhelming and, increasingly, I started to look forward to days off, because I knew I could have a little binge. It's no way to live your life, and I can't think how it must have been for Lucy. My medical notes around this time indicate I was 'very low and depressed' and even entertaining 'some self-harm thoughts', and I suppose what happened in this period fits both theories.

I was in the apartment, on my own, after another day's training that had confirmed to me that I was still all over the place. I reached into the fridge for a bottle of beer and flicked off the cap. I glugged it down and went back for another. I felt desperate. I was drinking to block it all out, and I knew it. I sat down, stared into space and realised that I was crying. After a couple more bottles, I began pacing around.

I wanted it all to stop.

I paused and opened one of the kitchen cupboards. I knew what I was looking for and it didn't take me long to find it: a box of Anadin Extra. I removed the sleeve from the box and pressed out the pills, one by one. I threw the lot into my mouth and swilled them down with lager. I don't remember exactly how many there were. There could have been eight, there could have been a full pack, there might even have been a second pack. I wasn't counting. I was past caring.

Someone will find me. They'll take me to hospital. I'll be fine.

I had a few more beers, to help get me off to sleep, and eventually stumbled to bed. When I opened my eyes, it was morning. My mouth was dry but everything else was normal. I got up, walked into the kitchen and saw an empty box on the counter.

You prick.

Just as hangovers never troubled me, it turned out I was also resistant to a gutful of Anadins.

Great.

I wouldn't categorise it as a suicide attempt. I wasn't thinking as clearly as that. It certainly wasn't planned, and I didn't have any real idea what would happen. I just wanted whatever was eating me alive to stop for a while.

I should have been relieved that the pills hadn't done any damage, but I knew it had been another cry for help that nobody had heard.

Lucy: Living with Matt at this time brought such a mixture of emotions. Some days he would appear rational and focused in his thinking, the next he would be completely irrational.

He had a tendency to try to escape – that's where the beers came in – but found that the same problems would be there the next day. When he got dropped for the next Blackburn game it was like the world was ending and the walls were crashing down, but at the same time he couldn't get past the idea that there was something fundamentally wrong with him.

I felt we needed to move on from the accident, and deal with the here and now, but Matt still fixated on Rome. He expressed disbelief that it had happened at such a pivotal point in his career and began to torment himself over the fact he could have been at the World Cup instead of in Italy.

I tried to be patient with him, but there came a moment when I snapped. 'Enough with the poor-me act,' I said. 'If I could do it for you, I'd go out on to the pitch, but I can't. It's up to you.'

'You don't understand what I'm going through.'

'No, I don't. But I'm doing my best to try.'

I felt I had to make him see how difficult it was for me to deal with him. I needed to hold a mirror up, and somehow get across what it was like, trying to handle this loose cannon who was so different from one day to the next. I came to dread him coming home from training because I didn't know what the night would bring. Would it be the sad, crying little boy in the corner? The broken man? The anger, the frustration, the outbursts? I hated him going out to work and hated the thought of how he would be when he came through the door.

It came to a stage when I felt I couldn't take much more of it. I wasn't a psychiatrist or a psychologist. I was his girlfriend, and now his fiancée, and I wanted the best for him. When you love someone, you want to support them as much as you can, but when you start to doubt whether your efforts are doing any good, it wears your patience thin. I didn't feel like he was listening.

'I can't tell you any more times – you can do it. I've seen you play.'

'Yeah, but I don't feel right.'

'But you look right. Honestly you do. Is anyone shouting at you, saying you're not doing it? No. Is anyone calling you a wanker? No. You can do it. You're scoring goals.'

'I'm telling you – I'm not right.'

'Okay, what more can I say? If you can't do it, don't. Finish. Quit. Come home, leave it, draw a line under it. You're going round in circles.'

Graeme Souness: When Matt came back, he didn't seem the same as the boy who had finished the 2001/02 season. I can remember one of the earliest games of his return, when he scored twice in the FA Cup at Aston Villa, but it was clear, as the weeks went by, that he wasn't finding things easy.

We intended to give him as much time as possible to get back to his best. With a serious head injury, it can be very hard to know how much time is enough. Is it something that is going to affect you for a few months, or years, or the rest of your life? Working out the ramifications is extremely hard, but I had every confidence that Phil Batty and our physio, Dave Fevre, would make the right choices for him. The medical set-up at Blackburn Rovers was as good as anything I ever experienced in football.

Our eagerness to do right by Matt also had a business aspect. In hard-nosed terms, Matt was worth a hell of a lot of money, and it was very much in the club's interests to get him right again. Along with Damien Duff, he was the most valuable asset the football club had at that time.

I also had to maintain a ruthless side as manager. It was my job to look at the bigger picture, and focus on trying to keep

Blackburn progressing in the Premier League. As much as you want to be loyal to your players, and as much as I hoped something would happen in Matt's recovery to get him back to his best, it was my duty to my employers to field the best possible team I could. That's why I eventually moved for other strikers, such as Dwight Yorke.

I don't particularly remember Matt opening up to me about how he was feeling in those difficult times. He was never one of the louder voices in the dressing room, and after the accident he became even quieter. I knew that he was seeing people in the psychiatry field, but the nature of any patient-doctor relationship meant that I couldn't be told what had been discussed, which is the way it should be.

I had, whilst at Coventry, seen a sports science consultant called Neil Roach. He was a nice guy but a bit like a schoolteacher, and all his work with me was very practical. These sessions were based around repetition, the idea that I would do things so many times that I would stop overthinking, and everything would start coming naturally again. It was another idea and it didn't have much effect. Just like practising penalties has a limited effect when you are in the tense environment of a shoot-out, controlling a hundred awkward passes on the playing fields at Alsager proved to be limited preparation for doing it on a Saturday afternoon, with the fear weighing me down.

In November, after the Anadins episode, Blackburn suggested I might benefit from psychiatric help. I told Phil Batty I was happy to consider it. Another magic pill that I hadn't tried? Why not.

The following month, Phil told me the arrangements had been made. I was going to be seeing a man called Steve Peters.

FIFTEEN

THE CHIMP

Letter from Steve Peters to Phil Batty, December 2003

Matt's concerns are that he has lost his ability to play at his expected level of expertise and constantly 'chokes' when under pressure. Currently he doesn't enjoy football because he makes mistakes and therefore makes a fool of himself. When he's on the pitch he dreads receiving the ball and tries hard to pass it on immediately.

He is not currently on medication but has tried a course of Paroxetine for control of his anxiety and depressive symptoms. He wasn't happy with this and stopped medication rather abruptly, which resulted in some side-effects.

He displayed little evidence of any biological features of depression but did exhibit some anxiety when discussing the possibility of being selected for impending matches. He is also concerned about his contract ending in eighteen months' time and this raised an issue about money and his future.

He works from a basis that he knows best and will dispute or challenge advice offered to him. In this respect he is very defensive and sees everything as black or white, and success or fail. For example, he sees the fans as either hating or loving him, sees past performance as virtually faultless and current performance as invariably poor. He is hooked on the ego-massaging and elevated status from the crowd and his peers, but is in great fear this will turn into belittlement if he is not successful.

When playing football he should be operating from his parietal memory. Instead he perceives the training and game as currently beyond his abilities and sees a perceived danger. This belief structure results in him operating via his frontal lobe and linking into his limbic system, resulting in him going into fight or flight mode. As he has perceived the demon of perfection to be more powerful than himself, he continues to go into flight mode and engages in avoidance techniques. In the past he has always got round this by inventing a safety net, for example having a niggling back or a sore throat. Consequently his natural talent would come through without a problem and any small blips would be dismissed using his safety net as an excuse. Currently he has not got a safety net and cannot see the excuses as substantial enough for his current poor performance.

My first suggestion is to offer him a valid safety net that will effectively stem the demon that he feels he cannot beat, the comments from his teammates and manager. He believes that they think he has emotional problems and if he tries hard enough he will succeed. He believes if his teammates and manager understand this is an illness, it will remove that pressure from him.

The first time I met Steve Peters was at the Velodrome in Manchester. He had silvering hair, a friendly manner and a focused expression that suggested he was listening very intently when others were speaking. He didn't seem, at first glance, like the person who was going to open my mind and sort me out once and for all. Did that person even exist?

It was an introductory meeting at Phil's instigation, and the cyclist Chris Boardman was also there. I don't know how much Phil believed in psychology and psychiatry at the time – he was more of a 'pull your socks up, grit your teeth' kind of guy – but it was clearly felt to be another avenue worth exploring.

I hadn't heard of Steve before, but Phil had explained his background. His main work was as a psychiatrist at the Rampton Secure Hospital in Nottinghamshire, where he dealt with patients with schizophrenia and other personality disorders, but now he was also getting involved with sport. The reason we were at the Velodrome was because Steve had just started working with the British cycling team.

Steve spoke briefly, explaining a little about himself. He was, he said, an athlete himself – part of the Great Britain veterans team and also, it turned out, quicker than me at the 100m, even though he was in his fifties. He didn't look like an athlete, but his times were ridiculous. Maybe, if he knew something of sport, he could get inside my head.

Or maybe he couldn't. Plenty had tried before, after all. We arranged to meet more formally, and the first session was to be at Barry's house, which was mutually convenient. Blackburn were content to pick up the tab.

The moment Steve rang the doorbell at Claxby, he gave the impression of working everybody out. We sat down and he encouraged me to explain, as best I could, how I had been feeling. It felt like we were just having a conversation. He didn't lay out a plan for our therapy, or discuss his method – he just listened, popped in a question or two, and I found that I enjoyed opening up to him.

We had regular sessions from there. Early on in one of our next conversations, I told Steve that, whereas before the accident I had found playing football natural and instinctive, now I was having to think about everything, and that this was screwing up my mind.

'I think there's an explanation for this. Let me talk to you a little about how the brain is working here.'

The brain, he said, was formed of several different parts, the most important of which were two lobes, the parietal and the frontal. These were new terms for me, but Steve went on to put things in a footballer's language.

'Think about a penalty shoot-out in a World Cup,' he said. 'Do you ever wonder why some of the top players miss their kicks? It's because the frontal lobe has taken over.'

I'm listening.

'The frontal lobe is essentially your learning stage. When you become good at something, it passes into the parietal lobe, where your actions are automatic. In other words, if you practise penalties for long enough – or any skill for that matter – there comes a point where you don't feel you are learning it anymore, and it comes naturally, or instinctively. In a shoot-out, though, it's different, because there's pressure.'

In a stressful situation, he said, the frontal lobe can come back into play. That's because there is no obvious way of preparing for the stress of a shoot-out. You're back in an environment where you're learning on the spot.

Steve connected this with how I was feeling in training and on the pitch. Some people have innate ability and rely on off-the-cuff decisions rather than rote learning. Other players churn and churn away, practise and practise, and become perfectionists. I had always belonged to the first group. So when I came back from the accident, and had to learn my motor skills again – relearn how to do the things on a football pitch that had long been second nature for me – it confused me. There was too much thinking. *Receive the ball. Control the ball. Which way to turn? Take him on. Change direction. Bollocks, I've lost it. Now what?*

I was in frontal-lobe mode in everything I was doing on the pitch, and it was giving me immense worry and stress. I was fighting to get back into that natural state, and it was proving more difficult than I had ever imagined.

'So I scored this goal against Liverpool,' I told Steve. 'I knocked it over the defender's head, came back inside, beat the keeper. It looked like a worldy, but I felt completely out of control and really panicked. I don't understand why it didn't feel right.'

'You won't have realised,' Steve said, 'but it sounds like your parietal lobe actually took over at that moment, purely through fear.'

I was learning a lot.

When Steve left after a discussion like this, I found that I felt a little calmer. He seemed to know what he was talking about. He had listened and come up with what felt like intelligent and rational explanations.

Sometimes our meetings were at Barry's, sometimes they were at Steve's own house, where I had to step around a couple of huge dogs, bigger than Great Danes, to greet him. Usually, by the time we got together again, I was back to square one. I had fucked up in training, or at least thought I had.

'I just don't feel right,' I'd say. 'And I'm scared that people will see me and think I'm not the player I used to be.'

I talked about the adulation I had always loved, and how terrified I was of falling short in front of the public, and if only people would stop telling me to be patient, and to keep trying, and . . .

Steve said: 'That's your chimp.'

Chimp?

He sat back in his chair and set out his theory. We all have an 'inner chimp'. This was his term for the negative side of our personality. When emotion gets the better of us, when we're no longer thinking logically, when we lash out or get wound-up or feel that everything's going wrong – the chimp is in charge.

'Your chimp is getting the better of you,' he said. 'Over the last eighteen months, it's grown so much that it's very strong indeed.'

It sounded so far off-beam that I wouldn't have known what to make of it, had he not then explained some of the science behind the theory. The brain has different components: some that react to things rather than process information first, and others that do the opposite. It's a bit like a machine.

In my case, the challenge was all about finding a way to get me thinking rationally, rather than have one small slip bring my whole world crashing down.

Steve sent me away with these ideas and a few thoughts on how to block out certain negative reactions. Once, because I was so convinced the crowd were going to see a version of myself I didn't like, he encouraged me to imagine I was playing in a shirt without my name on the back, and wearing a hood over my head. Imagine I was an anonymous player, without an ego to protect.

'But I don't see how I can do that,' I said.

Because I didn't have any great faith in or knowledge of psychology, I was sceptical about some of these tricks. Especially in the beginning, I doubted whether any of it was going to work. As I drove home, though, I always felt inflated from having opened up to Steve. I found there was a boost from talking to this intelligent man. I chatted to Lucy about how much brighter he made me feel. The problem was that the boost only lasted so long. As the week went by, I steadily deflated. By the time I saw him again, I was back on the floor.

'Steve, it's not working. I'm just not getting it back.'

'Yeah, a goal, but I was rubbish.'

'I don't think this is right. It's not making any difference to me.'

'Steve, I honestly think I must be brain-damaged. I'm convinced of it.'

The sessions became my respite, replacing those five or six beers I had been drinking in the evening. In the short term, they silenced some of my cries for help and, in that sense, kept me relatively stable and my daily life became a little more comfortable.

They didn't make me play much better, though. Between February and May I had seventeen sessions with Steve. I looked forward to driving over to get that release. But my chimp was always waiting with a pin to burst the balloon. It was bigger than I or anyone else could have appreciated. It was a monster.

Letter from Steve Peters to Phil Batty, February 2004

```
Matt has distorted ideas, for example, that
before the accident, his play was virtually
faultless, and he can only accept being
```

virtually faultless or never play again. He can only be happy playing football and in his life if he is back to where he perceived himself to be before the accident. He believes he has lost none of his skills and does not need to revise. He minimises anything he does that is good and magnifies any errors and then self-denigrates with a corresponding loss of confidence.

He is very impatient for progress and believes his fear is the only reason he cannot play brilliantly, and that this fear can be removed instantly. He believes that no-one knows better than himself. He uses safety nets wherever he can and is prone to despondency and will beat himself up over trivia. He lacks confidence in anyone having the ability to help him and therefore constantly defends himself by saying it will not work.

I have worked with Matt to challenge the beliefs one by one and begin a behavioural programme. Progress is expected to be slow, but I expect to see changes steadily between eight to twelve weeks. Matt initially challenged much of the work and ideas I presented him with, and continued to be very negative until a couple of weeks ago, when he began to admit things had moved on and was beginning to see a change in his approach.

There were other problems at Blackburn beyond my own. One day in March we were playing a five-a-side competition – strikers versus defenders versus midfielders versus also-rans versus staff. It was lively, full of banter, and when the strikers went up against the staff we opened up an easy lead.

Cole and Yorke were really enjoying themselves, celebrating goals as if they had been scored at Ewood. Souness was also enjoying the challenge of stopping us, but didn't like it when Yorke nutmegged him. The manager turned round and appeared to swing a punch at Dwight, failing to make contact. There were a few cheers from the sidelines, but the red mist around our manager didn't lift. A minute later, Yorke received the ball and Souness two-footed him. It was a challenge from his Liverpool heyday, into the back of the leg, and Yorke was furious.

'What's your problem?' he said, limping away. 'Why the fuck are you making a challenge like that?'

Yorke walked off and later, in the canteen, presented his bandaged lower leg. 'What the fuck's that all about?' he said.

Souness, who saw this, was unimpressed. 'This is the problem with you guys today. Nobody's got the bollocks to put a tackle in. In my day someone came in with a gash on their leg every day at Liverpool.'

I wondered if the big characters of Yorke and Cole were making life more difficult for Graeme than he liked.

Life for me was no easier. A couple of games here and there, but no sustained run, and no lasting let-up from my demons. The longer it went on, the more upset I got. Steve, to his credit, didn't give up on me.

Letter from Steve Peters to Phil Batty, May 2004

Matt has improved steadily since [December] but after a period of relatively poor play, he catastrophises this and slides back. He demands reassurance constantly and phones regularly. It can be difficult getting an

objective point of view from Matt as he is
very self-deprecating and will minimise any
progress made.

I explained that if he felt no progress
had been made then there was little point
in him continuing with me as we clearly
were not getting anywhere. He then retracted
his statement and said he felt we were
progressing, and then went on to tell me that
he had had some very good sessions recently
and his anxiety levels were beginning to
settle during training and reserve matches.
He admitted having made good improvements in
many areas over the last three months.

Steve invited me for another meeting at the Velodrome. This
time there was someone else at the table: a young woman who
appeared almost painfully shy and introverted, barely able to
look up and talk when invited – even when Steve asked her to
tell the rest of us that she was now an international champion
in cycling.

Victoria Pendleton shared similar fears to mine. She was
scared to get on the bike and would even refuse to do so unless
Steve was also there. She had doubts, negative thoughts, visions
of falling off the bike and messing up. But if Steve was there with
her, just before the start of a race, it built her back up and gave
her positive reassurance.

It was another way of telling me that I could also get back to
top performance if I could find ways of overcoming my fear. It
left me wishing I could have Steve in the dressing room with me
fifteen minutes before kick-off.

The close-season then brought another period of relief. I could
park the worries again and let my mind drift away from football.

That May, Lucy and I got married. It was such a happy day and our honeymoon, on safari in South Africa, and in the Seychelles, was a wonderful escape. I felt free and content and, in the middle of it all, started to wonder . . .

No – the following season brought it all back again. When the squad numbers were finalised, I realised that I was no longer No.10. Because I'd figured so intermittently, my name was down at No.17. My sessions with Steve had given me the tools to rationalise this in a way that minimised the effect it had on my confidence and well-being.

A number's a number. Doesn't mean anything.

But my chimp was having none of that.

There are only sixteen players in a matchday squad.

We didn't start the season well, yet in September there was a dramatic change. Newcastle, who had rewarded Bobby Robson's achievement of turning the club around with the sack, came in for Souness. He accepted, and suddenly Parkes was back as caretaker. Not for long, though. Blackburn's choice to replace Souness was Mark Hughes.

I knew Sparky. I'd played with him, trained with him, and if anyone knew what I was capable of, he did. It should have been great news, but it terrified me. It raised the possibility that he might actually pick me.

Garry Flitcroft: At Blackburn we had a fantastic club doctor in Phil, and fantastic physios in Dave and Paul Kelly, but the mental side of football wasn't given as much attention as it is now. These days, clubs and players are bringing in their own psychological coaches, but back then you had your manager, assistant and first-team coach, and that was about it. Prior to Matt seeing Steve Peters, I had a meeting with Phil and Steve, who explained what was going to be happening. Because I was close to Matt, they asked if I could help give them some feedback on how Matt felt things were going. When I subsequently chatted to Matt, it was clear he felt that seeing Steve was doing him some good.

My own experience of Steve Peters is positive because, after encountering him through Matt's situation, I ended up taking my dad to see him. My father had a mental illness, and Steve was great with him, but he wasn't sure whether my dad was taking in some of the things he was saying. It works for some people and not for others, and I suppose it depends on how much Matt was taking in, too. I think Steve did get into his head, and Matt believed in him a lot, but he was still of the opinion that he was letting his teammates down on the pitch, and he wasn't going to get back to his best.

You could still see glimpses in training – more than glimpses, really – when he would bang the ball into the top corner and show other flashes of his ability. In the dressing room afterwards I'd say, 'You were outstanding today, Janny.' But he just couldn't seem to believe in himself.

Soon after his arrival, Hughes asked me into his office for a private chat. 'I'm going to build the team around you,' he said. 'We'll get you back playing your best.'

Build the team around me? *Oh no.*

Sparky let his coaches, Mark Bowen and Eddie Niedzwiecki, do most of the training and the talking, but when he added his own input, people certainly listened. I don't think, though, that he fully knew what I was going through. His first game was against Portsmouth at Ewood, and he named me among the substitutes. He brought me on for Morten Gamst Pedersen and, fifteen minutes from the end, I scored the winner.

It was a decent goal, but once again, I felt out of control. It might have taken some attention away from my mistakes, but I still couldn't enjoy it. My celebration was painful and my thoughts were bleak.

He might pick me again now.

He did – against Bournemouth in the League Cup. We drew 3–3 and it went to penalties. I put myself well down the queue to take one, but as the shoot-out reached sudden death, I realised I couldn't avoid it. When my turn came, I walked to the centre circle trying my best not to show how scared I was. I was breathing heavily. I wanted it over as quickly as possible. I placed the ball, ran up, and scored. Tugay and Jon Stead, another new striker, missed theirs, and we were out.

Before our next game, at Charlton, I approached Eddie near the dressing-room toilets and told him I was scared to play. By this point I was desperate enough to pour it all out to a first-team coach I barely knew. Eddie took time to listen and I appreciated that.

'You really don't need to be scared,' he said. 'Just go out there and give it your best.'

But what *was* my best? I played, but nothing much happened, and from there Hughes started picking me less. I also picked up a cartilage injury, which kept me out of a few games. I was delighted.

At some stage, Blackburn stopped funding my sessions with Steve. I wanted them to continue, so I paid for more myself. I still needed the respite, the drug, of talking to him. Hughes then gave me another start, in November against Birmingham. Apparently, in the fourth minute, Steven Reid crossed and I turned it past the goalkeeper Maik Taylor.

It was the last goal I scored in the Premier League. I wish I could remember it.

Lucy: Physically, Matt recovered quickly after the accident, but I don't think anybody realised how big a stumbling block the mental side was going to be.

Matt has always had an element of anxiety about his personality.

Until 2002, his football had mostly concealed it, but it was still there. This aspect of Matt had clearly been brought back out after the accident. Before it happened, life had been plain sailing – wonderful career, lovely family, people who would treat him like royalty – but then this event shook up his whole mindset. It triggered the doubt that he couldn't do it anymore.

When Steve Peters became involved, I felt relief. There was only so much I could do or say, and it was an important step for both of us that he could now get some independent, professional help. Matt could go off and see Steve for three hours, talk about himself, and Steve would take it in and respond to it rationally. He would tell things straight to Matt, and that meant he wasn't pouring everything out at home, leading to a big, fat row and us not speaking to each other for a couple of days.

I don't know how much of Steve's advice Matt allowed himself to hear. He is the sort of person who doesn't like to be defeated. I imagine he fought against some of it, and kept going back with different problems, because the alternative was to show some kind of weakness.

We used to live next door to a family with two small boys, who always wanted him to go round and play football. He used to nutmeg them in the garden. I would ask why he wouldn't give them a chance, and he'd look at me as though I had two heads. 'They won't learn anything if I just let them win.'

Maybe that's what it was like with Steve. Accepting everything was letting him win.

Steve asked to see me a couple of times too, and I loved it. It was like this big release. Don't get me wrong, I'm not the sort of person who craves attention, but I had been taking a lot of Matt's troubles on my own shoulders and I needed an outlet of my own. With Steve it felt that I could talk and talk, and not be judged. I can completely identify with what Matt says about feeling inflated and boosted after one of his sessions.

I used to joke with Steve: 'Can you not come and live with us?' I actually felt that if he had been there, every minute of every day, Matt would have got there. He was such a positive influence. But when you left Matt for too long, the self-doubt crept back in.

Matt certainly had some really low spells. He said a few dark things – 'I'm going to kill myself' – but almost in passing. It never felt like it was a serious possibility, even though the words on their own were awful to hear. There were another few occasions when we'd go out for a meal, and he'd have a few drinks, which reacted with his antidepressants. Once, I had to call Jay and ask for his help, because Matt had slumped on the stairs and I couldn't get him up.

A few times, things like this would happen almost at random, while I was out. I would get the call and rush back to make sure he was all right. I have since wondered if some of this was about control – testing me, seeing how I would react.

I found, though, that I would forgive most of it, because of the situation he was in. I don't know how bad things have to get before you think, 'Okay, enough's enough', but it would have felt like weakness to give up on him. I was so caught up in it emotionally that I wanted to keep him buoyant whenever possible.

A couple of people asked me why I was still there, why I was putting up with it. My response was always that, if you love someone, you don't walk away in that sort of situation. I was rooting for him, trying to get him through it, trying to help him find some sort of light at the end of the tunnel. It would have done him no favours whatsoever to face the rest of that journey on his own.

Barry: I found Steve Peters remarkable. You learn so much about yourself just by talking to him. Over the course of his time with

Matt we became good friends. I marvelled at how he spoke and how he had such command of his subject.

If Matt had been able to see him more often, particularly before a game, he may have been all right. As part of Matt's recovery, Steve also wanted to address the dressing room at Blackburn, as a way of getting the other players to understand his situation. This was arranged, but, by all accounts, Souness didn't take it especially seriously. Despite this, a number of Blackburn players said they also wanted sessions with Steve.

Steve's view, ultimately, is that he got to Matt too late. The problem was that nobody knew the ideal solution at the time. When you think of the work that Steve has done in sport since then, you have to conclude that, if he couldn't turn Matt around, nobody could have.

Matt was one of the first athletes Steve worked with, and certainly the first footballer, and that work helped to establish his career in sport. Yet he regards Matt as one of his failures. When people were referred to him subsequently, he subjected them to the 'Matt Jansen Test' – designed to ascertain whether or not there was a good chance that the athlete would be responsive to Steve's technique and a positive outcome could be achieved. Matt got a lot of benefit from working with Steve, but it came too late for him.

SIXTEEN

SORRY

Despite my sessions with Steve Peters, I remained under a dark cloud: depressed, upset, frustrated, confused. I tried different medication, but I was going around in circles. The stronger pills messed me up. Michael Gray, who joined Blackburn in 2004, told me what I was like on away trips during this period. We'd be on the bus, a game of cards would be under way.

'Janny.'

No response.

'Janny!'

Nothing.

'Fucking hell. *Janny!*'

Eventually I turned slowly towards him, half-smiling, barely registering what Micky and the others were saying. I was in a trance, and it wasn't just the pills. I was paralysed by fear.

Without there being a single tipping point, it became clear that I had to come out of football completely. Steve Peters approached Phil Batty with the suggestion that a break might be the best option, and then Barry – who had taken over as my agent because Jay had got another job that required more of his time – went into Ewood to discuss the details with John Williams. Soon after, a statement was released by the club. It confirmed that, following advice from doctors, 'Matt's ongoing rehabilitation will be taking place away from the club until the end of the season.'

That was vague enough to obscure the full truth. A franker statement might have read: 'Matt can no longer cope. It's tearing him apart and he's begging for a way out. He has to get away from football, otherwise it's going to destroy him.'

I couldn't admit that to the supporters and soon I refused to admit it to myself. The decision was made before the end of the season, when I put my head back into the sand and told myself I'd be fine when I returned for pre-season. It hurt to watch a Premier League game and see others on the stage when I was stuck in the wings, but for the most part I distracted myself and kept fit and told myself that it would all be different next season.

Hughes made it clear that I was welcome to go back for pre-season, so I drove to Brockhall feeling fit and fine, ready to give things another go. Blackburn wanted to give me a new contract. My situation had clearly changed in the three years since the accident and the lucrative deal I'd signed before the best twelve months of my career was now up. Something different was on the table. I'd never seen a pay-as-you-play contract before but that changed when I realised how far down the pecking order I'd fallen. My basic wage in Blackburn's new offer was no more than a couple of hundred quid a week. Only if I started a game would I get Premier League money – twenty-five grand. A substitute appearance would mean a few thousand. If I could get the old magic back, I'd be rewarded. If I couldn't, the club wouldn't be paying for a talent that had been mysteriously lost. There was a little negotiation, but it seemed like the best offer I was going to get. I signed and looked forward – if that is the right term – to pre-season.

It didn't take long for the demons to return. As soon as training moved towards a game situation, I was groping for those old, instinctive feelings and they weren't there. The lads were fine with me – although they didn't see the full picture – but I couldn't engage with the group like I had before. I couldn't take the piss in training. I was no longer the big fish. I didn't feel special. Days on the training ground were to be endured rather than enjoyed.

I played in some of the pre-season friendlies, including against the Spanish team, Espanyol, when I bent my knee back in a challenge with their goalkeeper. I went off the pitch in pain and an appointment was made to see a doctor in Cumbria, at Sedbergh. Dad took me, because I couldn't drive, and it was there that the bad news was broken: it wasn't as serious as first feared. An inch either way and the damage might have been more severe. Instead, I only had a couple of weeks out. Two weeks with the relief of not playing instead of the months I'd hoped for.

How had I come to think like this?

I kept seeing Steve, hoping he could somehow find the switch that would relocate the old me, but I was clinging on. Dad came to one of our sessions, but I don't think he, or the rest of my family, fully understood the extent of my problems. Steve, Barry and Lucy were the only people I leaned on, because I saw them the most. They saw me at my worst and took the brunt of my moods. I doubted that anyone else could understand what I was going through. Unless they were living it, how could they know?

I also continued to give interviews that disguised the truth. I told reporters that I was in a much better place, that seeing a psychiatrist had made a world of difference, and that I was ready to prove this, that and the other thing.

'Look at me, everyone, I'm still trying.'

Look how hard I've got to try. There's got to be something wrong with me.

I wasn't involved in our first two games of the season, then I made a sub appearance against Aston Villa. Under my new contract, that meant my earnings plummeted and a couple of the lads asked why I wasn't getting more game time. I now had twenty-five thousand reasons to get into Hughes' starting line-up. If I sat on the bench and came on here and there, it would cost me a fortune over the course of a season. But that was fine with me.

September came round, and a game against Bolton at the Reebok Stadium. Hughes told me I would be starting. *Shit.* Back into the old routine: a call to Phil, telling him I wasn't sure if I was up for it. A call to Steve, who did his usual best to reassure me. I played for an hour as a lone striker and then came off, with no idea how I had performed. It was the last start I made for Blackburn.

Hughes had started to rely on other options. His job was to win games. Every time my name wasn't on the team sheet, the club saved thousands, but what right did I have to complain? I didn't once consider knocking on his door to demand more game time and by the middle of December I had mustered the grand total of three substitute appearances since the Bolton game. The season was happening around me, sometimes I wasn't even making the squad, and I was as pissed off with life as ever.

Barry was more focused than I was in the search for answers and he asked the club why I wasn't playing more. Then, shortly before Christmas, a window opened. A few extra injuries had hit the squad, and a trip to Fulham was approaching. John Williams called Barry and assured him that, because so many players were out, I would surely be involved this time. When we got to London, Sparky named the squad. I wasn't in it.

I experienced the familiar combination of relief and frustration, but Barry's mind was clearer. This, he figured, was the last straw. If I wasn't going to get a game when there was virtually no one else to choose from, what hope was there?

'I'm not prepared for Matt to suffer in this way anymore,' Barry told John. 'I don't care about contracts, breaches, or whatever you want to say. He's not coming back. That's it.'

The media sensed that something was up and stories appeared that I was looking for a move. That wasn't true, as there was time for one more attempt to find a solution. At Barry's instigation, a meeting was arranged with Mark Hughes and he invited Steve Peters to chair it, in his office, at the Manchester Velodrome.

It was supposed to clear the air – a chance to discuss things thoroughly and try to establish where I stood. Phil also came and he did most of the talking for Blackburn. Sparky didn't say much, which hadn't been the idea. We'd hoped that, as manager, he would set out his own position and get into a proper conversation about a possible way forward. Instead, the conversation went round in circles and when we shook hands at the end of it we hadn't achieved anything. Sparky and Phil got up and left. Steve waited a while before turning to Barry. 'You did your best,' he said.

There was nowhere left to turn. I didn't get back in the team and when I talked things over with Barry, we agreed that there was nothing more to be gained by going through the motions: not playing, barely getting paid and, worse, knowing it wasn't going to change. The terms of my departure were agreed amicably.

We knew the club would have their own say, so Barry put together a statement and made sure it got to the press first. I had got to know James Fletcher of the *News of the World* well over the years and, as Blackburn played QPR in the FA Cup, he wrote the story which would also be sent to the *News & Star* in Carlisle and the *Lancashire Evening Telegraph*.

The next day, everyone knew I was a former Blackburn Rovers player.

'This is the hardest and yet probably most sensible decision I have ever made,' Jansen said. 'I love the club and its fans but what is happening there is tearing me apart.

'I'm not a troublemaker and I don't kick up a stink if I'm not in the team, but enough is enough. I cannot take this anymore and I know I have to leave.

'For months I have kept my head down, worked hard and, in my opinion, produced some of my best-ever training sessions, but it is like I'm invisible and no one is watching.

'I respect Mark Hughes's decisions, but I want to be playing.'

The last five words formed a neat little fib. And what was that about 'best-ever training sessions'? I certainly didn't believe that. But it struck the right tone, and the rest was fair enough. I'd loved my time at Blackburn before the accident, and the club had always been good to me. The fans were brilliant too, and in normal circumstances it would have seemed crazy to think about leaving – but that's where I was.

When the news broke, I received lots of supportive messages: from players, coaches, managers, fans. The day I took my belongings out of Brockhall for the last time, I had no intention of going to another club. I wanted to drift away and disappear. Others, though, had different ideas.

Within a day or so, Barry had fielded approaches from Manchester City and Everton. I suppose I wasn't brave enough to walk away for good, and that interest lured me back. We went to meet the City manager, Stuart Pearce, but he didn't give the greatest sales pitch. Our meeting was squeezed into a short period of time before a training session and he was quite disorganised, and not particularly enthusiastic. We left underwhelmed.

Later, there were reports in the press that I'd been due to sign for City, but had failed to show up for training. That was rubbish. Nothing came of the Everton interest, but then there was another call. Bolton Wanderers wanted to know if I would talk to them. I had no greater desire to be there than anywhere else, but in the absence of a better idea I agreed to meet them. Barry and I arrived at the Reebok and made our way into Whites Hotel, attached to the stadium. As agreed, we headed into the restaurant and settled at a table overlooking the pitch.

Ten minutes passed, then fifteen, then twenty, and nobody had turned up. Eventually, the doors swung open.

'Sorry, fellas!'

Sam Allardyce strode to our table like the king of the realm. He was immaculately dressed in a tailored suit, clean shaven, with his hair shower-damp, and he smiled as he offered a firm handshake. He appeared to fill the room by walking into it. Sam sat down and put me at the centre of his world. He explained that he had always admired me as a player, and that something had caught his eye when I had played against Bolton a few months ago.

'We looked at the stats,' he said. 'Yours were right up there at the very top. Distance covered, passes completed, you name it.'

I didn't believe any of that could be true, but Sam was known for his attention to detail. He had also, at Bolton, revived the careers of a number of players who needed a restart: Kevin Davies, Ivan Campo, Youri Djorkaeff, Jay-Jay Okocha.

'I'd like you to come and play for me,' he said. 'Do you think you could give it a go?'

After my medical, I was asked to undertake a psychometric report, where I was asked to describe myself in my own words.

What made me tick, in layman's terms. My summary was more honest than I'd been for a while.

'Determined, low on confidence and self-esteem. Love to show off if I believe I'm good at something, and quite like being the centre of attention when things are good.'

Things had not been good for nearly four years, but Sam was something new. He was big on psychology and sports science before many others in the game caught up. He also made it clear that he'd do his best by every player at Bolton. He had two psychologists who everyone had to see for forty minutes each week, and after each training session we were asked to jump into ice baths to help our recovery. He had masseurs and acupuncturists and harvested as many stats as he could from each individual's performance. If he thought something could move the team forward another inch, he would try it.

I didn't know whether it would help me, but I had nothing else to lose. I'd done the hard part by getting away from Blackburn. If this worked, it worked, and if it didn't, well, that would probably be that. Once I started playing again, it would soon be obvious.

Bolton's next game: Blackburn away.

Sam was very chilled about it. 'Listen, if you don't want to play, you don't have to,' he said. 'I'll put you on the bench, and if you feel okay, I'll give you a run. Are you all right with that?'

It sounded like he was concerned with how I was feeling, concerned with me as a person rather than simply trying to manage his way around an awkward problem.

'Yeah, I'll be all right with that.'

It was incredibly strange to go into the away dressing room at Ewood, and just as strange to watch the game from the away dugout. Midway through the second half, Sam turned to me.

'Five minutes? Ten minutes?'

He winked at me, and I took his invitation to warm up. As I stood, and jogged down the touchline, the Blackburn fans started clapping. A few minutes later, Sammy Lee, Sam's assistant, whistled me over. Sam was waiting for me and, after I took off my tracksuit top, he called me towards him. He put his arm around my shoulder and started pointing towards the pitch.

'Now listen,' he whispered in my ear. 'People watching this will think I'm giving you all sorts of instructions, tactics and all that bollocks. It's just for the cameras, this. All I want you to do is go out there and enjoy yourself. Okay?'

I wanted to laugh a little, and I appreciated that he was trying to keep me settled. I played the last fifteen minutes of a goalless draw. At full time I acknowledged the Bolton fans, and then went round the pitch to salute the Blackburn supporters, who stood and applauded. It was my goodbye to them. We had enjoyed some good times, hadn't we? I appreciated that, in better days, they had put me on a pedestal, and they had never been hard on me when I failed to relive those days.

In a sense, I left Ewood that day happier than I had for many months. I came on against Man City the following weekend, then against Arsenal in the FA Cup. Fifteen minutes or so, but I felt okay, quite natural, which was surprising. Adrenaline, maybe. Sam then started me at Portsmouth. I won a penalty, and didn't come off the park feeling miserable, which was progress.

Three days later we played Wigan at home. I started again, but this time it didn't feel right. I lost the ball a couple of times and that was enough. The demons came back with a vengeance and Sam brought me off at half-time. I was heading for the showers as the others went back out for the second half. Sam came across and looked crestfallen.

'Sorry, Janny,' he said. 'I've asked too much of you too soon. I shouldn't have gone with you today. It's my fault.'

It was good of him to say, but I knew whose fault it was. The chimp was all over me again.

We went to Dubai for a short mid-season break. We trained in the evenings, and I was shocking, as bad as I'd felt for ages. For the first time since signing for Bolton, I didn't want to be in the team for our first game back, against Arsenal. If Sam's eyes were in working order, there was no chance he'd pick me after I'd trained like that.

We landed back in London and then travelled together to The Grove hotel in Hertfordshire. At breakfast the next morning, Sam convened a team meeting and announced the side.

I was starting on the left wing.

Oh no.

Maybe this was another of his tricks, keeping me in the dark so my anxiety wouldn't build. I suppose a few hours of worrying were better than several days, and I admit that I did feel a bit less terrified when kick-off arrived. But I still had no perception of how well I played. For me it was about trying hard and avoiding fuck-ups. This I did until, with ten minutes to go, I picked up the ball and went past someone in midfield. I took it on further, but an Arsenal player then dispossessed me.

Well, that was shit.

It wasn't long before the board went up and my number was on it.

Thank God.

By the time I reached the touchline, I was consumed by the fact I'd just lost the ball. I couldn't think of anything else. I must have had a beast.

I held up my hands. 'Sorry, Sam, sorry.'

He looked at me and frowned.

'Sorry? Fucking sorry? What are you on about?'

I put on my jacket and sat down. I later met Dad, who gave me a hug.

'Well done, lad,' he said, with a beaming smile. 'You were quality out there.'

'Really?'

The papers agreed with Dad, giving me 'star man' ratings, while that night Sam had also called Barry, urging him to watch *Match of the Day*. 'He was the best player on the pitch,' he said. Also on the pitch were Thierry Henry, Cesc Fabregas, Freddie Ljungberg and Robert Pires.

'We've got him back,' Sam added.

Wishful thinking. I just couldn't accept that I had played well, and nor did games like that help me go into training feeling any different. I didn't feel excited and couldn't get back that sensation of showing off and being the best. Sam and his staff seemed to understand that I had a problem, and because of that I wasn't constantly trying to convince them that I was struggling. But I wasn't 'back' – nowhere near. I was only a couple of steps further up from the bottom of Everest.

A faint click I'd felt in my knee during the Arsenal game turned out to be more than a niggle. A scan proved that I'd torn a small piece of cartilage. An operation was booked, another couple of weeks out were guaranteed, and how did I feel about that? You can probably guess.

I spoke to Steve a few more times, but because the injury had taken me out of things again, there wasn't a real need to see him so often, and eventually our sessions stopped completely. I also think that, deep down, I'd accepted that this was my last chance, and I wasn't straining quite as hard as I had been at Blackburn.

I came back in April for Bolton's game at Anfield, and walked through the tunnel where Souness had told me I was going to the World Cup. I sat in the dugout for an hour, came on for the final stages, and then came off. My final appearance in the Premier League left barely any trace.

If only my football life had gone in the same direction as my life outside the game, I would have had half a chance. Late into my time at Bolton, our plane landed in Manchester after a game against Tottenham, and Lucy, despite being heavily pregnant, was there to collect me.

That night, her waters broke.

I received a new perspective on hard work over the following day. In Macclesfield Hospital, Lucy went through a very tough twenty-four-hour labour. I'm sure she's thrilled to know that one of my most vivid memories of the night is the telly in our private room showing the final of the World Snooker Championship. Eventually the doctors told us that, because of a couple of complications, they would need to perform an emergency caesarean.

And I thought I had problems?

Minnie Rose eventually arrived, at 8lb 11oz, and Lucy, thankfully, was okay.

I was a dad and, for one night at least, the chimp took the hint.

The longer things went on at Bolton, the more hopeless it seemed. I was still thinking too much, still hesitating on the ball, and if there was one aspect of Sam's regime that I didn't particularly like, it was the fact he was so meticulous with his plans. In training, he broke the game down into small details, always stressing the importance of working to his system. It must have worked for him, and for many of his players, but it didn't encourage me to play as freely as I liked, the way Venables had. In all honesty, though, I was too far gone for that to make much difference.

I spoke to Sam a few times in his office and told him how I felt. As ever, he listened and appeared concerned. The season drifted to a close, and soon afterwards, a bulletin on *Sky Sports News* reported that a host of players were being released by Bolton. Okocha was one. I was another. A letter arrived to confirm my fate. After seven appearances, my contract wasn't going to be renewed. I would have preferred to have been told in person, but what did it matter? The message was clear: even Big Sam couldn't turn me around. I drifted out of Bolton as surely as I had drifted in, another little failure under my belt.

I was twenty-eight, and unattached.

What next?

It was far too early for answers. I went home, threw my bag down, opened the fridge and pulled out a beer.

Sam Allardyce: At the time we brought Matt to Bolton Wanderers, we knew he had some post-accident mental issues, because we'd linked very well with Blackburn Rovers and their medical staff prior to signing him. The extent of it, though, was never going to be completely clear in the early stages. It's not something that would be flagged up in a medical, and nor would you expect a player to go into maximum detail about it when you're offering him a deal.

He hadn't been as involved at Blackburn as he wanted to be and we just felt that a fresh start, coupled with the staff we had at Bolton, could benefit him. We used to get criticised for having thirty-two backroom staff, which was bigger than our playing staff, and my chairman also used to moan like mad about it. But that support staff was why we achieved so much. Every little helped and with two people in our medical department who were particularly equipped to deal with anxiety and mental problems, we believed we had the best people in the country in terms of that side of the game. Other clubs might have had sports psychologists, but we were the only one who had a clinical psychiatrist.

Our aim was to ease Matt back into life as a professional footballer, to the point where he would start to enjoy it and deliver the goods again. Above all, it was a case of trying to get him back to where he used to be, which was as a wonderfully talented player.

As he settled in during the initial weeks, it looked like we might have a chance. As a person, he was a dream come true. He trained hard and appeared to enjoy being around the lads. On the training pitch it was obvious he hadn't lost his talent or fitness. When I spoke with some of the other players, they said the same. 'This is looking good,' I thought. I felt that if we could get him right, it would be like getting a £6-8million player – at least. He was a goalscorer, after all, and I didn't get another of those until I signed Nicolas Anelka. We paid £8million for Anelka and, after a season and a half, Chelsea bought him for £16million. Had Matt started scoring his goals again, something similar would have happened. At Bolton we were brilliant in terms of punching above our weight and getting into Europe, but the directors were always looking to sell somebody. So we'd have been selling a fully restored Matt Jansen, I'm sure of that.

Unfortunately it just didn't happen. There was a stage when he sort of half-ducked out of a game for what seemed to be no reason at all. In reality, there was a very good reason. He was so fearful of the game he couldn't perform.

It took a long while, and quite a bit of probing, before Matt really opened up with me and we got to that realisation. In the meantime, other signs of his frail mental state had started to emerge. The Arsenal game that he describes, when he came off the pitch apologising, sounds very familiar. We were telling him, 'Look, you were brilliant, you were fantastic today,' trying to be supportive. He couldn't see it and that was clearly a consequence of his accident.

Looking back with a more up-to-date perspective, you would say it was more than anxiety with Matt, and he was almost clinically depressed by the fear of playing. The brain is such a key factor in allowing a player to perform at his absolute best, because the brain will maximise the physical skills. Someone might appear to be a wonderful player with a high level of ability, but if he hasn't got the brain to maximise that ability, he ends up in League One or League Two.

Matt certainly had that brain power before the accident, because he was rightly recognised as one of the top young players in the country. Afterwards, his brain just wouldn't allow him to recapture certain things.

At Bolton we'd turned a lot of players around who'd been broken, whether through being blown out or mistreated by other clubs, or by different circumstances. It was never quite the same with Matt, because of the horrific injury that he'd sustained. He was fit and well in terms of living his day-to-day life, but it seemed like any real pressure from playing first-team football in the Premier League was a problem for him.

In the end, I suppose he accepted that. I believe he recognised that he felt no enjoyment in being selected and he couldn't get over those fears. As much as we all wanted him to get there, and as hard as we tried, it came to a point where there wasn't much sense in continuing. I hope he at least felt that, while he was at Bolton, we did our best for him.

SEVENTEEN

DRIFTING

Sam had said after the Arsenal game that I was the best player at the club but I was the only person who couldn't see it. He was right about the last part. I couldn't see what others apparently could. Any thought that my ability might have been intact was swamped by the doubt and the fear.

However, in football people tend to judge with their eyes rather than their ears. Sam had signed me because of how I'd played against Bolton and now, regardless of what they had heard about me, there were still plenty of managers who believed they had seen enough of the old talent to take a chance.

That summer, I didn't know what I wanted to do. Try again at another club? I didn't know if my heart would be in it. Give up altogether? That felt a little . . . final. This uncertainty, added to my existing depression, resulted in an intense frustration with no end in sight.

What would people think if I called it a day at twenty-eight? The dilemma plagued me. And what would I do? I had no idea. This led me back down a familiar route, of trying to do what I thought I *should* be doing – what other people *expected* me to be doing. I decided to get back on the horse.

1. *June 2006*

Phil Smith was a prominent football agent who ran the First Artist agency. He got in touch, asked to meet Barry and me and explained that he was keen to represent me. I didn't want to go down that route. I was happy with the trust and care I had from Barry, and I didn't see anything to gain from adding another unknown at a time when I barely knew my own mind.

However, Phil had one interesting idea I hadn't considered before: America. Major League Soccer was starting to grow and there was concrete interest from a couple of clubs: Columbus Crew and New York Red Bulls. The latter was managed by the former Celtic and Rangers striker Mo Johnston. Columbus, meanwhile, came recommended by my old Blackburn teammate Brad Friedel, an Ohio native.

Half-heartedly, I boarded a plane with Barry. New York Red Bulls had arranged the flights, sorted hotel accommodation for a few nights and made plans to involve me in some training sessions at Giants Stadium. Although I loved New York, I quickly discovered that football there was more than a little different. Training was quite basic: small-sided games, passing drills, old-school routines on an artificial surface that took a little getting used to. The players seemed very fit, and genuine athletes, but not as football-smart as they might have been. In my first session, I received the ball and saw one of the New York players moving towards me. He came lunging in with a tackle that could have been seen coming from outer space. I sidestepped him easily and left him on the floor.

'Oh, unlucky man,' someone called.

Unlucky? It was shit defending, mate. You sold yourself.

There was a lot more of this sort of thing and, while you

couldn't fault their energy or their enthusiasm, it was clear that playing in the States was going to mean a drop in standard.

I stayed to watch a Red Bulls game. The Giants Stadium had a capacity of about eighty thousand but the night I was there, at the most four thousand were rattling around inside it. The arena was magnificent, but it had been built for American sports. How was I going to show off in front of so few people?

When I discussed money with New York, there were other aspects I found unsettling. There was a wage cap in the American league, around the $3,000 mark. New York said they would pay me up to that limit and then top up my earnings with endorsements, appearances and so on. I had hated that stuff at the best of times in England, let alone in a place where nobody knew who I was. A few extra grand to cut the ribbon at a new Walmart? No thanks. I'll take my $3,000 and stay at home.

I couldn't dismiss the idea outright, though. There weren't a lot of better offers on the table. We'd just had a baby, so moving everyone to the USA would be a fairly big deal. I had lots to think about as I flew home.

Soon, it was time for the next trip: to see what Columbus Crew had to offer. Dad joined me for that one and, before the flight, I popped a pill that I'd been given to ease my anxiety. It was supposed to be a placebo but, determined it would work, I took one and then two others.

They weren't placebos. Just one would have been powerful enough to floor a farm animal. They sent me halfway into the next world and I spent part of the flight with my mouth agape, dribbling. I must have been great company.

Thankfully they'd worn off by the time I reached Columbus. Training was similar to how it had been at New York and I left after the final arranged session with a promise that I'd meet the club for formal discussions. In the meantime, we found a nice golf course and teed off. I was so relieved to be there, on the fairways, not trying to impress a coach or chairman at a football club. We had several rounds, extending the trip into a holiday. Every so often, my phone rang. At first it was the Columbus Crew coach, then their owner.

I ignored the calls. 'Come on,' I said to Dad. 'Let's keep playing.'

Dad knew what I was up to.

'You're going to have to speak to them eventually, son.'

'Do I have to?'

The thought of going back there had made me uneasy. Dad practically dragged me to the meeting that Columbus wanted. As I walked into the restaurant, I made a lame excuse that I had left my phone in my hotel room while we were out exploring the local area.

Over dinner, they made it clear they wanted to sign me, and we shook hands with a promise that I would think it through. On the way back, Barry called. New York had been back in touch and, though Mo Johnston had been sacked and replaced by the former USA coach, Bruce Arena, they wanted to meet me again. Could I meet them at the airport?

Dad said: 'You've got to meet them.'

'I don't want to. I just want to go home.'

'It'll only take an hour at the most. I think it's the least you should do.'

'No.'

I didn't want to meet anyone else to talk about football. It was completely ungracious, and probably disrespectful, but I had had enough.

We flew home. It's a long way from Ohio to Cheshire, and when you're airborne, nobody is there to put any pressure on you. My mind settled over those few hours, and inevitably the switch was flicked again.

You know, maybe I can do it. If Lucy is prepared to come over, with the baby, we could cope with it for a year or two. It'll be a life experience. I'm out of the limelight, so nobody will see if I struggle. America's a nice place. New York's a nice place. And easier to get to than Columbus. What the hell. Let's do it.

By the time I got home I had pretty much convinced myself of the idea. Then fate stuck its oar in. I had been unaware that in America, the first club who registered formal interest in you had the option to take complete priority in negotiations. New York, apparently, hadn't recorded their interest in this way and so Columbus had jumped in. They were the 'official finder' and this gave them the right to stop me going anywhere else. It was a bizarre set of circumstances but, essentially, if I didn't want to sign for Columbus, I couldn't go anywhere else without the sort of complicated fight I simply wasn't up for. I didn't want to sign for Columbus, so that was that. I quietly withdrew from the possibility of continuing my career across the pond.

As I went back to no-man's-land, Barry explained the 'official finder' scenario to the BBC. He said: 'Matt wants time to train and play without the pressures that a contractual environment provides . . . so he can progress at his own pace and in his own time.'

My own pace, my own time . . .

That, ultimately, is what I'd achieved in America: I'd bought a bit of time. Occupied myself. Gone through the motions. Done something different. Shown people I was still trying and hadn't given up.

Pretended.

2. September 2006

After America, there was nothing for a couple of months. I thought I'd be happy with that – happy to drift along without the pressure of another comeback. I'd stay at home, with the baby, play more golf and try to enjoy life for what it was.

I assumed that it would bring me a little bit of happiness and, to begin with, it did. I was relieved to be away from it again. But doing nothing can't keep you happy for long. As the weeks passed, I started to get bored. I got out of bed knowing that I had no purpose in life. I wasn't keeping myself busy with anything that you could call a focus. I didn't want to play and at this stage I had no urge to try to be a coach.

When you have time to kill and nothing to kill it with, you torment yourself in different ways. At home, little things started to nag.

That stain on the carpet wasn't there before. Where did that come from? Who put that there?

And what's that – who put that mark on the wall?

Minnie's toy shouldn't be left out like that. Can we not put things away?

Is there any chance we can look after the place?

Tiny things, trivial things that I never noticed when I was happy and playing – now I couldn't take my eyes off them. They wound me up, made me irritable. The monotony was awful.

Come September, there was an escape. A call from James Fletcher, the journalist I'd entrusted with the news of my departure from Blackburn. Big Sam had been in touch with him and, indirectly, had suggested that if I ever wanted to go back in to Bolton and train – use the facilities, keep ticking over – I was more than welcome.

It was something else to do. I took up the offer.

It was strange being back at Bolton, but I realised I'd missed the club environment. I threw myself into training without any real worries. They also took me off the horse tranquilisers I'd been on since that flight to America, once they realised how powerful they were.

In one training session, we were required to do sprints which were measured by lasers. Ten metres, then twenty, then thirty, then forty. I whipped through them and was later told my times had been the quickest in the squad. I was never the fastest player, so that was something. Bolton had just signed Nicolas Anelka, who was known for his pace throughout a career at many top clubs, and when we teamed up in five-a-sides, we ripped it up.

Anelka's agent watched one of these sessions, and later called Barry.

Barry: I was immediately struck by the way Anelka's agent spoke. He'd gone to Bolton to watch his client train, but had been left agog by how well Matt had performed. He explained to me that he knew about Matt's post-accident problems and wished me to know how good he had looked, adding that he had never seen a player perform so well on the training ground. He was not speaking as an agent – more as an observer, and I thanked him for taking the trouble to call me. I was naturally encouraged by this, and relayed the conversation to Matt.

Barry remains adamant that Anelka's agent had simply called to let him know how well I was doing in light of how I had struggled since the accident, with no ulterior motive. I have a different suspicion about this and have often wondered whether it was an attempt to butter Barry up, in an attempt to add me to his portfolio. Even if that was the case, it would never have happened. I was happy going into Bolton and going home again without any further demands. No contract, no expectation, no pressure, no chimp. Not yet.

Eventually there was talk that it might come to something with the club. The thought troubled me. I couldn't go through with it. One day I left the training ground and didn't go back.

3. July 2007

More aimless months, more monotony, more wasting away. Then – another invitation, this one from the past.

A call from Neil Dalton, the physio at Carlisle. Was I up to much, and did I fancy coming up to join in pre-season training? The door was open if I did. I grabbed my boots and drove towards the M6.

Going back to Carlisle was a comforting thought, but not necessarily because of the football. It was a chance to go home, see Mum and Dad, my brother and sister, and some friends like Giles and David Jenkins, the Carlisle chairman's son, who lived in Wetheral. A change of scenery. A chance to escape the mundane for a while.

At Brunton Park I was reassured by some familiar faces. Dolly was there, so was David Wilkes, and so was Eric Kinder, the youth-team manager who had been at Blackburn for many years before moving to Cumbria. 'Fucking hell, what are you doing here?' Eric shouted when he saw me, a big grin on his face. I then met Neil McDonald, the manager.

'Thanks for letting me come and keep fit,' I said. 'I'm happy just to train.'

Neil was an excellent coach, and pre-season training was very snappy. Carlisle had a decent young group of players who had come off a promising season in League One. Although I hadn't trained with a club for months, I still felt fit and sharp and it was good to be part of a squad again.

I suppose it was inevitable that the local media would pick up on the fact I was back. I was photographed on the training ground and the picture was front-page news. Carlisle, two years earlier, had helped turn around the career of Michael Bridges, who had come to the club after a rotten run of injuries. Could they do the same for me?

If that was their plan, it certainly wasn't mine. I was filling time, nothing more – there in body but not really in mind. I trained for a few days, dragged it out, then picked up a problem with my toe. The club sent me to a chiropodist, then I came back and trained some more. The first pre-season friendlies were on the way, and Neil told the media that he would have a chat with me to see if I fancied playing in the first of them, against Kendal.

It didn't get that far. It was Carlisle, and it was home, but the thought of actually playing brought the chimp back with a vengeance. I couldn't do it, wouldn't allow myself to. After a week or so, I packed my things and went home.

Initially, there was some confusion at Carlisle about where I'd gone, and Neil said he was disappointed it hadn't led to anything. Maybe I hadn't made it clear enough that I'd never been looking for a contract. Maybe, like all the others, he thought he could tap into what I used to be. He had the same chance as the rest of them.

I knew that the people at Carlisle would have rallied behind me. But I also knew they'd have had questions.

'What happened to him?'

'Why has he ended up here?'

'He used to be great. Where did it all go wrong?'

How would I have explained to them that my bubble had burst, that I was afraid to take the plunge again – that, no matter how I looked and played, it just didn't feel the same anymore?

4. November 2008

Arthur, our second child, arrived in September 2008. We were now living in Alderley Edge in Cheshire and, as far as a personal focus was concerned, I didn't have to look any further. Professionally, though, I was still bereft.

I'd turned thirty without any sense of what I was going to become next. The phone rang from time to time, and I kept in touch with old teammates, but there was no hook, no drive.

In October I went back to Cumwhinton School to open an extension building. When asked by a reporter how I was occupying myself, I was suitably vague.

'I'm keeping fit and I always keep the door open on football,' I said. 'You never know. But at the moment I'm into property development and currency dealing.'

The accurate answer would have been: 'Well, I'm playing a bit of golf, bumming around, and not much else.' But I wasn't going to admit that. The truth wasn't going to justify my existence.

The interest in property and currency was not quite the new path I had suggested. Put simply, Barry and I had done a deal with a bank that allowed the mortgages on the properties I owned to be multi-currency loans. This meant we could switch the loans to, for instance, US dollars, Swiss francs or Japanese yen, depending on which exchange rates were most favourable at the time. Barry took the lead on this, and while I did take an interest – following the markets and researching the situation – it wasn't what you would describe as a career choice. I was 'into' it to the extent that it was something to say to people who asked what I was doing with my life.

As the months passed, I played in a few charity five-a-side tournaments. No stress, no ties. I was usually the best player. 'Why aren't you still playing?' someone would ask me. I didn't know how to answer. But who would understand?

Steve, inevitably, put it best. He likened it to being told Father Christmas isn't real, and then trying to believe in him again. No matter how hard you try, you can't. The spell is broken. That was my invincibility. Gone in a puff of smoke.

On I meandered. When Blackburn played West Bromwich Albion the following season, I was invited to appear in one of the executive boxes. There was a question-and-answer session that also involved the West Brom legend Cyrille Regis. After the game, I met up with some of my old Blackburn friends. I shook hands with Phil Batty and we caught up on life. I'm not sure what made me do it, but I found myself asking if I could come in and train.

'I'm bored at home, Phil. I feel like giving it another go. If you like me, great – if not, I won't waste your time.'

'Hey – of course you can.'

Phil said he would speak to Paul Ince, who'd been appointed manager that summer, and make the necessary arrangements. He was as good as his word and I went in the following week.

It was Groundhog Day all over again. Training was fine, there was a kind of purpose to my days, and I gave a couple of optimistic interviews where I said I was getting 'itchy feet' and had felt my old hunger return. Ince, when asked, said he would be silly to rule anything out. As ever, Lucy and Barry encouraged me to give it my best shot. Throughout all these 'comebacks' they didn't want to see me give up on what I had without a fight.

I don't know who I was kidding the most. Ince soon got the sack, replaced by, of all people, Sam Allardyce, but that didn't make any difference. I trained, and tried, but steadily began to find the drive to Brockhall more of a pain than it should have been. I also picked up a little knee injury and spent more time in the gym than was good for my mind.

Sam had only been in the club for a short while when I went to see him and explained that history was repeating itself. After a few pointless weeks at the club where I'd had the time of my life, I wouldn't be sticking around.

5. February 2009

Steve Watson, a good friend who was on the coaching staff at Huddersfield, invited me to come down to train with them.

Okay, I said, I'll come.

Would I like to give it a go for the reserves against Rotherham? Yeah, why not?

The game was at the Don Valley Stadium in Sheffield. The Huddersfield team had a couple of old stagers, David Unsworth and Andy Booth, mixed in with a load of younger lads. I wasn't match-fit, and although I scored a header in the first half, it still didn't feel right.

I wasn't terrified of getting the ball, exactly, but I wasn't comfortable with it, either.

No, it wasn't for me. I hung around for a while then went and had a word with Watto. Off I went again.

6. March 2009

This time, a call from Dean Saunders, now manager at Wrexham, in the Conference.

'What are you up to? Come down for a game, let's have a chat.'

What was I up to? Well, let's see . . .

Not much, as usual. Certainly not playing. Certainly not *wanting* to play. Thinking of doing my coaching badges, though. I should probably make a start on those.

I went to the Racecourse Ground and met Dean. When I sat down with him, I made it clear that I wanted to do some coaching. Was there an option to work with the reserves, or the youth team?

'Yeah, don't worry, we'll sort it,' Dean said. 'Just come down here and we'll work something out. We do want you to play, though.'

Dean, in his own bright way, did his best to big me up. He asked me to give it a go against Woking that weekend. I played in a 1–1 draw, and afterwards he was full of beans.

'Oh, you were on fire, brilliant, amazing.'

Wrexham weren't in great shape on the pitch and Dean was struggling with some of the paranoia of a young manager. He confided his fears and asked for my insight.

'What are they saying about me in the dressing room?'

'If I'm honest,' I said, 'they're saying they've had twenty-seven days in here without a single day off.'

'Right, right. Okay.'

Lo and behold, the players were given two days off and I became an instant hero in the dressing room.

He picked me again to face Northwich, which didn't start well. We conceded early and, from the restart, I tried to spray the ball out to the wing. It didn't go quite where I intended, and the Wrexham fans on that side of the pitch started booing.

Fucking hell, I thought. What am I doing here?

Fortunately, I got the ball a minute later and sent it into the stanchion. I missed a sitter later on, but we won 2–1 and I'd played my part. I didn't enjoy it, though.

In some ways it was the worst thing I could have done. Because of the level I had come down from, I was expected to put in a performance and be a class above everybody else. It's like a cup tie, where the bigger club has nothing to gain but everything to lose when facing an underdog. I was getting by, but there was nothing for my ego to feed on.

By the time I played again, against Crawley, I still hadn't done any coaching. It was always around the corner, never quite happening, and although Dean threw as much money at me as Wrexham could justify, that wasn't why I went there.

It became clear that what I wanted to happen at Wrexham was never going to happen. That summer we called it a day.

7. July 2010

On I drifted, on and on. I spoke to another old Carlisle teammate, Darren Edmondson, who was now manager of Workington. Another passing thought, never likely to go anywhere.

I was then invited to appear on the Sky Sports show, *Soccer AM*. They got me involved in one of their skill challenges outside the studio, where you had to aim the ball into a small target as many times as possible in a certain period. One of my flicks is still on YouTube if you can be bothered to search.

Back inside, the presenters asked what I was doing with myself these days. That old question. Once more, I said I didn't want to shut the door on football despite everything I'd been through. I suppose it was half true. In almost the next breath, though, I shut one of the main doors. I approached Gordon Taylor at the Professional Footballers' Association to discuss the financial implications of retirement.

I was insured for £10 million but, having come off a motorbike in Italy, there was never any prospect I would receive a full payout. Taylor said he would do his best to get a little bit together for me, but I would need an official letter from a club doctor first. I wrote to Phil at Blackburn and asked for his help. It was, at the time, just part of the process, but down in black and white my words must have seemed very final.

'I am afraid I will never fully recover from the accident and it has been dragging me down,' I wrote. 'With that in mind I have decided to officially retire from football. I believe it will help me draw a line under the accident and try and move on.'

When Phil got back to me, he said I would have to pay for the knee scan I'd had when I had last trained with Blackburn. If I was prepared to do that, he would then write the letter to the PFA. I wasn't expecting to be asked that, but I wrote the cheque and Phil contacted the PFA. Gordon Taylor proved very helpful, and on 14 July 2010 I received a payment of around twenty-five grand. It came with a stipulation. My 'retirement' applied to football in the Premier League or Football League, or the equivalent levels in another country. If I ever changed my mind, I would have to relinquish the money. Not that it was quite the ten million it could have been.

I knew that there was little chance of that happening. There had been too many attempts, too many chances that I hadn't been able to bring myself to take. The fear had beaten me, and I couldn't keep trying to rewrite the same chapter time and again.

The snowball was no more.

There was also something else.

EIGHTEEN

NEW START

There was a time, in the months and years when I was meandering through life and looking for some sort of purpose, that Steve and Barry had a difference of opinion. Not an argument as such; more of a debate. Barry had always done his best to help me find a new focus, encouraging me after each failed effort but eventually coming to the correct conclusion that I was just doing things to be seen to be doing them, and walking away when it came to a point of commitment. Barry was one of life's workers, and the thought of me idling along without anything to do didn't sit well with him.

I remember the discussion well.

Barry: 'Well, he has to do *something*.'

Steve: 'No, he doesn't. It's his choice. He can do what he wants.'

As ever, with Steve, it was a line that made you look at a situation from a less obvious angle. Surely everyone needs a reason to get out of bed in the morning, something to aim for? Not necessarily.

Steve explained that he had a relative who was extremely intelligent and went to Oxbridge, and yet now he was content to sit in his bedsit and spend a great deal of his time just playing the drums. That's all he wanted to do. It made him happy.

'I'm not going to say Matt is wasting his life,' Steve said. 'If he wants to do nothing, that is up to him. Just because he's not living the life you want him to live doesn't mean he's not living the life he wants to live. He's an adult. He can make his own choices.'

It was a reasonable point, which I suppose came back to what Steve did best: got you thinking more open-mindedly about life, stressing that you didn't need to put pressure on yourself, because what would that cause but damage? The chimp might be dancing on your shoulder, telling you to stop loafing around, but what if you were allowed to be happy loafing?

We're all different, I guess. In football, there are those who, after retirement, continue to devote their every working hour to the game: coaching, management, the media. Others go into different lines of employment entirely. Then there are those who drift, do nothing, live a comfortable life and are perfectly happy. Equally, some try an existence of no work and no stress and find it detrimental to them. They find themselves on a spiral.

I have a split personality. I can chill, but I'm also a hundred-percenter when I'm engaged with something. At my worst, I just wanted to get out of football. But then, I found that I wasn't happy doing nothing. It was a frustrating and, at times, excruciating way of learning about myself. Having time on your side can be both a blessing and a curse.

My main problem, as I faced the retirement decision, was that I didn't know what exactly I wanted to do. But by the time I wrote that letter to Phil, another opportunity had come forward.

I had accepted it, even though I couldn't be certain that it was going to lead to anything substantial. But I had no better ideas.

Going on *Soccer AM* had been another front. When the presenters had asked me if I was planning to go back to Wrexham with

Deano the following season, I played it with my pads, saying that I hadn't decided yet, but I'd be sure to let him know.

Later that day, Garry Flitcroft called, my old Blackburn skipper.

'Janny, how do you fancy coming in with me at Leigh?'

At Ewood, Flitty had always been a confident, popular character. He was a strong voice, a straight-talker, a figurehead on the pitch who had the respect of Souness and also took the lead in organising the players' parties and piss-ups. We'd kept in touch, although not with any great regularity. After packing it in as a player, he'd gone down the coaching route, and that spring he'd been appointed manager of Leigh Genesis in the Unibond Premier League.

Flitty was someone I instinctively respected. I didn't know anything about Leigh, but I agreed to meet him. He explained that a handful of rich businessmen were throwing some money at the club, and how did I feel about going in as player-coach?

I didn't know how I felt about it, but the idea of taking my coaching badges was still on my mind. Flitty would probably look out for me more in this way than Deano had at Wrexham. Maybe it was something I could try. Something I might enjoy. One step at a time.

I also felt that Gaz, as much as any teammate, had a bit of a handle on what I'd been through. He'd been at Blackburn during my good times and bad and I got the impression that he understood things, at least to a certain degree. Flitty had gone through a hard time of his own because his dad, John, had committed suicide the year before, having suffered from depression. Later, Gaz told me that he'd taken his dad to see Steve Peters a few times, after Steve had been into Blackburn following my accident.

It was the sort of story that gives you a strong degree of perspective. It also encouraged me to think that Gaz would be a good person to be alongside. He said that it would help him if I would also consider playing – which I was still allowed to do in non-league – but I would certainly be able to get stuck in with coaching.

It was, I figured, a purpose of sorts, something I could fix my mind on and plan my time around. It was going to be low-key but that's what I needed by this point. It would also satisfy my ongoing anxiety to show people I was actually doing something and not wasting my days away.

Garry Flitcroft: After Matt left Blackburn and my own career came to an end, we remained in touch and I kept an eye on his movements. At one stage we did a couple of property deals together, and later I heard he'd gone to Wrexham in non-league. I'd just taken the manager's job at Leigh Genesis with my best mate, Mike Quigley, when I saw Matt on *Soccer AM*. As I watched the show, I sensed that he didn't seem entirely happy.

I phoned Quigs up straight away. I said I was going to call Matt and ask if he'd fancy coming to play for us. I did, and Matt immediately said yes. I wanted him to come in as a player, to help raise the profile of the club, and to feel his way into the coaching side of things, but also to try to get him a bit happier again. Maybe it would benefit him to play for someone who knew him well.

The club's home was the Leigh Sports Village, a state-of-the-art facility with a 12,000-capacity stadium. It held a few hundred when the Genesis played but the big idea was to keep building, and gradually more people would come. It was two levels below the Football League and, in certain respects, a change of culture. Flitty was very much in charge and wasn't shy in how he addressed the players. I took a couple of training sessions and chatted to them as we went along.

It was, to begin with, a departure from the kind of training I'd been used to. My first instinct was to get the ball and ask the players to pass, pass, pass. But quickly I realised this was the wrong approach. Pitches at that level varied a great deal, and so did the standard of player. I could see there was talent in the team, but all the circumstances pointed towards relying on pace and power and knowing when to go direct.

This was the environment most Leigh players had come through, and I recognised I had to learn about *them*, not the other way round. When I spoke, I sensed the players were listening. They knew who I was and where I'd played. I'd worried that they wouldn't accept me, but that wasn't really a problem.

I discussed things further with Gaz. He would do the bulk of the planning, the coaching and the organising, and I would be his sounding board. He wanted my input on training, but he wasn't expecting the world from me.

Because Gaz was such a strong-minded bloke, I imagined a role where I'd put an arm around the players and be the one they'd come to if they were feeling upset or unhappy. The traditional number two, more or less. But this was early days and to begin with I was only helping out with bits and pieces. That suited me fine. It was manageable. Because of the money that was being invested in the club, I received a decent amount just for turning up twice a week for an hour or so. It was part-time, not particularly intense, and I was working under the wing of someone I felt was sincere. I reckoned there were probably worse things I could be doing.

It didn't take long before Gaz asked me how I'd feel about playing a few games. I could have managed without it, but he didn't force me into anything. 'Just say if you don't fancy it,' he said. 'If you're not feeling it, let me know.'

That gave me more comfort than at Wrexham, where Deano basically just wanted me on the pitch.

'Yeah, I'll have a game,' I said.

I can't say I enjoyed it all that much.

I knew the crowds would be small, so that didn't come as any surprise. I knew Flitty would expect me to produce at least something decent for the team, and I also knew there would be a few players who would like the idea of introducing me to the real world of non-league football. But I'd taken a Gary Brabin clothesline and survived, so there was nothing to be scared of there. There was, though, a culture shock I hadn't prepared for. The referees.

In my professional career, I barely picked up any bookings. The only one I can remember is the night at Deepdale when I whipped my shirt off when celebrating, but that all changed when I started playing for Leigh.

One thing about small crowds is that you hear individual voices more clearly. When some opposition fans saw me in the Leigh team, the welcome was traditional.

'You're just a fancy dan, Jansen!'

'Big-timer!'

That sort of crap. Players threw similar stuff my way, but that was nothing. Once, near the touchline, I saw some old boy spit at me. Thanks for that. But even that didn't get my goat like the refereeing.

They seemed completely blind to a lot of things that were going on. Decisions I naturally expected to be given just passed them by. They were also very reactive. If a partisan crowd shouted for a foul, the whistle usually went. 'Oh, it must have been a foul,' you could see them thinking. Not all of them, but a lot more than at professional level.

I shouldn't have let it frustrate me as much as it did, but I had such little tolerance for playing by that point that I boiled over. In a game at Harrogate Railway, I got halfed with a tackle so late it nearly missed the Christmas post. Flat on the turf, I looked at the ref.

'This isn't the Premier League anymore, you know,' he said, not bothering to break his jog as play continued.

'Are you serious?' I said, getting to my feet. 'That's a foul!'

'Well, I didn't see it.'

It wasn't the rough challenge that bothered me – it was the total ignorance of the official. A few minutes later I was chopped down again. I kicked out in frustration at the Harrogate player and the red card came straight out.

It wasn't ideal for Flitty, and neither was the time against Marine when I headbutted somebody in retaliation. It was completely uncharacteristic, but, as I sat out my suspension, I realised that there was nothing more I wanted to achieve as a player. That's why I had no restraint in these situations.

In March, I scored a hat-trick against Rossendale in front of sixty-one people. It wasn't the Millennium Stadium, or a packed-out Ewood, but I wasn't bothered about that anymore. Playing was now a means to an end rather than a stage. I was much more interested in what happened on the training pitch.

Leigh hadn't filled the void completely. It was part-time and my role wasn't all that crucial. It still left plenty of days where I didn't attempt or achieve a great deal. There was no immediate transformation in the way I was feeling. It did, though, allow me to dip in and out at my own pace, to come up for air every so often, and make my own rules about what I could do.

It was something. A start.

Garry Flitcroft: He ended up breaking my wage budget, but it was worth it! The other players couldn't believe how good he still was, and they also looked up to and respected him because he was never a big-head or a show-off around them, despite it being a much lower level than he was used to.

There were a couple of times when I was on the sidelines, Matt was on the bench, and it looked like he was staring into space a little bit. 'What's he thinking here?' I wondered. There were occasions when I'd turn to him and say, 'Janny, I'll need to put you on if we're a goal down,' and I'd get the sense that he didn't really want to go on. But he did, and invariably performed really well for me. There was no doubting his ability, even if there was maybe something still lingering on the mental side.

There were other occasions when he'd want a rest, or not want to play, and a couple of times when he got sent off, which I'd never seen before with Matt. You would get big centre-halves wanting to make names for themselves, and on a couple of occasions he retaliated. Otherwise it was a really positive experience for him and it did seem like he was enjoying his football again.

On the coaching side, I first asked Matt to put on a session for the strikers. He had clearly learned from his coaches in the professional game, and the lads enjoyed the work he did with them. Although he can be quite shy before he gets to know people, he soon settled in, and people certainly listened to him. Along with Quigs, and Jonathan Smith (Smudge) as chief scout, we had a really good management team and Matt became a big part of it. There was a bit of good-cop, bad-cop in how we operated – as a manager you can't get too close to your players, but Janny and Quigs could, and they would tell me if anything was going on in the dressing room, or if any of the lads needed an arm around them.

The lower you go in football, promises that sound too good to be true usually turn out that way, and not every supposed benefactor turns out to be like Jack Walker. At Carlisle, selling all the players who could have taken the club to greater heights proved the end of Willy Wonka's dream. In the years after I and many others left, the club was in a mess. It became very bitter and divided and eventually, in 2002, Carlisle United changed hands and by the time he left, Knighton was hated. I'd also lived through Goldberg's quick rise and steep fall at Palace, and in non-league there were dozens of stories of clubs who were going to be the next big thing, only to crash and burn when the money ran out.

By the winter, it had become clear that Leigh's big future wasn't going to be so big after all. There was a dispute over the club's use of the stadium, which was also occupied by Leigh Centurions for rugby league. Next, an expected instalment of money from the people backing the club wasn't forthcoming. At that level, you can quickly realise that your castle is built on sand.

Put simply, we didn't have enough funds to pay the players. Half the team left, and the rest carried on until the end of the season, sharing what little money remained. Flitty wrote cheques himself to keep paying some of them. It's a story I'm sure many people who follow the non-league game can recognise. I couldn't help but admire the lads who were playing for next to nothing. Given the circumstances, we did well to finish just outside the play-offs as we battled through to the end of the season.

Chorley, who were in the same division, then approached Flitty to be their new manager. Would I go with him? There wasn't a great deal to think about.

At first glance, Chorley appeared to be built on more solid foundations. It was a traditional club with an old-fashioned ground, and while the pitch wasn't brilliant, this was the Unibond League, so it was hardly going to be a bowling green. The people seemed honest and straightforward: a non-league club trying to make its way.

As at Leigh, I played a bit, while assisting Flitty. It still wasn't full-time, or something that occupied my every waking moment, but it was okay. I found myself enjoying the challenge of helping Chorley progress, without any major stress.

Our first season developed strongly and we progressed to the play-offs. We beat Curzon Ashton in the semi-final to set up a home tie with AFC Fylde where promotion would be decided. The day before, I was in bed with a horrible fever. It wasn't as bad as the time I had sat with Sven, in my pants, but I still felt like shit. I rang Gaz.

'I've got the flu, mate. Rough as hell.'

There was no softly-softly approach from my friend and manager.

'Fucking hell, Janny, are you serious? How bad is it, really?'

It was almost as though I was making it up.

'I'm not good, mate.'

'Come on. Just give me what you can. It's the fucking final.'

'I will if I can.'

This time, I could. I also knew how much it mattered and I knew how much Gaz had looked out for me. I managed about sixty-five minutes and watched the rest from the touchline with a thick head. We won 2–0 and the Chorley fans in a crowd of nearly three thousand were in paradise.

I'm sure it was followed by a legendary night, but there was no Utopia for me this time. As the players hit the beers, I went straight home. The next day the party continued at Haydock Races. I went along but had to leave after an hour.

The following season in the league above began under a different kind of haze. Cheques had kept bouncing at Chorley and things seemed strangely tighter than they should have been. Eventually, the directors found evidence of financial irregularities, and in September, the club's accountant, Phil Haslam, was arrested.

As I had learned at Leigh, when things are tight at a small club, it doesn't take long for the reckoning to come. In no time at all Chorley were in peril and struggling to pay wages. Again, Gaz paid some of the players out of his own pocket. Others, understandably, didn't stick around to see what was going to happen.

It was looking very bleak for a while. As our predicament was made public, fans tried to raise money with auctions and raffles. Directors put some money of their own in, and eventually some local businessmen rallied around the club. Trevor Hemmings, the local billionaire business tycoon, then wrote a cheque for several grand which kept the club from the brink.

We still had debts, tax bills to settle, but that at least gave us some breathing space. It helped us survive that worrying time, and when the matter came to court, two years later, the reason for the sudden jeopardy into which the club had fallen became clear. More than £70,000 had been illegally taken from the football club, its social club and the club lottery. Haslam pleaded guilty to three charges of theft and two of burglary and was jailed for twenty-one months. Another man, Ian Daniels, also admitted his involvement on the day he was due to stand trial and got two years.

Gaz and I had encountered serious financial problems at two clubs in the space of a couple of years. It was an education you didn't get on the B Licence coaching course.

Although I was off the radar in terms of elite football, not everyone had forgotten about me. Occasionally a journalist from a national newspaper would call, intrigued by the fact I was now working in non-league and wondering how I got from there to here.

Earlier that year, I went back to Ewood Park. A decade had passed since the Worthington Cup final and, to commemorate the anniversary, I was invited to the club shop to sign a few autographs and meet supporters. I found it enjoyable to reminisce and flattering when the fans said nice things. The old ego got a nice boost. If the event had taken place four or five years earlier, I doubt I would have gone. I'd have been too depressed to compare that feeling in the Millennium Stadium with what had happened since. I would have dwelt on the moped, on Rome, on being on the brink of the World Cup and then ending up too scared to play football.

Time had healed me in part, and I had a different focus now. There weren't so many clouds over my head as I drove away from Ewood, because I wasn't going home to a state of complete depression and torture.

I was trying to be a coach, not relearning how to be a player. The more I helped Flitty, the more I tried to understand how Chorley could win games, the less I was asking myself the recurring questions: when will I get it back? Why can't I get it back? Why can't people see I'm brain-damaged? I had something else on my mind, and it felt a little lighter.

The same couldn't be said for my old club. In 2010 Blackburn were taken over by the Indian poultry firm Venky's. At the start they seemed positive and bold and hopes were high that these overseas owners would invest heavily in the football club. The swift sacking of Sam Allardyce, though, raised eyebrows, and hopes that the club would make a daring appointment to signal the dawning of a new era were dashed by the promotion of the first-team coach, Steve Kean, to the top job. Later, the new owners hired Shebby Singh, a Malaysian with an unremarkable football CV, as their 'global advisor'. Singh lacked credibility with supporters, who regarded him as a clown. The new regime appeared clueless about the realities of Premier League football. They signed players left, right and centre, some of them kids on inflated wages who wouldn't have got into Carlisle's reserves.

Kean's tenure went from uncertain, to troubled, to outright mutinous as far as the fans were concerned. The club tumbled into the relegation zone and, after an extremely bitter stand-off, Kean eventually left. A series of successors followed, some of them lasting weeks rather than years.

It was difficult to watch what was happening. This was Blackburn Rovers, the family club I'd been proud to belong to in the days of Jack Walker. He'd given the town its greatest days, yet it all collapsed so quickly.

I went to watch a couple of games, and did a bit of radio commentary, but you couldn't fail to notice how crowds were shrinking as supporters' protests rose in volume. It couldn't have been further from that night at Deepdale, or in Cardiff, or those other great days at the top.

I also felt the turmoil at Ewood gave some players an excuse. Some players can hide behind bad situations and you learn about character in adversity. But it all comes from the top. If the support needed by the manager, his players and everyone else isn't as it should be, it doesn't take long for a solid football club to come apart at the seams. It wasn't a happy thought, but not for the first time, I felt relieved to not be at the heart of Blackburn Rovers.

That summer, my first coaching qualifications were under way in earnest. I was surprised by the workload but recognised the benefits.

'They have to be done because it's part of what I want to do,' I said in an interview. Then I surprised myself. 'I'm ambitious and I want to progress in the game. One day I would like a go at management.'

Would I?

I didn't really know for sure, because I was still enjoying the freedom of being second in command. It was a good thing to say, but could I seriously be a manager?

In the autumn I went back to Carlisle to play in a testimonial for Peter Murphy, who had been at Blackburn before building a solid career in Cumbria. It was a reunion of sorts and I quite enjoyed being back. Not much had changed.

The urge to show off with a ball at my feet was still there, but in a lesser form. I accepted invitations to play in more charity and exhibition games – one was at Macclesfield, another club in crisis. To raise funds, they invited a legends team to face a team of Macclesfield Town heroes. I scored twice but Macclesfield won 5–2, so everyone was happy.

A few weeks later, I attended another event, at Old Trafford cricket ground. Bryan Robson, who had played in the Macclesfield game, was also there. He saw me in the bar and turned to his friend.

'See this bugger,' he said, pointing at me. 'He should still be fucking playing!'

If you're going to have your ego stroked, pick a legend to do it.

I was now in my thirties, getting towards the point when I would naturally be retiring.

Could I still do it?

No. Pointless thinking that way.

These games, these cameos, were more chilled and I found that I enjoyed them more easily. I was appointed captain of a British all-stars team against a Germany select XI in the grounds of Highclere Castle in Berkshire, otherwise known as the setting for the TV drama series *Downton Abbey*. We had a tour of the building, there was a car rally and rides for kids. The game, staged to mark the anniversary of the start of the First World War, raised money for the charity Help for Heroes. The kids came to watch – now including Freddie, born in 2012 – and I scored in that one, too.

At Chorley, we were denied a second straight promotion in the play-offs in 2012. The following season we missed out again, but by 2014 we were on the march. It was a great season – the financial situation had improved with new businessmen on board and a bit of investment coming in. We hit the front and won the title with a 2–0 victory at Buxton in April to reach Conference North.

The club had kicked on in a big way. Crowds had quadrupled – we were pulling in more than a thousand as our season gathered pace. There was a real sense of achievement and also focus for me as I progressed with my badges.

At home, Lucy encouraged me further. 'Are you just going to stay as a number two, then?'

I didn't know. Things seemed to work well enough with Flitty. I still wasn't all that heavily involved, yet we were starting to come in for some attention as a double act. Gaz hadn't done his badges, but there had been interest from other clubs. He got quite close to a couple of bigger jobs, but he remained in charge at Chorley as we prepared for the 2014/15 season.

Momentum is a powerful thing. In our first season in Conference North, we reached the play-off final, taking a 2–0 lead against Guiseley before the Yorkshire club came back to win 3–2. It was a bittersweet day, one that spoke volumes about how far we'd progressed, but it also hurt.

It was a pivotal moment, not just for Chorley, but in my life.

Garry Flitcroft: When we moved to Chorley we had great success, winning three promotions and also doing well in cups. We built the club up from averaging crowds of two hundred to about a thousand. It helped the profile of the town and as far as Matt was concerned, he was relishing being back in a club environment with people he knew. We had some great nights out as a group and, in our training sessions – Tuesday and Thursday nights from 6:00 to 9:00 p.m. – it looked like he had the buzz of being involved again. It was nice to see him laughing and joking with everyone.

I spoke to both Preston and Accrington about the possibility of taking charge. The Accrington job seemed a realistic prospect, but they wanted me to work with their own staff. I was loyal to Matt, Quigs and Smudge, so it wasn't an option.

The following season at Chorley, after we narrowly missed out on our fourth promotion, to the National League, I felt it was time for me to step back from it. I'd missed a lot of time watching my two sons play football over the years and I wanted to support them. I also knew I needed to develop the building company I'd had since I was eighteen. I spoke to Janny and Quigs about it, mulled it over for a couple of weeks, and then went to see Ken Wright, the chairman, to explain my decision. There were a lot of tears from him before he asked what we should do about the manager position. I instantly recommended going with Matt, with Smudge and Jamie Vermiglio – my captain at the time – as his assistants.

Ken had said things had been going so well at Chorley that he didn't want to change anything – and choosing Matt meant he didn't need to. He was totally respected at the club, knew what the players were all about, and like any young manager, he just needed an opportunity, the same as I had received a few years earlier.

A month or so after the final, Gaz announced he was stepping down. It was unexpected, but no more so than what came next: a call from the chairman, Ken Wright, who asked if I would meet him. When I did, both Ken and the vice-chairman and secretary, Graham Watkinson, made it clear they were of the same mind. Gaz had recommended that they should invite me to step up and, in his words, 'finish the job'.

I wouldn't say it felt like the moment I'd always been waiting for. It felt sudden, strange and a little bit scary. Then again, if I wanted to find out if I could be a manager – if I had any curiosity at all about what might come of it – where else was the chance going to come?

'So, what do you think?' Ken asked.

In that moment, when I thought about the opportunity and the challenge, I was excited.

'I'd love to do it,' I said.

NINETEEN

GAFFER

Do I want to be a manager?
Do I feel like a manager?
Can I be a manager?
Can I be the bad cop?
Am I too nice to give out a bollocking?
Did Flitty get out at the right time?
Can Chorley go to the next level?
Am I the man to take them there?

Before it all began, before I realised I could answer 'yes' to practically all those questions, this was the list I went through in my head. However, I also knew I had to give it my best – if not, I could be left with huge regrets.

Gaz had quit in early July, so I only had two days before the start of pre-season. It wasn't completely unfamiliar – I knew the club, the place and many of the players – but two days isn't enough time to come up with a grand plan. I just had to get things started and take it from there. I knew the guys who would be stepping up to assist me, and felt I could trust Jonathan Smith and Jamie Vermiglio, who had both played and coached at the club and knew the league and the level.

When the first day of training came around, there were the usual welcomes, the normal reunions, handshakes and hugs. I then gave a little speech, explaining that Gaz had stepped down and I had been asked to take over. I wouldn't be reinventing the wheel, but I hoped they would work their bollocks off for me and do everything possible to have another good season in a tough league.

'No problem, gaffer,' someone said.

It was a small thing, but I found it reassuring. The rest of the players started using the same word, which for some reason counts for more in football than in most other industries. From day one I was glad that people had made the distinction. In training, the lads did what I asked, and my initial fears passed, but I had to get to a place where I would be comfortable making all the decisions. Our captain, Andy Teague, was one of our biggest characters at the club, and I had spoken to him before the others.

'I'm going to be the new manager and I want you on board. I need you. I'm going to give you a bit more responsibility. I want you taking the warm-ups and I want your opinion in the dressing room. But when I speak . . .' – because he's quite gobby – '. . . you're quiet. How does that sound?'

'No problem, gaffer.'

I figured that getting the most influential people on my side was the only way it could work. Pre-season was fine, but in friendlies there's rarely any real pressure. I allowed the players to play, tried a few different systems and ideas, and used the games to figure a few things out. There was no stress. That came with the start of the league season.

We began with a home game against Nuneaton Town. More than a thousand people were in Victory Park and there was a sense of anticipation around the ground.

We lost 3–2. Okay, not the ideal start, but there were aspects of the performance I was pleased with.

Four days later we went to North Ferriby and lost 4–0. It could have been six or seven.

Am I a manager?

The questions returned as I chewed the game over at home that night. We'd been fucking terrible.

'I don't think I'm a manager,' I said to Lucy.

'You have to give yourself a chance,' she said.

I tried to calm down and look at the game more analytically. Clearly, we had to be better defensively. Teaguey was missing with injury, but there were a few tactical changes that could still tighten things up. I got the players to work on them in training and in our next game we drew 2–2 at Corby Town, and could easily have won. We'd taken one point from nine and were bottom of the table – but in the dressing room I felt as though I'd won the FA Cup and earned a lap of honour. My first point as a manager, and an improvement I'd been able to affect, as we'd been much more solid defensively.

Next, we were at home to FC United of Manchester, newly promoted from the Evo-Stik League. The club was formed by a sizeable core of Manchester United fans unhappy with the takeover of their club by the Glazer family and so they brought a big support. It was very early in the season for one of our biggest games, but it couldn't have gone better. On a warm Tuesday evening we stuffed them 3–0. It was a great night and we followed it with another victory, at Worcester. By the end of August, I already felt like I'd experienced every emotion in management.

Sam Allardyce once said that a golden rule of football is never to get too high or too low. He's dead right, but as a first-time manager, that was easier said than done. Everything felt different to how it had been as assistant to Gaz. I took every defeat home and worried about it for the rest of the night. If we won and played well, I was elated. I began to see why some managers described the job as an addiction. Games seemed to go by slower than before, and the responsibility was a heavy weight, but when things clicked, it was a seriously good feeling: less intense than playing, but very satisfying on a deeper level.

I had inherited an ageing squad and I recognised that I would have to move a number of players on before I could be completely happy with what I had. That process was quite stressful and meant results were stop-start as the season went on and I was still figuring things out.

In October, we faced Solihull Moors, who were top of the league. We drew 2–2 but I was disappointed with how we had played. As I walked into the dressing room, I felt I had to let the players know. I raised the volume and told them that I expected better. Afterwards, in the office with Jamie, we went over what had happened.

'Hey,' he said, 'where did that come from?'

Jamie observed that my rant, if you could call it that, had sounded natural. It hadn't felt forced. I was pleased to hear this. It told me that Jamie knew I was learning on the job and was looking out for me. It also put an extra skip in my step as I walked across the car park. On the way home I called Dad and Barry, and they must have sensed the excitement in my voice. My first few team-talks had felt a little false, because I was so unaccustomed to giving them. I also didn't know whether I would be taken seriously when I had to properly shout for the first time. Getting over that hurdle meant a lot. I could give a bollocking and the players, some of whom texted me that night, had got the message. It made me, I suppose, feel more like a manager.

I was never much of a thinking player. I probably should have paid more attention to the tactical side of the game but, as Venables,

Souness and others realised, I was all about freedom: getting the ball, taking people on, scoring goals. The only instruction I really had to remember was to be at the front post when we had a corner, because my spring was useful in winning flick-ons. As for the opposition, they didn't really occupy my thoughts.

That made the learning curve of management steeper. Although starting my badges had made me think more critically, the real education came by doing the job. A course can't really teach you when to gamble or play safe with your formation, because it doesn't replicate the pressure of the dugout. And there were other things I hadn't considered about the logistics of the job – arranging hotels, planning away trips, getting the schedule right, juggling the budget.

You only truly learn to drive once you've passed your test and the L-plates are removed.

I soon realised that hindsight fuels a lot of thinking in football, particularly on fans' forums. At the start, curiosity – and maybe a bit of insecurity – got the better of me. I logged on and had a look. There was a diverse range of opinions, in line with our results, but one remark held my attention.

Jansen – great player, but maybe too nice to be a manager.

A mind like mine was never going to brush that off. The chimp loved it. There were dozens of positive comments, but I spent the rest of the day dwelling on that question.

Am I too nice?

It was always worse if we'd lost. Fans generally don't hold back, and their criticism found my weak spot.

I'm not a manager. I'm really not.

Andy Todd, an old Blackburn teammate, was one of the people I confided in when I was feeling my way around all this. He was an assistant manager in Ireland, and a tough operator.

'Don't listen to any of that crap,' he said. 'You're never going to please everybody.'

He wasn't the only person to tell me I needed to have broad shoulders and not take things personally. Lucy was adamant I shouldn't be looking at the forums and tormenting myself just because one person was calling me a wanker. That same person, if I met them at the game, might say the exact opposite to my face, so I should stick to what I knew, and trust in my own strengths and weaknesses. Everyone has their opinion and you have to work out which ones to value.

They were right, but it was something I had to learn. Even in a crowd of a thousand, I would still hear that one negative voice.

A game, against Salford. It's 1–1 and we have the ball on the left. It is worked to our left-sided centre-half and is then patiently returned to the goalkeeper.

'Bloody too slow, Chorley,' someone shouts.

We then move the ball swiftly up the pitch, and a few passes later it's in the Salford net. As everyone jumps up in celebration, I can't help myself. I turn around and identify that voice.

'TOO SLOW?' I call. 'TOO BLOODY SLOW?'

I probably shouldn't have reacted. But you have no idea where the adrenaline takes you at times like that.

There was another game, against AFC Fylde, when we slipped two goals behind after less than twenty minutes. Quick as a flash, that traditional terrace song began:

What the fucking hell is this? What the fucking hell is this?

We then stormed back to lead 3–2, and the soundtrack changed.

Matt Jansen's black-and-white army!

Super, super Matt, super Matty Jansen!

After the game, three big points in the bag, I was interviewed.

'The fans were excellent today, Matt,' the reporter said. 'Wouldn't you agree?'

I sighed and bit my tongue. As diplomatically as I could, I made the point that it is one thing to sing when you're winning, another to support when we need it the most. Come on, I said – make Victory Park a fortress.

Criticism is given easily, but it can hurt for a long time. If my son misses a penalty in the playground, I don't lambast him, I support him. If your team is struggling, what will get a better response: abuse or encouragement?

I found myself thinking more about this psychology as time went on and my doubts about management progressively diminished.

Don't let the chimp win.

There was a message there. A message that wasn't just for me.

We finished the season in eighth position: never quite in the running for a play-off challenge, but better than I'd feared. If I was going to convince myself I could be a manager, it wasn't the worst of starts. The squad had changed considerably, and I hoped the upheaval would put us in a better place for the following year.

What had really hooked me, though, was the challenge of dealing with the players as people. Working out what was happening in their heads. Inevitably, as a manager, I often spoke to the group, but I found that I preferred talking to the lads individually. What made them tick? It depended on the person. That season we had one player, quite an experienced lad, who had bags of ability but no self-confidence. It had been the same story throughout his career. I enjoyed the challenge of trying to make him think more freely.

'I don't care if you try to dribble past your man seven times and lose the ball seven times. Go back and do it an eighth time, because that time you might go on and score.'

It was too late in the day to turn that particular player into a fearless animal. But I didn't want to be the sort of manager who dished out bollockings to people who tried and failed. I realised, by now, what fear had done to me.

One of Steve Peters' lines that always stuck with me was: 'You'll never succeed if you're not prepared to fail.'

Another person who helped open my mind was Michael Finnegan. He's a brilliant psychologist who's worked with business people and elite sportsmen. He helped Darren Clarke win The Open and worked with Jimmy White in snooker and Sam Allardyce and David Moyes in football. He also happens to be a lifelong Chorley fan who regularly came to our games. One day he introduced himself. 'If you ever want me to do anything with any of your players, or give a talk, I'll be happy to help.'

Twenty years earlier I'd have looked at him as though he had two heads, but now it felt like a gift. It would have cost a few hundred quid to book Michael for a session, but he agreed to talk to the lads for free. I bought a load of pizzas and brought everyone together to listen to him. Later, he sat down with my staff and me as we talked more privately. Another player, I explained, was struggling with his state of mind. It wasn't uncommon for him to walk off the pitch having been named man of the match, but by the time he was on the team bus he'd be worrying himself into a corner again, doubting that he was good enough for our level.

I recognised traces of myself in that, apologising to Big Sam after the Arsenal game. This player's chimp was also off the scale. Michael agreed to see him, one-to-one.

I met Michael regularly and, at home, worked my way through a book he'd devised. It was full of little nuggets, and exercises which showed how the mind worked without you realising it. On one page, for instance, there was the following bunch of words with spaces removed:

opportunityisnowhere

Now, what does that say?

Opportunity is nowhere.

Wrong.

Opportunity is now here.

Also in the book there were arrangements of images, which differed depending on whether you focused on the black shapes, which revealed negative images, or the white, positive ones. It is all about your mindset, about how you want to look at things. The idea is to teach us to challenge our thinking, especially if we're naturally inclined to look at the pessimistic side of life.

I was fortunate that Jamie, my number two, also bought into what Michael did. He loved it. And, in due course, Michael's written work became a basis for some of the ways we tried to get the players to think about their challenges.

We spoke regularly on the phone and Michael also came in to talk to the board. It was the sort of thing I wanted to spread right through the club.

In our pre-season of 2016, the club came up with another idea to try to get supporters on our side. For £20 a ticket, the 'Manager for the Day' scheme gave fans the chance to win a place in the dugout for our friendly against the Welsh team Airbus UK Broughton.

'You'll take part in all aspects of the match day, from team selection and pre-match tactics to the half-time team-talk and substitutions,' our club website announced.

By now I was more comfortable in my skin and in the job. I questioned myself less and was more assured in my decisions. A year earlier it would have been strange to try to explain the ins and outs of management to someone else. Now I quite liked the idea.

A couple of days before the game, I drew the lucky winner out of a hat and, on Saturday, welcomed Julien Robb into Victory

Park. Julien was a proper die-hard supporter who followed us all over. I showed him the ropes of matchday preparation: how we researched the opposition, the stats we looked at, the videos we watched, the heart-rate monitors our players wore, the whiteboard where our plans were drawn up.

Then, as the players came in, it was time for the team-talk, which he was expected to give.

'Are you nervous?' I asked Julien, as I prepared to address the lads.

'Bricking it, mate,' he said.

I reassured him that I'd do most of the talking. It was a pre-season game, so there was no need for too much detail. I told the lads how I wanted us to play, but stressed it was mainly about fitness and trying different things.

'Oh, and boys,' I added, 'make Julien welcome, because he's going to be our manager for the day. Now, would you like to say anything to the boys, Julien?'

He looked at me.

'Er . . . just everything you said, basically.'

The dressing room collapsed into laughter. He came out and joined Jamie, Jonathan and me in the dugout. I hoped he'd enjoyed the experience – it was certainly an eye-opener for him – and that he would spread the message to the other regulars, the people who went on the bus, the supporters who had an influential voice. I hoped he'd tell them that we *did* know what we were doing, that we weren't just making it up as we went along.

Mentally, being a manager is relentless. When my friend Gary Caldwell was at Wigan, he said it didn't matter what level you were at – the demands were the same. He was no more stressed losing games in the Championship than when he'd been winning them in League One. That feeling of responsibility never dropped.

It didn't leave me, even as we started the 2016/17 season well. But the nagging doubt did lift. Results help, of course, and so do good players. But so does experience. It's one of the building blocks of belief. That probably made me easier to live with, too.

In October, I was named Vanarama National League North manager of the month, after a run of four wins and three draws. Recognition like that is for everyone, really, not just the individual. But I can't pretend that it didn't feel good.

We were coping well with a daunting challenge. We'd been forced to replace Darren Stephenson, our top scorer, who'd been lured to Tranmere Rovers in the division above, while some of the other budgets in the league far outweighed ours. Fylde's wage bill was five times the size of Chorley's, Kidderminster were full-time, Solihull Moors were benefiting financially from an arrangement with Land Rover, and Stockport, Darlington and Halifax were still clubs of decent stature, despite falling from a height.

Other clubs who had risen through our levels had come by a few quid. Forest Green, a tiny club, had serious backing and were heading for the Football League. Barrow were taken over by a Texas-based millionaire with local roots. These were the clubs who, in an ideal world, we'd try to catch. To make that transition, you need serious investment, yet football doesn't always lend itself to patience and realism. If you overachieve, which I felt Chorley had, people can see that as the new norm and expect it to be maintained regardless of the situation.

That's fine, as long as you have the tools. How much should I be expected to achieve if a rival could throw a few grand at a player while I have to beg someone for a free loan signing?

A lot gets put on to a manager's shoulders – too much in some respects. You need a united effort and a collective vision; a plan and a focus. But hunger can still take you a long way. It was something I felt now almost as clearly as I had as a player before the accident. I had something to prove and something to aim for.

Not long before I became Chorley manager, I played in Sir Alex Ferguson's charity golf day at Mottram Hall in Cheshire. Afterwards, in the clubhouse, I got a beer and sat down at a table with Jim White, the Sky Sports presenter. Sir Alex was circling the bar, and eventually spotted us. He walked over. 'Hey,' he said, pointing at me, 'I would never have tried to sign you if I knew you drank.' He then pulled up a chair and asked how I was keeping. I explained that I wasn't playing anymore, and was getting into coaching.

Sir Alex smiled as he took a sip of his wine. 'You're a bugger for not signing for me, you know?'

Jim chipped in and asked why, in all seriousness, I'd turned down the biggest club in the land all those years ago. I explained, as I had at the time, that I went to Palace because I thought I'd have more chance of playing.

Sir Alex: 'Why would I have tried to sign you if I wasn't going to play you? Think of all those trophies you missed out on.'

He was in good spirits and I could share his mood. I'd never dwelt on that scenario. I'd punished myself over all sorts of things since I came off that moped, but that question – whether I'd go back to the boardroom in Carlisle, aged twenty, and make a different decision – wasn't one of them. The honest answer, as I explained to Jim, is that I would do the same all over again. It's too easy to imagine that one change of heart could have mapped out a perfect future. How can anyone truly know that? The fact is that, until the accident, I was as content as anyone could be. I'd scored in a cup final, made the England squad, set myself up for life and had bigger clubs watching me all the time. Rome changed everything, but can I blame that on picking Palace over Man United? Of course not. That would be crazy.

Sir Alex Ferguson: My first and lasting memory of Matt was when he was a player at Carlisle, and his form and ability alerted our scouts, who strongly recommended that we sign him. We then made a bid for him and were surprised when he turned us down and signed for Crystal Palace, at which point we all questioned his sanity! But he went on to have a good career – and I sincerely wish him every success.

Working over what was, what is and what might have been, is destructive and pointless. Sometimes the temptation is strong, and I can't say I have always managed to resist it. But you can't affect the past. Should I have got on the moped? Probably not. Was my recovery handled in the best possible way? Possibly not. Did I, and others, take decisions rationally, and for what we thought was the best at the time? Yes, I think so.

I spoke to Sir Alex a few more times after that golf day. I felt he recognised I was sincere in what I said about the day I turned him down, and he was always happy to talk about coaching and management. He urged me to be ambitious, to always think bigger. 'If another opportunity comes along, and it looks like a better one, you'll need to think very hard about taking it,' he said. He should know – he'd gone from East Stirling to St Mirren, to Aberdeen, then to Manchester United and the absolute peak of his profession.

I had no idea, when speaking to him, what I could achieve at Chorley and where I might be able to go from there. Would I have a long and successful career as a manager? Would I only get so far and then settle into a different position, as a coach, or maybe even a scout? Would I build a second career in the game, or become another statistic?

I was desperate to find out – and that in itself was a remarkable feeling, given where I'd been since the accident. I wanted to try and to learn. I'd found a drive and a motivation that I presumed I'd lost.

The last time I spoke to Sir Alex, and shared a little of this, he left me with another pearl.

'Son, it's not about where you start – it's where you finish.'

TWENTY

GOOD AND BAD TERMS

Footballers who are having a good time of it carry themselves with a bit of a swagger. They give the impression of thinking they are better than they really are. I knew that feeling well. So, when my career unravelled, and I was around friends and teammates who still had what I had lost, I couldn't bear it. I recognised that part of me was missing, and it hurt.

That swagger tends to go when you retire. In most cases, the end brings us all back to the same level and so it helped me when I reached an age when my peers began to hang up their boots. I stopped looking at them with envy and hating what I'd become.

Every player has a few regrets when it's all over. The challenge is to keep them in their place, in a box. I'm lucky to have had a few years of practice with this.

You also need a plan, a focus, and after drifting around for so long, I'd found mine. I enjoyed being a manager in ways I could never have imagined. It helped me move on from a lot of the torment I suffered.

One reason for this is that it gave me an outlet to use a negative experience for good. If you don't have setbacks in life, how can you relate to people who are struggling? In management, solving problems and dealing with players whose minds might be in all sorts of different states is a daily challenge. Before I became a coach, and then a manager, I didn't have this outlet. I was at war with myself, and losing the battle.

The other, bigger reason is that I was no longer trying to live up to Matt Jansen the player. That's what had crushed me: trying to get back to my best, and failing to deal with the fear that grew when it wouldn't happen. My nerves became unmanageable. Any time I tried to reach those heights again, it felt like an invisible hand was pushing the bar up, and up, and up again. I stopped believing I could clear it.

What I felt was an enormous positive – my ego, the snowball at its biggest – proved to be my worst enemy when I tried to build it again from scratch. Thankfully that chapter is now finished, and as a manager, I'd stopped comparing myself to a previous version. I was no longer trying to live up to what I used to be.

That helped me look forward. I still got nervous, but not because I was scared, or worried people would think less of me than they used to. More often, I just experienced the clearer emotions of management, and did my best to embrace the extremes. I hated the pressure of being on the sideline and watching my team go a goal down – that stress is worse than anything you normally experience as a player – but the adrenaline rush when we turned it around was so powerful.

There is rarely any middle ground, so it amused me when I was named manager of the month another time and among the messages I received on Twitter was this one:

Admiring the calm and professional management style of @mrmjansen of @chorleyfc #ManageroftheMonth

Professional? I was certainly trying my best. Calm? Nowhere

near! Maybe I've got a good poker face, and it's also easier to project calmness when you're winning. That season, we were. Although we finished just outside the play-off places, we gained a reprieve because Darlington, who finished above us, fell foul of stadium regulations. This gave us a two-legged semi-final at Kidderminster, who beat us 1–0 at our place – and celebrated as though they were already through – only for us to win 2–0 in the second leg and advance on aggregate. I felt the players really responded to my team-talk that day.

If that was my most satisfying experience as a manager so far, the final, against FC Halifax Town at their ground, The Shay, was comfortably my biggest occasion to date. The crowd was 7,920, a record attendance for our league, with nearly two thousand from Chorley, and the prize was the highest position in the club's history: the top tier of non-league football.

Kick-off was delayed for fifteen minutes as traffic piled up because of roadworks. I reminded the lads of the need to be clear-minded, to focus on the game, and to remember everything that was important to us: team, belief, work rate, ability.

Halifax got in behind us to take the lead early in the second half, but Adam Blakeman brought us level with a special free kick. There is no coaching course that can replicate the tension of a day like that – and certainly nothing that tells you what to do and think when you go on to lose. Halifax got the better of us with a header in extra time, and, after a pitch invasion by their supporters, I found it hard not to shed tears – for the players and the people who'd backed us. We had come so close.

I felt proud and my resolve to go one better next time was strong.

Losing that final was a big blow, but Chorley may not have been ready to move up to the National League. At that level, everyone is pretty much full-time and there is a lot of travelling to the south of the country. For Chorley, that would have meant overnight accommodation for part-time players with day jobs who might struggle to secure the time off work. Whether or not it would have been a good thing for the club is an interesting question.

However, if you're competing in a league system and not aiming for promotion then something is wrong and the bottom line was that we had improved once again. That summer I brought in a couple of players I thought would make us stronger still, for a league that was going to be tougher. Salford were investing heavily and Harrogate went full-time, but we were still in decent shape.

That was reflected in the best FA Cup run Chorley had experienced in twenty-seven years. It took us to the first round proper and a tie with Fleetwood which was televised live and attracted a capacity crowd. This generated a six-figure sum for the club – all of which got swallowed up by historic debt, apparently – and we put on a good show, taking the lead against the League One club before they came back and nicked it in injury time.

That winter was one of the worst for a long time and it led to a backlog of fixtures. We had something like thirteen matches to play in the space of six weeks, and ground to make up in the table. But the lads were brilliant and took us on a roll. We secured a play-off place again and turned Stockport over at their ground in the quarter-finals.

Then it was Harrogate, on their artificial pitch, against a side I felt was the strongest in the league. We went ahead, but had full-back Lee Molyneux sent off in the first half, and the home side eventually came back and won 2–1 in the dying minutes. It was hard to take, and I felt we had come off poorly with some of the refereeing decisions. As the disappointment slowly faded, though, I could reflect that we had embarked on another good run. That close-season I worked hard on recruitment and, as the summer went on, I felt we would start the new campaign with the strongest team in the club's history.

That May, Barry received a phone call from Phil Smith, the agent who had lined up my potential move to America.

'You're Carlisle United's first choice . . . would you be willing to go and speak to them?'

My first club had recently parted company with Keith Curle. The sense was that Carlisle needed a fresh start. Was I interested?

I didn't particularly want to relocate – I was very settled at home and I hate being on my own, so the thought of becoming a commuter, staying part of the week in accommodation owned by the club, did not appeal to me. Still, Barry urged me to speak to them. I'd never had an interview before and it would be good experience at the very least, as well as courteous to hear what they had to say.

Barry and I met the club's directors in Wetheral, at the chairman Andrew Jenkins' house. I was apprehensive but, by the time it was over, I felt good about it. The interview had gone very well. I came out thinking, 'Well, if I am their first choice, I've got the job.' In which case, I'd have a serious decision to make.

Carlisle had an obvious pull for me, but the club didn't appear to be in the best possible shape. They had backed Curle financially but had failed to get out of League Two. That summer they had clearly decided to do things differently and this came across in the interview. Chief executive Nigel Clibbens had explained that the budget had been cut, some of their big earners had gone and they would be trying to get rid of others the following summer. He asked me how I'd attract players to Carlisle who wouldn't cost significant amounts of money.

My first thought was: 'The only reason they'll come to Carlisle is if we pay them a little bit more, because it's not exactly the geographic epicentre of English football.' However, I said that I had many contacts in the game from the Premier League right through the divisions, as well as a good knowledge of non-league – where I believed there were more players like Jamie Vardy who, given the opportunity, could cut it at a higher level.

I left Wetheral in good spirits. Amusingly, there had also been a supporter representative on the interviewing panel who could have been my biggest fan. He kept asking if I remembered this game I'd played in, or that goal I'd scored. Good for the ego, of course. But on the drive home I shared my concerns with Barry. 'Is this a sinking ship? Do they just want to pull all the money out and let the manager deal with the fall-out?'

There was a delay of a couple of weeks before I heard from them again. In that time the Livingston manager David Hopkin was strongly linked with the job, with Morecambe's Jim Bentley another in the frame, but there was no news of a decision. Eventually Barry heard from Phil Smith again. They'd 'decided to go down a different route', but still wanted me to join, as a number two.

A different route – what did that mean? And a number two to whom? They didn't know yet, or, at least, weren't saying. I felt it was a strange request. What if the prospective manager didn't want me as a number two? What if he turned out to be someone I couldn't work with?

I couldn't figure out why they did it that way, and I didn't feel they were being completely honest with me. Did they want me to work with someone more experienced, with a view to me taking over down the line? If so, it was never said. I declined the offer and, after more time had elapsed, they finally confirmed John Sheridan as their new manager.

I don't know whether he'd been on their radar to start with, but I remembered that I'd locked horns with him in the past over a loan player I wanted for Chorley when he was at Oldham.

He wouldn't have been the first manager I'd have chosen to work under and the feeling may have been mutual. Either way, it had been a bizarre situation. Back at Chorley, meanwhile, a series of issues began to threaten the smooth progress of my fledgling career as a manager.

The chief executive, Dave Riche, had come in on a wage which I felt would have been better spent on a couple of players, or on the pitch, which was not in the best shape. I found it hard to warm to him.

Before our FA Cup tie with Fleetwood, we found ourselves short of a goalkeeper, because our main No.1, Matty Urwin, was on loan from our opponents and not allowed to play against them as part of the agreement. Without my knowledge, the chief executive put out an SOS on social media, asking anyone who could get us a keeper to help. This unorthodox plea was picked up by the national press and it made us look really amateurish.

Then, in April, a radio commentator, Ian Livesey, was heard making sexist comments about a female referee at one of our games. 'You should be at home doing the ironing, love,' was his alleged remark. It also made the national news and the club took the decision to ban him. Dave Riche said it was a 'regrettable' incident but the club 'had ground regulations which needed to be followed,' also citing Football Association policy.

His commitment to fairness and equality was not so obvious when, that summer, Riche was in Blackpool and took a photo of two unsuspecting women, posting it on Instagram and fat-shaming them. This led to a flurry of complaints on social media. Riche eventually apologised and claimed he'd 'had a few drinks' when he posted the picture. But he kept his job.

It seemed hypocritical and some people connected me with the controversy, arguing that, by working as manager under Riche,

I was condoning this behaviour. This idea of guilt by association made me very uneasy.

There had been other issues. On the way back from away games, I would be the one to buy the lads and everyone else on the coach a drink – on a wage that barely covered my travelling expenses. The chairman and board members on the bus, knocking back the wine I paid for, never seemed to think that this kind of initiative should come from club funds.

On another occasion, when arranging pre-season friendlies, I was urged by one of the club owners to play against opposition from a lower level rather than a side that would have given us a much more competitive test, because it might help advance his personal business interests. My role as manager was to make Chorley as successful as we could be, and I was not prepared to be compromised in this objective.

Another issue that was hampering our development was the aforementioned condition of our pitch. The previous year, the club had brought in a young groundsman, yet the playing surface at Victory Park remained in a poor state. During training, the players complained that it was dangerous, and I was concerned that its condition also made it much more difficult to play the style of football I wanted. Instead, it had become a leveller for visiting teams who were technically inferior to us.

When I raised the matter with the club owners, they countered that the young lad was there all the time and was doing a good job, but I'd been given different information by others inside the club: that he perched on his sit-on lawn tractor for a while, spent half his time on the phone and then left.

The owners suggested the situation would be reviewed in the summer, but I stressed that it had to be dealt with now, because it was adversely affecting our game and there was a risk of players getting injured. Jamie, my assistant, had a friend who was responsible for some school playing fields in the area which were extremely well maintained. We invited him down for a chat, and were very impressed with his proposals for getting the pitch back to an acceptable standard in the short term, and then giving it serious attention at the end of the season.

Perhaps the fact the groundsman had an indirect connection to one of the club's sponsors got in the way of reaching the right decision, but it wasn't until around Christmastime that I was able to put this clearly positive solution in place. It was then left to me to break the news to those involved. I presented it to the young lad as a need for a little more expertise and thanked him for his service. The new guy started the next day, and it didn't take long before everyone at the club was commenting on the transformation of the pitch.

There was also a serious problem developing with my wages, in the sense that, that summer, I wasn't receiving any.

Barry: In discussions with Chorley the previous year, I negotiated that Matt would be paid on a fifty-two-week basis, rather than terms that would run merely for the duration of the season. I assumed that, at the end of the fifty-two-week period, this would simply continue, but instead they stopped paying him altogether. He worked through the close-season, putting a new team together and planning for the new campaign, without any remuneration. In lieu of further discussions on this I asked the chairman to authorise Matt to be paid on the basis of the package that was already in place, but he then disappeared on his holidays without getting back to me. It was this that brought matters to a head.

I felt that I wasn't being appreciated, that I was being taken advantage of. The club weren't prepared to bring my wages up to date despite the success we'd had and the revenue those results had generated. Although it wasn't my direct responsibility, I'd helped contribute to the club's financial situation in other ways, such as negotiating a cheaper deal for a Premier League-standard team bus. Despite all the problems, I turned down interest from other clubs to stay with Chorley. Yet they weren't showing the same level of loyalty to me.

When they repeatedly refused to acknowledge Barry's requests to speak to them, in order to sort out my terms for the forthcoming season, I didn't have anywhere to turn. I'd worked hard and brought success for eight years and now I didn't feel like they were acting toward me with honesty or respect. They'd often suggested that money was tight, and there was a sense that creditors had to shout louder than others in order to get paid in a decent time frame. Was it the same with me? Had I not shouted loud enough for my wages?

When Barry canvassed the opinions of other people he and I trusted – Dad, Jay, colleagues in the game I knew well – every single one of them agreed with the course of action I felt was now inevitable. Barry drafted a resignation email on my behalf and sent it to Chorley on 22 June 2018.

Barry: Matt recognised that he had to leave Chorley but, nevertheless, it hit him hard. He'd worked tirelessly throughout the summer, putting together what he considered to be a league title-winning team : the strongest Chorley had ever had, and one with an even greater chance of success given that the division's bigger-spending clubs had by now moved up to the National League.

He didn't leave the club with a distinct idea of what to do next, but there is a crucial difference between this and the way he was when he finished playing. Then, he was content just to drift for a while. Now, he knew he needed to be doing something.

I don't want to drift. I know I have to satisfy my ego. Management did that, especially when it was going well, and I hope the next opportunity will do that, too. It might be management, it might be coaching, it might be working as a chief scout, working with young players, working with adults, or working with the Professional Footballers' Association, who are interested in what I have to say about mental health. What I need most is the focus and purpose that would come with the right role.

In management experience, it's still early days for me – the equivalent of knocking on the door of Carlisle's first team all those years ago, wondering how good I could be and where my limits might lie. Maybe it's the start of a new snowball. Perhaps I'll only know if my mind has truly healed if I succeed at some level and then crash and burn again.

I can at least say that it helped me come to terms with all that happened after Rome. It brought a bit of the ego back. It gave me something to concentrate on and be proud of. I'm more level-headed than when I finished playing and I know my own mind in a much clearer way. I trust that this will keep me moving in the right direction.

TWENTY-ONE

BELIEF

Lucy: It would be nice if Matt's career in management or coaching progressed and he regained some of what was taken from him when he was a player. He sometimes jokes that I never saw him when he was at his peak, and I suppose it's true. I only went to a handful of games before the accident, and then everything changed.

I never really looked at him as 'Matt Jansen the footballer', even though I steadily learned more about that world – and these days, I can barely see him that way at all. Our local gym is occasionally used by football teams and you can spot them a mile off, strutting around like peacocks. I just can't imagine Matt ever being one of those people.

I hope that, having been thrust into the Chorley job and done well at it, this line of work will be the making of him. I saw him grow into it, and I do think he is ten times the person he was before he made that step. Matt needs a focus. He's a driven, able man, who shouldn't be sitting at home doing nothing. He's got a brain and a lot of talent. If he can channel that into other people, teach them what he has learned, it'll be good for him.

There was, at the beginning, a lot of frustration in terms of the level he was working at. It's a league he never knew as a player and because of that he had to pick things up as he went along – knowledge of players and how a club the size of Chorley works, day to day.

It brought him out of his shell. On holiday, when we saw another high-profile footballer, Matt would try to avoid making eye contact with them. If the other person approached us and said hello, he'd be fine, but he'd be reluctant to make that first move. After becoming a manager, he seemed more open. He bumped into Mark Hughes a while ago and they were just chatting away about management.

He learned gradually that just sitting around is no good for him. At first, he simply wanted to be away from football, but there was no anchor to his days, and this became a frustration in itself. It was obvious, too, that he was missing something.

Footballers don't realise the banter they get in the dressing room isn't something available on tap at home, nor is the acclaim. 'Well done, you cooked a great meal. Ten out of ten – Dream Team Star Man!' I don't think so. Real life doesn't provide that kind of constant adulation and I think that is why a number of players struggle to adjust when they retire.

He doesn't like looking back on what happened after Rome, and so a new focus is very healthy. But in other ways, it'll always be there. There are times when we will argue about something trivial, and it'll escalate and escalate, and eventually it's: 'You made me get on that bike.'

It doesn't happen very often, but my response – whether I say it or keep the words in my head – is that, if everything had gone swimmingly, if Rome hadn't happened, who's to say what life would have brought instead? We might have a host of different problems. You just don't know.

He does realise this, and he looks forward rather than back these days. There is nothing I would have wanted more than for him to fulfil his dreams and ambitions as a player, but we both decided to get on that bike. It was an incredibly stupid decision, and we've both paid the price with what we've been through. But you have to find a positive slant to put on it if you possibly can.

It has been very easy for me, over the years, to say, 'It's happened, deal with it,' but that's not always what the other person wants to hear. Pointing out that there are always people worse off than you is the worst thing you can say to someone in that situation. It must have been gutting for him, plain and simple, and as his girlfriend and his wife I have tried my best to understand how he's been feeling at all the stages since then.

The early years after the accident were tough. At one point in his life I think he thought he was going to be the best footballer in the world. I think, to some degree, they all have to think like that to reach the heights they do. The flipside is that, when everything is taken away, it casts a huge shadow.

It upsets me to think of the what-ifs he must have struggled with. We've had three beautiful, healthy children, bought a beautiful home, were surrounded by lovely families, went on nice holidays, and yet there was this long-lasting depression, this low feeling, the suspicion that nothing was going to make up for what he had lost.

I've seen Matt with the lowest self-esteem you could imagine and that side of him is still there. When he had his sessions with Steve Peters, and my father sat in with them, they'd come back and discuss it and invariably Matt would completely disregard all the positives and focus on a single, negative thing.

I guess that's human nature to an extent, but as a manager he had to be careful to guard against it. He has a Twitter account, which I was sceptical about for someone in his position at Chorley. One person tweeting criticism or asking whether he was the right man for the job, could outweigh dozens of compliments. I once deleted the Twitter app on his phone, knowing he wouldn't be able to reinstall it. But he managed to put it back on his iPad. I think he felt that if he came off it completely, the critic would have won.

I used Twitter to follow the Chorley scores. Someone uploaded an interview with Matt after every game and I always listened to it. I tried to go to as many matches as I could, even if the kids struggled to take a lot of interest. If Daddy is on the pitch, playing, it seems to be different – when they've been to watch him play in exhibition games they've enjoyed it. If Daddy's standing on the touchline, waving his arms around, less so. But I felt that it was important to support him, as I always will.

A lot of time has passed since our lives changed dramatically. I don't know if I would ever like to go back to Rome and see where it happened. Arthur would like to see the Colosseum and all of that, while Matt seems totally fine with the idea, because he can't remember anything about it. But I worry that I'd be a bit freaked out. For a long time after it happened, I'd wake up with a gasp. I'd like to think we could enjoy the city again, because we had such a nice time until the accident. Maybe we could make new memories of Rome.

Sometimes, when I meet someone for the first time and we have the usual conversations about our lives, what our husbands do and so forth, I say it all quite flippantly: 'Oh, he used to play football . . . Blackburn . . . we went to Rome and came off a scooter.'

So many years on, I rarely stop and consider what a big deal it is. But when I do reflect, I end up thinking that we're really lucky to have come through it together and survived.

I've been reading a great book recently. It's called *Legacy* and it's about the New Zealand All Blacks rugby union team. As I went through it, I found myself highlighting phrase after phrase, because it summed up many of my own philosophies about sport and life, how it's all about the team, not individuals. The idea that character trumps talent. The image of the manager and captain sweeping the dressing room having just won the World Cup. Humility, dealing with people, setting an example. Mindset.

The idea that the mind is the most powerful tool in your box could not have been further from my thoughts at the start of my playing career. Psychology? A load of rubbish. A shrink? Do me a favour. I played on my instincts and the game came naturally. What else was there to consider?

What did I know?

At Chorley, where we had to punch above our weight and think on our feet, it was my job to find every possible advantage. In setting out our aims at the start of a season, I'd introduce to the players the principles I'd formed as a result of everything I'd been through.

The first buzzword was 'team'. Our togetherness, our unity. How we get on, how we fight for each other.

The second was 'belief'. Not only in yourself, but in the team; believing in our direction, and committing to it with confidence.

The third was 'work rate'. Look at the stats in the Premier League or other elite divisions. The team that covers the most distance and works with the most intensity tends to win the game.

It was no accident that this came before the fourth factor: 'ability'. I used to think I was the dog's bollocks. I didn't need to be told to adapt to defensive shape, or to sacrifice my individual qualities. I didn't care to be told there were things just as important as a shimmy, a dribble or a shot. Ability was king, I thought. I was wrong. It still counts for a great deal, but it cannot come before the others.

The fifth was the unwritten extra, the dusting of icing sugar: 'luck'. We all need a little bit of that.

To illustrate what can be achieved when all this is in place, we looked at Leicester City, Premier League champions in 2015/16. If you studied Claudio Ranieri's team, it was apparent that they were all prepared to die for one another. They appreciated that they could only reach their goal together. That belief was as potent as rocket fuel.

The following season was markedly less successful for Leicester and it was as though that belief had diminished, like air inside a leaking tyre. You can try to inflate it, but it won't be fixed without a fundamental repair, and the nagging idea remains that things might never again be the same.

Believe me. I know.

Look at Wales in Euro 2016, going all the way to the semi-finals. Look at Iceland – on paper, vastly inferior to England, but, in that tournament, capable of humiliating us. Look at England's transformation under Gareth Southgate in the World Cup two years later. What was at the core of these success stories? Belief. Those players bought into each other and they were immensely strong of mind.

After the accident I quickly regained my ability but lost the belief I needed to return to my peak. It took me until now to fully understand exactly what effect this had on me.

The boys at Chorley took my message in different ways. It breezed past some of the younger ones. I could see them thinking, 'I don't need this'. They laughed through it. I couldn't criticise or reprimand them, because that's how I used to be. In my teenage days at Carlisle, when we were introduced to the sports psychologist Bill Beswick – a man of strong credentials in his field – I'd scoffed.

Some of the older Chorley players considered what I said. A few appeared to be half in, and half out, and half a dozen seemed completely sold on it and told me the talk had helped them. Wherever I go in football, I'll stick firmly to these principles. I have lived, suffered and negotiated with the mind at its very worst. Now I can repackage the whole experience as something irresistibly positive.

How important is experience in coaching and management? Some believe there's no substitute for having been there and done it. Others think that teaching and playing are so different that your appearance tally and your medals don't matter much.

I'm willing to consider both sides of the argument, but you're never going to convince me that true football experience is no advantage. As a basis for coaching, it must surely be a head start and it can be frustrating that not everyone thinks that way.

Coaching badges are important, but as a former player I've found much of the studying process long-winded. When I completed my FA Level 2 qualification, and subsequently my UEFA B and A Licences, I found certain aspects very useful, but other elements had the feel of a box-ticking exercise.

When I started my A Licence in 2015, there was a pre-application process, spent in a classroom in Nantwich, Cheshire. I was the only footballer there.

'This course might take you six years, seven years, even longer, but this is the start,' the leaders said. That may be a reasonable prospect for someone new to the game, but it left me dismayed. I asked, as an ex-player, if I had to go through the same initial process. Yes, I was told, the £60 charge was intended to show you were serious about going to St George's Park – the FA's national football centre – to take the course in earnest. I'd already committed four grand, but now another sixty quid was needed. Box – tick.

A couple of months later, I was formally accepted to go to St George's, near Burton-on-Trent. It was a sprawling place of contrasts. Its facilities were state of the art, its pitches and indoor equipment superb, a Hilton hotel conveniently on site. But too much of it lay dormant. Every day I saw empty pitches. I knew certain league clubs used it, but the cost was steep and so it was a treat, at best. Why not cut the prices by a quarter and have the pitches full? The sense of waste was hard to avoid as I began my course, which entailed a nine-day residential period in the first year, eight days in the second year, and a pack that had to be worked through and on which students would be assessed. My challenge was also to balance these commitments with my first managerial job.

I was with a good bunch of lads, having a laugh, enjoying the best facilities in the country and working towards something important. But I also found that we were going over the same topics, over and over. The days started at 9.00 a.m. and finished at about 8.00 p.m. Then we all got pissed, woke up the next morning, and started again. Groundhog Day. There was so much padding. It felt like they could have condensed the nine days into three or four without any trouble.

I heard stories from people who'd taken the course in other countries. Someone described Ireland as a stag do – two weeks, and you've got your B and A. No Level 2 to bother with. By comparison, my Level 2 took me a year, the B Licence eighteen months and the A Licence just over two years. How can that be right?

I also had an assessor visit Chorley to watch me coach. He talked to me, monitored me, checked how many boxes I had or hadn't ticked. Sometimes this was helpful, other times it got in the way. On one occasion, I was required to put on a session around defending with a back four. Having played with a back three for a long time, having to drill my players in a different system wasn't just a nuisance, it risked disrupting my team. Why should I confuse my players for the sake of ticking another box? Why should I jeopardise our form? Why should I put my own position at risk in the process?

Recalling these pointless exercises leads me to the pack, one of the requirements of the course. There were all sorts of questions in there, so many blank pages that you had to fill in, many of them for good reason. But one particular task stood out. It required a description of a scenario involving a fictional player who was suffering from psychological problems – nerves, anxiety, issues at home, stuff like that – and how you would deal with it. You write down your imagined story, a psychologist reads it, and that's another box ticked. What could I have gained from this exercise in creative writing? How about my personal experience? Nerves, anxiety, depression, suicidal thoughts – I had the full house. If you need a case study, I'm your man.

On the B Licence course, I'd already set this out when, at a seminar held at Curzon Ashton Football Club, the tutors asked if anyone in the room had heard of a man called Steve Peters. One or two murmured, thinking of the psychiatrist who had become renowned for his work with elite cyclists, athletes and footballers. I coughed and said, well, yes, I kind of know him. Having spent upwards of 120 hours with him, as Steve tried to untangle my mind in the years after the accident, I considered him a friend.

A few eyebrows went up. They asked me to stand up and talk about my experience. I described how I'd met Steve, how he'd tried to get me back to my best, how his sessions were so powerful that they became like a drug. How I'd wished he could have been in the dressing room before each game. How I'd wished I'd been exposed to his methods much sooner. How I now reflect on the work he did, and the way he tried to nurture me, as a positive, something I can use with my own players. It was only a brief speech, but it allowed me to give some background to the basic story that many people in the room already knew: that I'd had an accident, and was never quite the same again.

There are areas where real-life experience should always count for more. To be fair to those running the A Licence course, they listened. I made it clear that I'd attended every seminar, done all the demonstrations, filled in everything else that was needed but, really, all things considered, was this particular part worthwhile? They let me off without completing that one section, and I passed the course. If there is anyone at the FA who still doubts how I would deal with a footballer who is going through the psychological mill, I hope they will accept this book as my submission. I hope they will agree that I have sat the test.

Graeme Souness: I'd never encountered anything like Matt's predicament before, and haven't since. Our paths didn't cross after I left Blackburn, although I've always looked back at my old clubs, and I kept an eye on what was happening with Matt. It's a great shame that he could never recapture his best form, and I suppose the big question of how good he could have been, were it not for the accident, is one nobody can ever answer.

I am sure that his willingness to be so open about everything can be of great benefit now. I don't believe there is enough advice out there for players who find life difficult after retiring, and Matt would be the perfect counsellor. He's in an ideal position to talk about those thoughts you have when things don't pan out the way you wanted, yet the majority of your life is still ahead of you.

I was lucky not to fall off that cliff, because, after playing, I dropped straight into management and, nineteen years later, moved into television. I've always had my football fix. There are many players who find the transition difficult and, as someone who has real and raw perspective on the challenges that come through being interrupted in your prime, Matt can speak with authority.

His story should be something of real value to the game and beyond.

Occasionally, I've been back to my old clubs as the years have gone by. At Carlisle, I put my boots back on for Tony Hopper, one of the Cumbrian lads who made the grade a couple of years before me and who, in January 2017, was diagnosed with motor neurone disease. A charity match, at Brunton Park, brought dozens of old faces back together, and Tony himself came on to play in the second half, flanked by his two brothers. There wasn't a dry eye on the pitch or in the stands when he walked off through a guard of honour. It was a really emotional day, full of memories, and nice to be back again where it all started.

Seventeen months later, Tony died. He was one of the nicest guys in the world, such a good and genuine person. I couldn't think of anything more unfair. It's a horrible reminder that none of us know when our time is coming, and to make the most of all we have.

I've been back to Palace the odd time, too, including a testimonial for one of the coaching staff who'd been there forever. Selhurst Park will always mean a lot to me. So will Ewood Park, where I've been more often, but I've never particularly enjoyed just going to watch games. I follow the results of the teams I played for, and look out for mates who are still in the profession. I won't turn off a decent game on the telly, either. But I'm not sure I could just be a fan. It's not enough for me.

I keep in touch with old faces from my playing days, many of whom I consider to be good friends, and I try my best to take as much money off Dwight Yorke and Mickey Gray as I can on the golf course.

Everyone moves on and does something different, but I do my best to look back more comfortably now. Occasionally I catch myself on Sky Sports when they show footage of an old game. One day, the lads at Chorley came in and said they saw me scoring a goal on TV last night. Sky had shown Blackburn's 5–0 win over Burnley.

'Hey, I scored two in that one,' I replied.

I've got a DVD called *There's Only One Matt Jansen*, which has footage of all my goals at Blackburn. The kids watch it sometimes and I can usually sit and look at it with pride, rather than regret.

Years ago, I'd have watched that stuff and tormented myself about what might have been. Now I'm older and have more perspective.

The one thing that still frustrates me is the certain knowledge that, without the accident, I would have played for England. I just know they'd have given me a try, and sometimes it pisses me off to imagine people thinking I can't have been that good, because I didn't get an international cap.

But I've taught myself not to linger on that thought.

I've kept bits and pieces of memorabilia from my career, but I've given a lot of it away to charities. Probably too much, but I don't like to say no. I've retained a few treasures, though: my Worthington Cup final shirt, my Carlisle shirt from Wembley, my England Under-21 caps. A few player of the season awards. There's a couple of manager of the month trophies alongside them now.

If you ask me right now, though, I couldn't even tell you exactly where my England suit is – the grey number that I was fitted for in 2002. I've never worn it, because I didn't get to go to the party. It will be in the house somewhere, gathering dust. I didn't go to David Beckham's party, either, and that invitation will be in a box somewhere too. What would be the point of digging those things out?

I hadn't looked back on the accident and everything that followed it in great detail until writing this book. It was a horrible time in my life and it can't be healthy to relive it over and over again. I want, as best I can, to keep it locked away, and to a fair extent I think I'm doing that. It doesn't affect my mindset from one day to the next.

I'm still convinced that, in terms of a complete recovery, I'm not yet back to a hundred per cent. I still find it weird that some memories are so vivid but others are a complete blank. Seeing Solskjaer on the plane is crystal clear, despite it being so close to the accident, yet the day I made my first-team comeback is so hazy.

Phil Batty sent me an article a couple of years ago about the consequences of head injuries – depression and so on. There was some new German research into head trauma, and he suggested it was something I could maybe look into. I never did, but I wonder if, twenty years from now, scientists will reveal something else that might explain things better. I'm aware of the 2015 film *Concussion*, starring Will Smith, which is based on a true story about American footballers and the neurological impact of the blows they receive to the head. There have been many cases of degeneration, depression and suicide amongst former players. I find it fascinating but, at the same time, I don't want to keep coming back to the subject. I don't want to immerse myself in it. I'm much happier moving on.

The kids are still relatively young, and they only know small parts of what happened. They know I was a football player who did well, and they're aware of other aspects of the story, but not in great detail. If and when they grow more interested, I'm sure I'll explain what happened.

In the meantime, I find that I'm thinking more deeply about the emotions they're feeling. Arthur is good at rugby and, when he was slightly younger, was known to cry if something didn't go his way.

'The referee was wrong, I didn't pass it forward,' he'd say.

I tried to explain that it won't always be fair, it won't always go your way. 'In those few minutes when you are being upset, you could have helped your team get the ball back and score a try.'

I try to work out what he's thinking all the time, the same with our other two. Freddie is still very young, but Minnie is old enough to make it very clear that she absolutely hates losing in anything she does. I quite like that. I can't stand the idea, which some schools and clubs encourage, that it's all about taking part. What's the point in just taking part? Where will that get us?

That's not going to breed determination. In any walk of life, you can't settle for being okay. You have to strive for something.

There's certainly a strong Jansen trait in all this. I think of myself, as a boy, seeing Dad shaking his head after I'd had a bad game. The will to win is very powerful, almost ruthless. It's certainly in the genes. At one of our first Christmases together, Lucy and her family were taken aback by how seriously the Jansen men treated a simple game of Trivial Pursuit. It was win at all costs, no quarter given. When Mum started whispering some of the answers to help the others, we couldn't believe it. What's the point of playing if you're going to do that? Poor Mum felt it was only a game, something for everyone to enjoy. Dad and I saw it as something to win. It's just the way we're wired.

Lucy and I are different in this way, but we get on brilliantly. She's not as driven as me, but she's more practical. Her family take the mickey out of me a lot. They say I know how to kick a ball around, but I don't really know how to do much else. Barry jokes that I don't know the difference between a spreadsheet and a bed sheet.

If you're lucky enough and good enough to play football at a high level, you get used to a certain way of life, and everything being done for you. Because I got there quickly, it probably conditioned me and I can be very impatient. I sometimes struggle to grasp all the little tasks Lucy does every day to keep our lives and our home ticking along. I frustrate her when I ask if certain things could be done quicker. This book, too, come to think of it. Could it not have been completed earlier? How long are these things supposed to take?

When we go on holidays, go on trains, book flights and so on, I basically just follow Lucy. It's what we're used to, but I know I'll never learn if it stays that way.

There's one foreign trip that I may have to take the lead on. I'd get on the plane to Rome tomorrow. It was a fantastic place that

I absolutely loved and, because I can't remember the worst of it, I can't imagine being traumatised at the sight of it all again. A while ago, one of my golfing friends said he was going there on his holidays.

'See if you can find my brain,' I told him. 'It'll be lying on a kerb somewhere.'

I can laugh about it. I'd even go back to the Hotel Eden and revisit the spot where it happened. It's the biggest event of my life, after all, and it was no fault of the city (other, perhaps, than the way they park).

It was a long time ago, and I'm not sure that it would feel raw in any way. It's the aftermath that I don't want to revisit, not the place itself.

I don't know if Lucy could go through with returning. I was wiped out, but she lived it. I was out cold, but she saw me lying there in a pool of blood. I was in darkness, but she held and squeezed my hand, fearing I might be dead. I have no memory of being lifted into an ambulance or being wired up in the horrible A&E ward, but she saw it all. She had to deal with things that I didn't. I have to respect that.

I'm still more of a pessimist than an optimist. I still question myself in different ways. But I've learned so much about myself and I realise that certain things take time. I'd like to imagine that I can be the happiest man in the world again, as invincible as I felt when I held hands with Lucy in the Italian sun and said those words out loud. On really good days, I can feel it creeping back. All I can do, along the way, is keep trying, keep hoping and keep believing.

AFTERWORD

BY PROFESSOR STEVE PETERS

I first started working with elite sports people in 2001. It began with cycling, but I also saw a number of footballers, as one-offs, in those early days. Matt was one of the very first.

I recall that it was Phil Batty, the Blackburn Rovers club doctor, who got in touch and asked me to see Matt. When I went to meet him for the first time, my assessment was to find out what this man wanted from me. Those around him felt that he was so anxious about going back out on to the pitch that he could no longer do it. It was my intention to explore things from Matt's point of view.

During that first interview, which was quite lengthy, I went into his history, right from square one: his career, the accident, post-accident, what he perceived had happened and what his beliefs were. When I pieced all that together, and listened in particular to his explanation that he felt he'd lost the ability to play well, I started asking if he was giving me answers that were defensive and frightened. My sense was that he felt vulnerable, and that unless he could attain his previous state of 'invincibility', he wasn't sure he wanted to carry on playing.

In psychiatry, you assess a situation like this in one of two ways. You ask if there is illness, or alternatively what I call dysfunction: there being nothing wrong with the brain, but the person is struggling to operate it well. In the latter instance you wouldn't go down the route of medication. Instead you would opt to talk the person through it.

There was something else to consider here. One of the common things you find as a consequence of serious head injuries is an increased anxiety state. That would be an organic illness, and nothing to do with Matt. People who have suffered such injuries can develop issues later in life, such as depressive illnesses and obsessive features.

I asked to see the scans he'd had. Although they didn't rule out microdamage, they didn't show much.

On the basis of my initial conversation with Matt, I had some reservations about the chances of him succeeding, and indeed wrote a sentence to that effect and underlined it at the bottom of my notes. I agreed, though, to keep going. It was made clear to me that he wanted to overcome whatever was preventing him from resuming the great career he'd previously enjoyed.

I went back to see him, conscious that my job was to explore things further but not to change his mind on what he did or didn't want to do (that is a misleading perception of what psychiatrists do. We give insights, not brainwash). When he spoke, I found that he was extremely open, never holding back. This, I soon learned, is the kind of man he is. As we talked, I found there was a clear lack of self-belief in Matt, and an inability to deal with what he perceived as less than perfection on the football pitch. I think it's good to be a perfectionist, as long as you can add reality – but he couldn't add that reality. Because of this, his thought process was very unforgiving.

I looked at matches in which he claimed to have been 'terrible' yet football experts rated his performances highly.

He was extremely hard on himself and steadfast in what he believed, against all the evidence. When Barry sat in on some of our conversations, his frustration was plain. 'Why can't he see what we see?' he said. It's a fact that, if someone has low self-esteem, they'll focus on negative points. Matt would persistently minimise, or play down, anything good that he did, and maximise – exaggerate – anything bad.

I then tried to lift him away from 'Matt', and suggested we look at football from a more general perspective. I was neither a football fan nor a football expert, but regarded it from a psychiatrist's point of view. It's a game in which an individual's performance is variable at best, and will always be judged by others. More so in football than other sports, the crowd are also extremely active and involved.

I then studied footage of footballers who made schoolboy errors. When they slipped up, the crowd went for them. But in every case, when that footballer kept going and produced the goods, the crowd swung back. They were expressing emotion in a very rapid way, and it was tidal.

I started looking at other factors too: the manager, the players, the press. We went through all that extensively as a way of widening the perspective.

It made no difference. Matt was quite fixed in his view of how he was. He was engaging, yet every time I said something that did resonate – and you could see it resonate – he would say, 'Yeah, but . . .'

This wasn't Matt being difficult. To me, he was saying, 'You're giving me the obvious. I know the obvious.'

I then took the route of asking what the advantages were of continuing to play – financially, for example – and the disadvantages. If he stopped, what would he do? That hadn't been thought through. Some people in elite sport will talk about their desire to go into the police, be a teacher, do a degree in biochemistry. They have an alternative career which we are thwarting, and you can then go down that route. Matt didn't have anything. In the event of things not working, he had no idea what else he might do or where he'd go. He was lost, and you could see the despondency setting in.

One thing I clearly observed in Matt is something I call 'Father Christmas Syndrome'. When you're little, and believe in Santa Claus, it's magic, but as soon as you know it's not true, you can't go back. Before the head injury, there were times when Matt wasn't invincible and collapsed within himself, but what he'd do in those moments is rationalise it. It was the ball's fault, the conditions' fault, the other players' fault, never his. The snowball, as he calls it, was total.

After the injury, his view was the opposite. He'd discovered the reality: that he was no different to anyone else, and there was no turning back the clock. From here I knew it had to be a case of managing his expectations, but from Matt's point of view he simply had to be invincible. It wasn't realistic.

There were two occasions when I asked him to demonstrate his football skills: once at my house, the other on a field with goalposts, with just the two of us present. It was very windy, and I asked Matt to shoot for the goal with either foot. This was simply an attempt by me to see him relaxed and kicking the ball, away from an environment in which his desire for invincibility was relevant to him. He indeed went about this in a relaxed and straightforward manner, but this was only a very small part of a much bigger and more challenging process.

I brought further rationality and practicality into it. I explained that a lot of us don't enjoy our work, but it's a necessity, and sometimes you have to do things you don't want to do. He'd buy into these ideas, and sometimes there were wry smiles when he ran out of, 'Yeah, buts . . .' When he could no longer argue, he'd suddenly see what the rest of us could see.

You can get out there and play, you can make mistakes – and you can get over them.

In all this, I was trying to offer a safety net that he could use to help restore reality if his thoughts started attacking him. The key was to enable him to gain enough insight to run his own mind. If someone twists their ankle on a walk, you say, 'Lean on me – but when we finish this walk, you've got to sort the ankle and start walking again'. The problem in my profession is that when you stabilise someone by giving insights into something that is upsetting and distressing, it isn't necessarily permanent and it's certainly not a magic wand. Matt started to grasp things, and when we got him back on the pitch there was a time that he was doing okay. The problem came when he went away from me and started getting on with his life, and his mind defaulted. There was a point where Matt, Barry and Lucy all joked that if only I could move into their house and be there 24/7, then the problem would go. I can understand why they would feel that, but of course it wasn't practical.

Matt has talked about loving the adulation of supporters, and this had also contributed to his view that any mistakes weren't his fault. The accident stopped this firmly in its tracks. Anyone coming back from injury has a state of vigilance about their own performance, and in this period a feeling of not being competent – the 'Impostor Syndrome' – is quite universal. People can often be talked through it, but Matt's belief that he was nowhere near his previous level, and therefore not invincible, hit him extremely hard.

Barry feels Matt returned to first-team action too soon, and also believes he'd have benefited from seeing me much earlier. There could be some truth in that. By the time I met him, it was a good year on from the accident, and all the behaviours and beliefs I've described were cemented. It wasn't a period in which I'd been in a position to advise, in conjunction with whatever approach his club took in those early days.

I talked about the chimp theory with Matt, as I do with other people I work with. By way of simplifying the neuroscience, I explain that a person has three different systems in their head. The first is effectively a very reactive system which is defensive and hypervigilant; that's the chimp, and it can be in fight mode or flight mode. If you look at Matt prior to his accident, he was in chimp mode with the unrealistic belief that he was invincible. After the accident, he was still in chimp mode, but this time with his belief that he would never be as good again.

The secondary system is a human system. This state is rational and logical, with executive functioning. We have to learn to switch to that in order to stabilise our mind, but Matt's chimp system was too powerful for this. It was constantly on high alert and exhausting him. When I managed to show him how to switch from chimp to human, he would go away walking on air. But, as time passed, the chimp regained control.

The third system is the computer; when behaviour is automatic. This is the state we try to get players into when they are on the pitch. The computer doesn't analyse or think; it just reacts to a situation, because it's programmed, or fully learned. Relevant examples in daily life are the acts of driving a car or riding a bike, where the routines, through extensive practice over time, become 'natural', without the need for further thinking. Matt's programming had become weak and disorganised, and he was defaulting back to chimp mode.

I'd say that he certainly related to this model, but not in a way that he could use it with any lasting effect.

I saw Matt on a good number of occasions before our sessions ended. The way I operate is that I allow the person to be in charge; I want them to be able to work things out and get in touch when they're ready. If someone is suicidal, that's different and I set the pace. Matt wasn't suicidal. He was really down, but he did the pacesetting. I saw him over a long period, but eventually I had a meeting with Barry to suggest that it was wrong of me to keep going. It was always Matt's prerogative, though, to engage or disengage, and it was his decision to stop. While he was lifted by our sessions, his belief that he'd been brain-damaged – and that this made a permanent cure impossible to attain – had to a strong degree proven unshakable.

There were times when I also saw Lucy, and she took the opportunity to unload a little. They are a lovely couple, a lovely family, but Matt had become the centre of everything. This was necessary, but on the other hand those who are trying to support people in such situations can become neglected. Effectively, the wife is the silent hero because, whilst trying to support, her own frustrations, worries and concerns are never addressed. So it's quite nice if you encourage that person to say anything they want, in the knowledge that it's going nowhere and doesn't leave the room. It can be cathartic. You're listening to yourself, which is often really helpful. Lucy did that.

I stayed in contact with Matt after the last of our sessions, but infrequently. It's not my role to follow everyone I see, but you do get to know people and their families, and, if they call or want to see me, I don't say no.

I'm so pleased for Matt that he later found a different niche, and that he was energised by it. As a manager, he'll have faced similar pressures as a player, if not worse, because you're not just responsible for your own play but are reliant on many other people. You can be a perfect manager, but if you don't have the right calibre of player, or find that they're not engaged, you get slated. To me that's an immense pressure – yet Matt took it in his stride.

This shows me that pressure was never the problem with him. When we met quite recently, I asked how he was coping with management. He said, 'Oh, I can deal with all that'. It was different to playing, and that seemed to be a huge difference.

Everyone's unique. There's no fixed template for working with people. I work out plans for each individual, and Matt's is a unique story.

The reason I worked with him is that he was a genuinely engaging guy. I won't work with someone who isn't going to work with me, or who is aggressive, but Matt wasn't that way at all. He tried extremely hard to overcome things, and we had some small successes along the way.

Although the 'yeah, but . . .' was a regular feature of our meetings, he was always intrigued to listen and learn. We couldn't give him his invincibility back, but working with him was a good experience, and I will always wish him well.

ACKNOWLEDGEMENTS

'Would anyone actually want to read it?'

I first encountered the glass-half-empty side of Matt in our first meeting, at Victory Park, Chorley FC, in the autumn of 2014. Even though he'd long since emerged from the hardest time of his life, the chimp was still there and needed to be tackled.

It was over a longer conversation at his home, when the significance of his story was discussed in greater detail, that Matt embraced the idea. I'd always been convinced that his was a unique and powerful tale that could reach beyond football and, in persuading him of the same, I explained that the answer to his question was 'yes' – provided he was prepared to be completely open, and willingly revisit the most challenging of his memories.

This he has done unflinchingly. You hear of sports people who regard the writing of their autobiography as a chore to be endured so they can collect the cheque at the end, but with Matt it was never like this. I would like to thank him, above all, for being so committed, candid and sincere, and for entrusting me to put his thoughts into words.

I am grateful to many other people who helped along the way, and apologise if I have omitted anyone here. Nobody deserves greater thanks than Matt's father-in-law, Barry Corner, who assisted in more ways than it is possible to mention. This book would be a great deal poorer without his steadfast support, advice, wisdom, care and meticulous attention to detail at all stages of the process.

Lucy Jansen warmly welcomed me into the family home many times, and was also prepared to talk about her life with Matt, including what happened in Rome, frankly and in depth. It could never be easy revisiting that period, but the book benefits hugely from her candour. Her account of the post-accident days is both riveting and essential – as are the contributions of Jay Bevington, Matt's brother-in-law, who gave generously of his time and knowledge.

Matt's parents, Mat and Judith, shed light on their son's childhood and career, and the early chapters in particular are testament to the time and help they kindly offered.

Thanks are also due to those in football who were happy to give their perspectives on Matt, significantly Mervyn Day, Garry Flitcroft, Sam Allardyce and Sven-Goran Eriksson. The arrival in the post of a letter from Sir Alex Ferguson, meanwhile, underlined the greatest of managers' admiration of Matt.

I am hugely grateful to Professor Steve Peters for an afternoon spent listening to his detailed professional insights, and his correspondence since.

Thanks, too, to Dean Eldredge, for supplying a crucial contact.

Two outstanding football journalists, Oliver Kay and Simon Hughes, offered invaluable advice at the outset, and also both pointed me in the direction of David Luxton, who as our agent has been a reliable and friendly source of help and reassurance. His belief in the value and potential of the book was thankfully matched by Pete Burns and Neil White, whose enthusiasm, faith, skill and care from the outset have made Polaris the perfect home for Matt's story.

I would also like to thank my colleagues at the *News & Star* for their support, particularly Chris Story and Alison Sisson, and good friends both at the newspaper and elsewhere for their discretion and encouragement. My regular work travelling companion, BBC Radio Cumbria's James Phillips, was kept waiting in a café for far too long one evening en route to a Carlisle United game while I met Matt and his family in Alderley Edge. I owe you a brew, mate.

A number of written sources were essential to the act of compiling a timeline of Matt's life. Where not directly quoted in the book, these include: *News & Star*, *Cumberland News*, *Lancashire Telegraph*, *Croydon Advertiser*, *Bolton News*, official programmes and club websites of Carlisle United, Crystal Palace and Blackburn Rovers, the *Five Year Plan* fanzine, and several national newspapers, news websites and news agencies.

Josh Vosper's photography of Matt's time at Chorley, meanwhile, is outstanding and appreciated.

Writing a book involves many sacrifices and it is inevitable that most of these are felt at family level. Above all I would like to thank my wife, Tess, for her boundless support, patience and love. The encouragement offered by my brother, Clark, and mother, Noreen, has never wavered, while the bittersweet feeling at the completion of the book is in knowing that my father, Jeff, will not be able to read it. He was the wonderful man who took me to watch Carlisle United for so many years, and hence introduced me to the magic of Matt Jansen; he was delighted that we were now teammates.

He died in May 2019 and is deeply missed. In so much as it is possible to dedicate someone else's life story, this one's for you, Dad.

Jon Colman
September 2019